# Computer Communications and Networks

The Computer Communications and Networks series is a range of textbooks, monographs and handbooks. It sets out to provide students, researchers and non-specialists alike with a sure grounding in current knowledge, together with comprehensible access to the latest developments in computer communications and networking.

Emphasis is placed on clear and explanatory styles that support a tutorial approach, so that even the most complex of topics is presented in a lucid and intelligible manner.

*Also in this series:*

An Information Security Handbook
John M.D. Hunter
1-85233-180-1

Multimedia Internet Broadcasting: Quality, Technology and Interface
Andy Sloane and Dave Lawrence (Eds)
1-85233-283-2

Information Assurance: Surviving in the Information Environment
Andrew Blyth and Gerald L. Kovacich
1-85233-326-X

UMTS: Origins, Architecture and the Standard
Pierre Lescuyer (Translation Editor: Frank Bott)
1-85233-676-5

OSS for Telecom Networks
Kundan Misra
1-85233-808-3

The Quintessential PIC® Microcontroller 2nd edition
Sid Katzen
1-85233-942-X

Intelligent Spaces: The Application of Pervasive ICT
Alan Steventon and Steve Wright (Eds)
1-84628-002-8

George Roussos (Ed.)

# Ubiquitous and Pervasive Commerce

**New Frontiers for Electronic Business**

 Springer

George Roussos, MSc, PhD, Birkbeck College, University of London, UK

Series editor
Professor A.J. Sammes, BSc, MPhil, PhD, FBCS, CEng
CISM Group, Cranfield University, RMCS, Shrivenham, Swindon SN6 8LA, UK

British Library Cataloguing in Publication Data
A catalogue record for this book is available from the British Library

Library of Congress Control Number: 2005929865

Computer Communications and Networks ISSN 1617-7975
ISBN-10: 1-84628-035-4        e-ISBN 1-84628-000-0         Printed on acid-free paper
ISBN-13: 978-1-84628-035-1

Printed in the United States of America        (MVY)

9 8 7 6 5 4 3 2 1

Springer Science+Business Media

springeronline.com

To Theano.

# Preface

At the core of this book is the interplay between technological and business innovation and social practice. Although the benefits of 50 years of rapid advances in digital telecommunications and computing technology have not benefited everyone equally, they have nevertheless transformed almost every aspect of the way we live. One area where technology has had a clear impact is in the way we conduct business. The rate of change that brings about modernity has been considerably strengthened by technological advances applied to product manufacturing, distribution, financing, and management, which arguably form the substrate for globalization and consumerism.

It is thus no surprise that businesses closely monitor advances in technology and invest considerable resources in exploring possible new applications and market opportunities. Yet, consumers' acceptance of new ways of buying and selling depends as much on business and technology as on our society's culture and the culture of the material environment that defines our values, sensibilities, and thus our commitments.

Moreover, the rate of technological innovation is such that to the consumer, technology implementation is fully opaque. Nonetheless, opportunities to carry out commerce in novel ways also introduce risk to established social structures, conventions, and institutions. In modernity, risk management is one of the core functions of society and to be successful in this, societies depend on their trust of experts. Experts take risks on behalf of society and are responsible for evaluating the full extent of a particular set of hazards including those associated with a particular technology.

With the deployment of ubiquitous and pervasive computing for business, technology becomes indistinguishable from everyday objects and thus disappears from public view, so that even its mere existence is not immediately obvious. Unlike previous technology generations, its operation is silent and its inner workings less accessible than at any other time in the past.

But technology and business do not always combine seamlessly either. Often, technologists have limited interest in the business implications of technology which they view as being dominant over all other aspects of commercial activity. This was illustrated in the 1990s during the boom of electronic commerce when business startups expected to dominate the market often on the basis of a single technical innovation, frequently without a viable business case.

This was also the period in which the concept of ubiquitous commerce was born: Throughout 1999, Anatole Gershman and his team at Accenture Labs were looking at mobile telephony as a channel for commerce. Most of the ideas they initially considered they rejected because of their narrow focus on the technical capability of the mobile phone and their limited appeal to consumers. In August of that year, while waiting a flight out of O'Hare Airport at Chicago, they observed different people using their telephones and it became clear to them that what is truly different with mobile phones is that they offer ubiquitous opportunities for negotiation and transactions, thus for ubiquitous commerce.

While this interpretation of ubiquitous commerce became a core theme for the work carried out at Accenture Labs, others also arrived at a similar concept starting from a technological perspective. Indeed, by the late 1990s computing research was turning its attention to a concept that first emerged earlier in the decade and while referred to by different names it was increasingly known as ubiquitous computing. Many asked what would be the applications when this technology could be used for commerce.

Another development that contributed in making ubiquitous commerce the focus of different research programmes in the early 2000s, has been the increased interest in Radio Frequency Identification. This technology allows for the augmentation of artifacts with computational and limited wireless communications capability at very low cost, thus providing a viable solution to one of the core concerns of ubiquitous computing. Recently, RFID has been used in a variety of practical deployments with businesses increasingly interested in implementing ubiquitous commerce at a large scale.

These different views came together in October 2003 at the first ubiquitous commerce workshop organized in conjunction with Ubicomp 2003 in Seattle, WA, USA. During this workshop different aspects of ubiquitous commerce were discussed and the tensions highlighted above surfaced. This book is the extension of the discourse that started with that workshop, enriched with contributions from several more authors. I hope it provides useful insights into the technological, business, and societal aspects of ubiquitous and pervasive commerce.

Hampstead, April 2005                                    *George Roussos*

# Acknowledgements

Alessandro Acquisti would like to thank Hal Varian, George Roussos, and the Information Technology department at HEC Montreal for help and discussions about the topics and models presented in Chapter 7.

Tony Salvador, Kenneth T. Anderson, and John W. Sherry would like to thank Edgar Whitley, London School of Economics, for his assistance in developing Chapter 10.

Gregor Hackenbroich, Christof Bornh, Stephan Haller, and Joachim Schaper would like to thank Tao Lin, Brian Mo, Uwe Kubach, Rama Gurram, Peter Ebert, and Hartmut Vogler for their valuable contributions to the Auto-ID Infrastructure project. We also benefited from fruitful discussions with other colleagues in SAP including Bernd Sieren, Bernd Lauterbach, Christoph Lessm-llmann, Ami Heitner, Alexander Renz, and Kai Morisse.

Large parts of Chapters 4 and 6 have been funded by the M-Lab (`www.m-lab.ch`), a joint research initiative of ETH Zurich and the University of St. Gallen, Switzerland. The M-Lab is working with several international companies on business applications based on ubiquitous computing technologies.

Roger Till and other staff at GS1 UK (visit `www.gs1uk.org`) provided input in Chapter 2 regarding the supply chain standards that constitute the EAN.UCC and the EPCglobal systems.

Project MyGrocer discussed in Chapter 8 has been partially supported by the European Commission under research contract IST-1999-26238. The MyGrocer Consortium consists of the following members: Nokia Corporation, Procter and Gamble, Unisys Corporation, ATMEL Corporation, Pouliadis Associates Corporation, Athens University of Economics and Business, Helsinki University of Technology, S-Markt, and Atlantic Supermarkets.

# Contents

## Part I Technology

## Part II Business

# Contributors

**Alessandro Acquisti**
H. John Heinz III School of Public
Policy and Management
Carnegie Mellon University
5000 Forbes Avenue
Pittsburgh PA 15213-3890, USA
acquisti@andrew.cmu.edu

**Kenneth T. Anderson**
Intel Corporation
2111 NE 25th Ave.
Hillsboro, OR, USA 97229
ken.anderson@intel.com

**Christof Bornhövd**
SAP Research Center LLC
3475 Deer Creek Road
Palo Alto, CA 94304, USA
christof.bornhovd@sap.com

**Elgar Fleisch**
Institute of Technology Management
University of St. Gallen
Dufourstrasse 40a
CH-9000 St. Gallen, Switzerland
Elgar.Fleisch@unisg.ch

**Simson Garfinkel**
CSAIL, MIT
The Stata Center
Building 32 - 32 Vassar Street
Cambridge, MA 02139, USA
simsong@mit.edu

**Anatole Gershman**
Accenture Technology Labs
3773 Willow Road
Northbrook, IL 60062, USA
anatole.v.gershman@accenture.com

**Gregor Hackenbroich**
SAP Research
CEC, Vincenz-Priessnitz-Strasse 1
D-76131 Karlsruhe, Germany
gregor.hackenbroich@sap.com

**Stephan Haller**
SAP Research
CEC, Vincenz-Priessnitz-Strasse 1
D-76131 Karlsruhe, Germany
stephan.haller@sap.com

**Andrew Fano**
Accenture Technology Labs
3773 Willow Road
Northbrook, IL 60062, USA
afano@techlabs.accenture.com

**Panos Kourouthanassis**
Department of Management
Science and Technology
Athens University of
Economics and Business
47A Evelpidon & 33 Lefkados St.
11362, Athens, Greece
pkour@aueb.gr

**Matthias Lampe**
Institute for Pervasive Computing
ETH Zurich
ETH-Zentrum
IWF D41.1 CH-8092 Switzerland
lampe@inf.ethz.ch

**Olli Pitkänen**
Helsinki Institute
for Information Technology
P.O.Box 9800 HUT
Finland
olli.pitkanen@hiit.fi

**George Roussos**
School of Computer Science
and Information Systems
Birkbeck College
University of London
Malet Street
London WC1E 7HX, U.K.
g.roussos@bbk.ac.uk

**Tony Salvador**
Intel Corporation
2111 NE 25th Ave.
Hillsboro, OR, USA 97229
tony.salvador@intel.com

**Joachim Schaper**
SAP Research Center LLC
3475 Deer Creek Road
Palo Alto, CA 94304, USA
joachim.schaper@sap.com

**John W. Sherry**
Intel Corporation
2111 NE 25th Ave.
Hillsboro, OR, USA 97229
john.sherry@intel.com

**Martin Strassner**
Institute of Technology Management
University of St. Gallen
Dufourstrasse 40a
CH-9000 St. Gallen, Switzerland
Martin.Strassner@unisg.ch

**Christian Tellkamp**
Institute of Technology Management
University of St. Gallen
Dufourstrasse 40a
CH-9000 St. Gallen, Switzerland
Christian.Tellkamp@unisg.ch

# 1

# Ubiquitous Computing for Electronic Business

George Roussos

## 1.1 Ubiquitous Computing and Networked Business

Many see ubiquitous computing as the next wave of information and communications technology to follow the era of the internetworked personal computer. What differentiates ubiquitous computing from previous paradigms is the fact that computation and (wireless) communications capability is embedded into objects, locations, and even people. In this way, it becomes possible to interact freely with digital resources at any time and everywhere rather than only through purpose-build information processing devices. According to the ubiquitous computing vision, access to information systems deeply embedded into the environment is mediated by objects or simply through the observation of users and the reflexive interpretation of their intentions by the system. Thus, computing devices become invisible and interaction is directly with the human sensory and affector systems.

At the core of this computational paradigm are mechanisms that make the physical and the digital worlds intimately related, and indeed to mirror each other [4]. Every object in the world we live in has a digital representation that follows the situation of its real self — for example, the supermarket shelf that is aware of the quantity, the price, and the brand of the cans of cola it holds. The same is true for spaces: the room that knows the types and locations of furniture as well as the identities of the persons that hold a meeting within it, their agenda, and their individual preferences. Digital entities also have physical manifestations: the mirror that displays weather predictions and the home that switches on the heating in anticipation of the arrival of its inhabitants. This unique linking of bits and atoms opens up numerous possibilities for new computing interactions.

Building ubiquitous computing systems has become possible because of several recent technological breakthroughs, including the miniaturization of electronics components, the massive reduction in their production and operation costs, and their ability to communicate untethered over a global ubiquitous network, often without the need for wires. These new capabilities are complemented by mature techniques developed in more traditional areas of computing, notably engineering mobile software systems, autonomic system and network management, low-power wireless, machine learning, and information management. Ubiquitous computing combines these techniques into systems that provide context-awareness and new interaction modalities often referred to as ambient intelligence.

Context-awareness in particular is intimately related to effective interaction with ubiquitous computing systems. Interaction is via objects and thus situated within the context of a particular activity. Detailed knowledge of the parameters of this situation is necessary to infer appropriate behavior. Context incorporates several aspects:

- The physical environment: for example, the user location, the presence of other persons or objects in the same location, and the environmental conditions observed. For example, knowledge of user location can assist infer their current activity.
- Time can also reveal considerable information about the current user activity — for example, whether a particular person is occupied by professional or personal concerns.
- Device and network characteristics, especially in the case where an information service must be delivered to the end user. In this case, service provision parameters must be optimized and the service adapted to meet the characteristics of its operating context.
- Information context is the semantic knowledge regarding the domain being investigated — for example, the short-term information needs of the user as they might be expressed in a query. Information context also includes the user profiles that reveal long-term interests, for example via demographic details.
- Social context is perhaps the most challenging aspect of context-awareness as it relates to information relevant to the characterization of a situation that influences the interactions of one user with one or more other users. Automated interpretation of a social situation is challenging and requires higher level abstractions than those provided by sensing, even more so in those cases where the user is part of a group.

This new computing paradigm has considerable implications for business. After an initial period of uncertainty over their direction, networked businesses are now coming into their own and are creating a radically inflated environment to conduct commerce. Contrary to the exaggerated declarations of the dot com era, which predicted that startups would dominate the market by capitalizing on the network effects of web-based communities, change is emerging from rethinking traditional business processes set within the new situation. Perhaps the area where most of the benefits have been observed is in forming dynamic relationships with trading partners as witnessed in marketplaces and integrated supply chains. To be sure, information technology can only be seen within the context of business innovation, which depends on the ability to manage material and human resources, their production process and their relationships with their customers [3].

Despite the benefits of the networked business model there are still significant discontinuities in the information flows within and across businesses that prevent a fully integrated network model. To a great extent, such data fault lines are due to the separation of digital and physical artifacts and thus the need for manual data entry, which is prone to error and consumes considerable resources at high cost. Ubiquitous computing, then, offers the opportunity to bridge this gap by providing unique information sources. For example, automatic identification[1] of product items can fuel production planning applications: stocking and inventory control is automated and does not require human intervention since assets identify themselves and their location. Subsequently, this information can be used to optimize enterprise resource planning. Moreover, collected data can move between trading partners mirroring the flow of products, which would allow for collaborative planning and forecasting. Last but not least, this physical/digital integration can transform the relationship between business and customer, including marketing, after sales support, replenishment, and payment options.

## 1.2 Ubiquitous Commerce Technologies

### 1.2.1 Automatic Identification

Although ubiquitous and pervasive commerce is primarily about business innovation, technology has a critical role to play as the enabler of new business capabilities. Evidently, the best established use of ubiquitous computing is in supply chain applications (discussed in more detail in Chapters 2 and 6), which benefit from the wider availability at very low cost of passive Radio Frequency Identification (RFID) tags (cf. Figure 1.1). RFID tags are computational devices that are small enough to be embedded in objects and living organisms and can transmit wirelessly the identity of the object or person,

**Fig. 1.1.** Radio frequency identification tags.

---

[1]Automatic identification techniques refer to methods of collecting object data and entering it directly into computer systems without human involvement.

**Fig. 1.2.** Radio frequency identification reader.

using radio frequencies. A typical RFID tag consists of a microchip — which contains the object identifier and other associated information but can also carry out simple computational tasks — attached to a radio antenna and mounted on a substrate. Data stored on an RFID tag require a reader to be retrieved, as seen in Figure 1.2. A reader is a device that employs an antenna to emit energy over radio waves and then receive signals back from the tag. The reader then passes the information on for further processing.

The main advantage of passive RFID systems is that they do not need an integrated battery. This is a critical fact as lack of a battery component means that passive RFID tags have considerably lower cost, much longer lifetimes as they do not require recharging to operate, and cause less pollution to the environment. The basic operating principle of such systems is that both energy and data are transmitted via inductive coupling: a magnetic field generated by the antenna of the reader induces a voltage in the coil of the tag and supplies the tag with energy (cf. Figure 1.3). Data transmission from the reader to the tag is carried out by modulating the parameters of the transmitting field (either amplitude, frequency, or phase). Tags collect the energy transmitted by the reader and respond by transmitting the identifier they hold by modifying the load of the field (amplitude and/or phase).

While passive RFID is the most common form of automatic identification today, it is by no account the only. One alternative is active RFID which differs in that it employs an on-board battery and thus does not require a

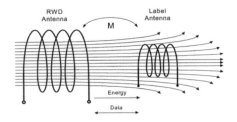

**Fig. 1.3.** Inductive coupling: principle of operation of passive RFID technology.

reader. Because active RFID tags can use more power to transmit data they generally also have much longer range.

The current use of RFID in supply chains is primarily as a replacement to bar code technologies (in Chapter 2 we discuss at length bar codes, their uses and their history). While bar codes also hold product identifiers, they have limited scope as an automatic identification technology because harvesting their data requires that a laser reader is appropriately aligned with the bar code symbol, a fact that dictates human involvement in the vast majority of use cases. Of course, the bar code must also be visible and thus on the surface of the object, a fact that has a clear impact on the design of the packaging.

### 1.2.2 Sensor and Actuator Networks

There are different automatic identification alternatives to RFID, notably video and biometrics. In both cases, objects and individuals are identified by comparing their captured image to that stored in a database. However, such techniques are error prone, and while used extensively in specific applications, they do not seem to satisfy the full scope of ubiquitous computing. A new generation of automatic identification devices with far superior capabilities compared to RFID has emerged in the past few years based on micro-electromechanical technologies. This technology has become known as sensor and actuator networks, and in addition to identification it can provide other context information collected via mechanical, chemical, or biological sensors [1]. More importantly, it can be used to build wireless networks on the fly and in an ad-hoc manner (cf. Figure 1.4 for an example of a sensor network node). In fact, sensor networks far exceed the capability of a simple automatic identification system, and indeed they can provide the information required to provide accurate models of the physical context.

**Fig. 1.4.** The Cube sensor network node by IMEC, Belgium.

Sensor systems have attracted the keen interest of the research community due to their ability to potentially satisfy the requirements of true ubiquitous computing systems. For example it is expected that within a few years sensor node size will fall below 1 $mm^3$ in volume, which will allow for it to be embedded in objects of any form or size. However, several core problems have

to be addressed before such systems become available for general use, such as
their limited life span and limited system robustness. Although software optimizations and other data-centric power management techniques have been
successful in extending their longevity, supporting industrial strength applications requires further improvements in efficiency of at least two orders of
magnitude. One promising approach seems to be harvesting ambient power
from the environment, but this is work still in its early stages.

Another problem that must be addressed before sensor networks become
a viable alternative is security. Access to the information collected by the
sensor nodes and reliable delivery of this information to the proper information systems is far from guaranteed by current protocols. It should also
be noted that implementation of security and trust management mechanisms
will further reduce the availability of the relatively scarce computational and
communications resources available on sensors.

Finally, programming sensor networks with thousands of nodes is far from
a trivial task. In fact, current embedded software development paradigms do
not carry over well to sensor networks and new approaches are necessary.
Although there are several interesting developments in this area, for example
employing a database abstraction [5], there still remain considerable challenges
to be addressed.

### 1.2.3 Location Sensing

Location sensing is a core component of ubiquitous commerce. Because there
are numerous technical solutions available, it is not possible to review here
all the different options. Instead, we will only briefly examine two approaches
which are characteristic of the general approach so as to provide useful in-
sight in the operation of such systems, namely the Global Positioning System
(GPS) and location beacons using RFID. A detailed discussion of location
technologies for ubiquitous computing can be found in [2].

The most common system for location sensing in use today is the satellite-
based Global Positioning System, which was initially developed by the U.S.
Department of Defence to support navigation for military purposes. GPS employs a constellation of 24 satellites, organized in three groups of six positioned
in orbit so that they provide best coverage of ground stations. GPS receivers
use time measurements of the arrival of the satellite signals to triangulate their
location. In this case, the estimated location is expressed in terms of longi-
tude and latitude coordinates and is accurate to within a few meters. Over the
years GPS receivers have been miniaturized to just a few integrated circuits,
becoming very economical, and have found their way into cars, boats, planes,
construction equipment, telephones, movie-making gear, farm machinery, and
of course computers.

An alternative way to determine location is as being proximal to a known
reference point within a specific, limited range. Proximity can be easily deter-
mined by physical contact, but more interestingly it can be estimated wire-

lessly. In the later case, proximity is identified as containment within the range of a wireless access point — for example when a mobile telephone registers with a particular base station (cell ID) — or more interestingly for ubiquitous computing applications, when an RFID reader records the tag identifier of an object at a known location (cf. Chapter 4 where Lampe, Strassner, and Fleisch present an asset management system that is built using such data). The accuracy of the location estimates clearly depends on the range of the technology employed and can be improved in some cases using signal-strength measurements.

### 1.2.4 Service Provision

Automatic identification and context sensing in ubiquitous computing systems produces massive amounts of data that must be recorded, managed and analyzed. Thus, there are considerable challenges for service provision architectures and ubiquitous computing applications: scalable and robust global-scale services, high throughput wireless networking, and multi-layered systems architectures. Regarding the last point in particular, it is necessary to control data streams proactively at the local level; otherwise business information systems will be overwhelmed by superfluous and meaningless data (in Chapter 3, Hackenbroich, Bornhövd, Haller, and Schaper discuss the issues related to the management of automatic identification and other sensor data). Moreover, putting together systems of this size and scope depends critically on common standards, regarding, for example, the semantics of the data moving across organizational boundaries. This is perhaps one of the most daunting tasks in preparing infrastructures for ubiquitous commerce (work in this area is well underway and discussed in detail in Chapter 2).

Last but not least, interacting with ubiquitous computing systems requires not only appropriate new interfaces (for example tangible input devices and embedded displays) but frequently the re-conceptualization of our established interaction paradigms with information systems. Indeed, until now we interacted with computers at specific service endpoints, for example terminals, mobile telephones, or digital TVs, but working with "everywhere, invisible" computing will require new frameworks to deal with the new situation (some work in the grocery retail sector that addresses these issues is discussed by Kourouthanassis and Roussos in Chapter 8).

## 1.3 Ubiquitous Commerce Case Studies

As noted earlier, the most successful application of ubiquitous commerce so far has been in the supply chain. Interest in this area was initiated by work carried out by the Department of Defense (DoD) in the USA after the first Gulf war. A doctrine for land operations was first employed in this conflict, which dictated the rapid advance of forces at an unprecedented speed in military operations.

This approach caused considerable problems in downstream information flows and upstream in the supply chain: intelligence about possible targets often had a lead time of over 12 hours and combat units often found themselves without supplies due to the inability to replenish materials, in many cases despite the fact that the required resources were available in storage nearby. This situation prompted the DoD to propose standard systems and protocols for the transmission of information in the so-called Network Centric Warfare model, but more relevant to this discussion, the management of the supply chain using RFID at the container level. At the time, this solution was not cost efficient for commercial use, but it did highlight the advantages of a system for automatic identification and tracking of products.

The falling cost of RFID technology over the following decade meant that by the early 2000s tags became cost effective in a variety of situations. As a result, several pilot projects highlighted the possible benefits of the technology [7] and subsequently some of the largest retailers decided to deploy: Wal-Mart in the US, Tesco in the UK and Metro in Germany are all actively implementing RFID to track products across their supply chains. These deployments focus primarily on tracking containers or stock keeping units (SKU) rather than individual items across open supply chains.

But this is not to say that there have not been attempts to use RFID for item-level tracking or in closed supply chains. For higher cost items especially it is relatively easy to develop an appropriate business case: Gillete is experimenting with RFID on razor blade packets as an anti-theft mechanism; M&S in the UK is deploying tags on men's suits to improve the accuracy of its stock keeping with a view to increase the availability of products on the shelves;[2] DHL is using RFID tags on clothing to guide robotic automation of its item sorting and warehouse management processes; and Prada uses RFID tags embedded in its garments to provide accurate information about product availability to the customer and to trigger the operation of the changing rooms at its flagship New York store.

RFID tagging has also found applications in commerce outside retail. For example, active RFID tags are used across the world in road toll collection systems, and indeed, RFID is increasingly used to tag individuals: during the summer of 2004 night clubs in Barcelona, Spain, injected punters with RFID implants that were used to control access to particular club areas and for collection of payment. While implantable tags are rather uncommon, tags that are carried by an individual have found many uses, primarily in public transport. The Oyster card in London, UK, and the Suica card in Tokyo, Japan, employ RFID to authenticate their users, provide access to the metro system, and deduct payment.

---

[2]M&S operates a closed supply chain, that is all its products are its own brand and manufacturers work exclusively for M&S.

## 1.4 Ubiquitous Commerce and Business Innovation

Undoubtedly, we have only just started to explore the possible uses of ubiquitous computing and the business opportunities they open up. Yet, the critical question is which of these applications will survive their encounter with the marketplace. This is exactly the question that Fleisch and Tellkamp attempt to address in Chapter 6, by examining the impact of these technologies on business processes and how such applications can create value. They also attempt to develop a framework for a costs/benefits analysis of different services looking closely at the effects and requirements for all business partners involved.

Of course, investing in ubiquitous commerce applications only makes sense if its benefits exceed the costs. In developing an evaluation framework for potential solutions, the main ingredient is the effective utilization of the data available due to the improved integration of the real and the virtual world. An analysis of the value proposition of RFID for the different actors involved in the retail supply chain is certainly useful to extract some early evidence in this respect: businesses have a choice between a reactive or a proactive approach. The analysis of Chapter 6 shows that due to the discontinuous nature of RFID implementations, business innovations based on ubiquitous computing technologies and thus competitive advantage are most likely when companies experiment with radically new ways of conducting business.

While supply chain applications are a relatively well understood area of ubiquitous commerce, the situation is more complex when one considers consumer applications, which are slow to emerge and remain largely ill defined. In Chapter 5, Gershman and Fano report on their experience with a variety of ubiquitous commerce systems and discuss the specific advantages that such systems have to offer. They argue that new kinds of services will result from three primary capabilities of ubiquitous devices: to provide a service channel for remote service providers through an "always on" connection, to inform these services about the local context of the user through an array of sensors, and to enable these services to affect things in the user environment through actuators and local communication links. These capabilities will enable an unprecedented degree of "customer intimacy" but will also require rethinking and redesigning of customer relationship management processes.

The provision of the ubiquitous commerce services envisioned by Gershman and Fano allow the combination of context, historical, location, and other personal data to dynamically alter the price of a product for each consumer in an approach known as price discrimination. This dynamic pricing has been used on the Internet before, but ubiquitous computing environments, because of their pervasiveness and transparent operation, offer sellers new powerful tools to silently implement such pricing strategies.

Price discrimination in a ubiquitous retail situation is the subject of Chapter 11 by Acquisti, where he discusses models of repeated interactions between sellers and their customers in which sellers use various ubiquitous computing to track customers over time. He extends such models to consider various cost specifications, multiple goods, and additional marketing strategies that may be natural applications in ubiquitous computing environments. The analysis developed by Acquisti indicates that the best opportunities for ubiquitous commerce are to be found where ubiquitous commerce transactions are combined with low marginal costs of providing products augmented with personalized services.

## 1.5 Ubiquitous Commerce and Society

While tracking and price discrimination strategies will be important marketing tools for ubiquitous commerce providers, they also present considerable risks for consumers – notably, the invasion of their privacy. This is the question discussed in Chapter 12, where Garfinkel provides an in-depth review of the issues in the particular case of RFID retail. Garfinkel reviews several case studies and relates it to the attitudes of individuals and modern culture. He also examines recent technical mechanisms introduced as a way to address the implications of RFID implementations. He concludes that a solution to assuring consumer privacy with RFID would be to use policy implemented through regulation and licensing requirements. He then proceeds to develop his so-called "bill of rights" that define the rights of consumers.

Regulation is also the subject of Chapter 9 by Pitkänen. Rather than concentrating on the implications of ubiquitous commerce for the consumer, Pitkänen examines the legal provisions that can affect the development and the structuring of this market. Indeed, legal systems must take into account numerous interests and seek to balance diverging and often conflicting principles. Their purpose is to develop structures to facilitate business by diminishing risks, establishing an environment of trust, and thus enabling effective business methods. Pitkänen concludes that legal challenges affecting the development of ubiquitous commerce systems will be related to aspects of use and ownership of personal data, intellectual property rights, and contracts.

Another part of society that will have to deal with the consequences of ubiquitous commerce are workers. In Chapter 10, Salvador, Anderson and Sherry note that where technologies have been adopted in retail establishments, they have been used primarily to rationalize operations but often the result has been to constrain human behavior. While Chapter 5 speaks to the potential for retail operations to profit by removing humans from the system, Salvador, Anderson and Sherry offer a complementary perspective: with the right attitude and perspective, ubiquitous computing systems can be designed explicitly to enable and collaborate with the worker, encouraging a human-machine retail system that values the clerk. They conclude by proposing a model for the design of such systems developed on the concept of agency and identify the specific types of actions that can extend its effectiveness.

## 1.6 New Frontiers for Electronic Business

This book is the first attempt to explore the ubiquitous and pervasive commerce landscape. While technology and business are seen by many as dominant factors over culture, it is a society's culture and the culture of the material environment that defines our values, sensibilities, and commitments. Ubiquitous commerce presents unique opportunities but also introduces considerable risk that must be managed. Managing risk is a core function of modern society and in doing so societies depend on their experts. Experts take risks on behalf of society and are responsible to realize the full extent of a particular set of dangers and the risks associated with a particular technology. Failure to do so compromises the very idea of expertise and their ability to act on behalf of the public [6].

For those involved in ubiquitous commerce, irrespective of their particular viewpoint, it is our collective responsibility to confront and address the challenges ubiquitous commerce introduces. How we deal with these issues will determine public perception of not only RFID but potentially of the whole range of emerging ubiquitous computing technologies and their chances of wider adoption.

Finally, while the initial entitlement of individuals to control their data is relatively well recognized, the economic mechanisms of coercion based on price discrimination are less so. Such mechanisms are mediated via the identities of the organizations and public institutions and this is where most of the tension will occur. Dealing effectively with misuse will become a priority in the near future.

While RFID use in the supply chain will soon become common at the SKU-level, item-level tagging will remain restricted to high value products for he foreseeable future. Yet, RFID is only one of a variety of sensor technologies that can be used to develop individualized consumer services, which are important in achieving high accuracy of differential pricing strategies. While businesses, individuals and societies alike struggle to cope with this plethora of new data sources and their numerous implications for privacy, new mechanisms for commercial use of private data will be introduced; the learnt behavior of shopping will change; and consumer activism will increase.

## References

1. I.F. Akyildiz, W. Su, Y. Sankarasubramaniam, and E. Cayirci. "A Survey on Sensor Networks". *Computer Networks*, 38: 393–422. 2002.
2. J. Hightower and G. Borriello. "Location Systems for Ubiquitous Computing". *IEEE Computer*, 34(8): 57–66. 2001.
3. J.W. Cortada. *Information Technology as Business History: Issues in the History and Management of Computers*. Greenwood Press. Westport, CT, USA. 1996.

4. K. Fujinami and T. Nakajima. "Towards System Software for Physical Space Applications. *Proc. 2005 ACM Symposium Applications of Computing*, 2: 1613–1620. 2005.
5. J. Gehrke and S. Madden. "Query Processing in Sensor Networks". *IEEE Pervasive Computing*, 3(1): 46–55. 2004.
6. A. Giddens. *The Consequences of Modernity*. Polity Press. Cambridge, UK. 1990.
7. P. Kourouthanassis and G. Roussos. "Developing Consumer-Friendly Pervasive Retail Systems". *IEEE Pervasive Computing*, 2(2): 32–39. 2003.
8. G. Roussos, S. Maglavera and A. Marsh. "Enabling Pervasive Computing with Smart Phones". *IEEE Pervasive Computing*, 4(2): 10–17. 2005.

# Part I

# Technology

# 2

## Supply Chain Management Standards in Ubiquitous Commerce

George Roussos

## 2.1 Introduction

On Thursday the 29th of November 1951 at the offices of J. Lyons & Co[1] LEO (Lyons Electronic Office) became the first ever software used to conduct business. The purpose of this software application was to calculate the amount and cost of raw materials required to meet the nationwide orders for bread placed with the company [5, 8]. Until then, the massive computing machines of the time had only been used for military or scientific applications.

To be sure, LEO was a far-sighted application of information technology for business that initiated a trend which resulted today in having computer systems embedded into and controlling many supply chains. Yet, it is also true that in other ways we have not truly met or progressed much further than LEO's aims. These laudable aims were for computers to support and improve the efficiency of business processes through a thorough understanding of the objectives of those business users.

Indeed, the Holy Grail sought by businesses and government alike in supply chain applications – ranging from supplying fresh food from the farm to the supermarket shelf to delivering uniforms from the manufacturer to the soldier in the desert – is to keep the process simple, standard, speedy, and certain [9, 10]. To achieve this goal, it is necessary that all participants in the supply chain exchange information frequently and accurately, that supply chain costs be minimized, and that all goods and services moving through the supply

---

[1] J. Lyons & Co. was founded in 1887 to became one of the largest catering and food manufacturing companies in the world. Lyons made its name as the provider of cupcakes served at its tea shops and Corner House cafes by their historic 'Nippy' waitresses. At its height, Lyons owned the ubiquitous Baskin Robbins and Dunkin Donuts brands. However, in the 1970s the company was severely affected by the high interest rates due to the UK being hit by recession and an oil crisis and in 1978 was acquired by Allied Breweries Ltd. Lyons survived for several years under new management but eventually was sold in parts to pay for acquisitions associated with the drinks trade, and finally became defunct in 1998.

chain be unequivocally identifiable at all times. An essential element to any solution that can meet these requirements is the use of open, worldwide data standards for globally unique product identifiers and product classification systems, combined with internetworked information services that can be used to track and trace goods and services.

The role of open supply chains is becoming even more important with the emergence of ubiquitous and pervasive commerce. Indeed, high product visibility and the free-flow of information across the supply chain are required elements of highly automated systems that can link physical product items to their associated information. Only this level of interoperability and internetworking can support the machine-to-machine interactions that form the basis of ubiquitous commerce systems. Thus, open shared specifications describing every aspect of business activity are at the heart of pervasive commerce systems and effectively compose the fabric of all types of business activity built upon ubiquitous computing infrastructures.

In the remainder of this chapter, we will first review the history of unique identifier and product classification systems and their use in supply chain management applications. Then, we will provide an overview of the EAN.UCC system, including its more recent specifications for the wireless auto-identification of products at the item level as well as related information services for tracking and tracing products on the Internet. Finally, we will examine global cataloguing schemes and standards for inter-organizational information exchange. We will conclude with a brief discussion of the role of standards for the development of open supply chains and how these contribute to the construction of value networks.

## 2.2 Unique Identifiers in Supply Chain Management

Unique product identifiers are not new: almost every person in the world is familiar with the use of bar codes and bar code scanners in retailing. It is already over thirty years since the first bar code was scanned on a 10-pack of Wrigleys Juicy Fruit chewing gum in a supermarket in Troy, Ohio, and the collected identifier used for a commercial transaction. Since then, supply chain automation has become ubiquitous and the use of bar codes has spread from retailers to suppliers and ultimately to the suppliers' supplier. Moreover, recent developments have defined other varieties of printed bar codes to carry additional information (for example, sell by dates or product weight) and to deal with different environments (including pallets, locations, and returnable assets). Of late, specialist formats have also been employed in specific situations, for example the datamatrix standard for small items used to mark surgical instruments, and new services have been introduced as in the case of global data synchronization (more on this in Section 2.3).

The most recent interest in radio frequency identification (RFID) and the use of electronic product codes through the EPCglobal system in supply chain activities is in essence the extension of the concept of unique identifiers to ubiquitous commerce. For example, TESCO, one of the largest UK retailers, are carrying out extensive trials of RFID for which they have already coined the term "radio bar codes"[2] while Accenture, a business and innovation consultancy, view the use of RFID in supply chains as the introduction of "silent commerce."[3]

### 2.2.1 The Early History of Bar Codes

The history of modern bar coding begins in the 1940s, when the president of an American food chain raised the possibility of a system that could read product information automatically at the checkout. Norman Woodland and Bernard Silver at Drexel University, Philadelphia, created such a system by encoding information in combinations of concentric circles printed on paper which they subsequently patented in 1949. However, a critical problem with this solution was the inability at the time to automatically input the encoded product identifier in a computer system. It was the advent of lasers during the mid-1960s that made reading bar codes practicable. For this reason the initial idea received little attention in the grocery sector until 1968 when RCA (which in the meantime had acquired the Woodland patent) developed a similar symbol and corresponding scanner. This early system was operational for 18 months in 1972-73 in a Kroger store in Cincinnati, Ohio [1].

Bar coding was also investigated in the rail industry as a means of tracking individual railway wagons. By 1962, Sylvania Corporation had designed a system using optical scanning devices to read orange and blue colored bars on a non-reflective black background. By 1968 the colors were eliminated, and by 1971 about 95% of all railway wagons had been bar coded. At that point only 120 scanners had been installed, and recession in the mid 1970s led to the system being abandoned.

Because of these and other efforts in this area, it became apparent that separate groups could develop different and incompatible systems for product identification that could considerably hinder the wider acceptance of a common standard in the long run. For this reason, in 1969 the American National Association of Food Chains (NAFC), assisted by McKinsey & Co, a business consulting firm, proposed a product marking system to a group of senior representatives of all sections of the grocery industry, including manufacturers, retailers, and retail associations. The result of these efforts was the recommendation in 1973 by the Ad Hoc Committee of the Grocery Industry of the Universal Product Code (UPC), a ten digit code (five digits for the manufacturer and five for the product line) and a symbol design that would be printed

---

[2]The vision of TESCO for RFID is discussed at: http://www.tesco.com/radiobarcodes/

[3]The vision of Accenture on silent commerce is discussed at: http://www.accenture.com/silentcommerce.

on products by the manufacturer. By the end of 1973 over 800 manufacturers had been allocated prefix numbers, and the following year scanners from IBM and NCR were supplied to retailers. History records the first commercial scanning of a UPC bar code took place at 8.01 am on 26 June 1974, when Clyde Dawson of Marsh Supermarkets bought a 10-pack of Wrigley's Juicy Fruit chewing gum in Troy, Ohio [4].

### 2.2.2 Bar Code Maturity

One of the main ingredients of the bar code success was indeed the development of UPC, a common standard for the representation of the information held in bar codes. A critical aspect of this work is the allocation of prefix numbers to companies, a task that was assigned to the Uniform Grocery Product Code Council established for this purpose in 1971. When in 1974 the council changed its name to Uniform Product Code Council it had over 3,000 members. Since 1984 the council is known under its current name, the Uniform Code Council (UCC). It is perhaps characteristic that typical American humility dictated naming this solution the *Universal* Product Code. The trouble was that not only was it not universal, but it did not even extend beyond North America. Soon after their introduction, Europeans took over these ideas, made them truly international, and improved upon them in several ways: where the UPC concentrated on the retail point of sale, Europeans took a supply chain perspective. Where UPC insisted on a code containing system identification, manufacturer identification and product identification, Europe decided on a "blind" identity number: one where you cannot read meaning into particular digits.

The decision to adopt this approach rather than UPC was made by a core group of collaborating companies, which formed for this reason as early as 1977 under the European Article Numbering (EAN) system. EAN worked closely with its national counterparts such as the UK based Article Number Association[4] (ANA). This collaboration was uncommon within the fiercely competitive consumer goods sector, and they clearly identified the necessity of collaboration on common open standards which would allow for a bar code to represent beyond doubt a particular product.

The output of the European work was the EAN system, which still has the idea of blind identity codes at its very core. This design decision has enabled the system to expand well beyond fast moving consumer goods into many different sectors, notably defence, healthcare and construction. Moreover, the separation of data from the data carrier has enabled the introduction of more types of bar code symbols in addition to the original EAN specifications. This flexibility extends to the new radio frequency tags (cf. Section 3.2), whilst maintaining stability in the standard and backward compatibility. The focus

---

[4]EAN has evolved today into GS1 (previously the e.centre) which is responsible for the EAN.UCC system in the UK.

on *item identity* rather than *product information* in automatic data capture has provided great efficiencies over the years, and yet it seems to suit well operation over the Internet.

The success of the EAN system extends well beyond Europe. In 1981, EANA was renamed to International Article Numbering Association (IANA), but is still frequently known as EAN International. Today, EAN codes are used across the world except North America, where UPC is still the dominant form, although several provisions ensure that the two systems are compatible. In 1990, EAN and UCC formalized this status-quo and co-managed global standards for identification of products, shipping units, assets, locations, and services, as well as a variety of other business standards that have become known as the EAN.UCC system (discussed in some detail in Section 2.3). In 2003, EAN International and UCC agreed on a 'sunrise' date of January 2005, after which time all systems in the USA should be able to scan an EAN-13 number. In addition, UCC formally joined EAN International and to complete the global integration of EAN International have re-launched globally as GS1, resulting in UCC being re-named GS1 US in June 2005.[5]

### 2.2.3 The Anatomy of an EAN Bar Code

At this point it is worth examining a typical EAN bar code (cf. Figure 2.1). An EAN bar code is a symbol which represents a unique identifier for a product following the Global Trade Item Number (GTIN) specification, as a string of 13 digits. This symbol can be read into a computer system using a (portable or fixed) low power laser scanner which can translate the sequence of white and black bars into the corresponding digits.

While the encoded number has no meaning, it follows a defined structure to ensure that each number for a product line is unique, including a unique number assigned to each user. The first two digits indicate the numbering system used (in this case EAN-13), the following five digits represent the manufacturer of the product, the next five digits are the product code, and the last digit is the checksum digit used to confirm that the code has been retrieved correctly. The manufacturer code is assigned to the particular business by EAN, while the digits corresponding to the product code are selected by the manufacturer.

It is important to observe that this number does not include any classification information in it – information about the industrial sector, the country or the region where the product was manufactured, or the type of product (for example clothing, food, electronic device, and so forth) cannot be retrieved from the code. It is simply a unique identifier (a key in database parlance), and to obtain associated product information it is necessary to query a related product information repository. Moreover, the unique identifier characterizes the product (one can of orange juice made by the Squeezed Juice company)

---

[5]Visit www.gs1.org for more details.

5 012345 678900 >

**Fig. 2.1.** A typical example of an EAN-13 bar code.

rather than a particular instance of the product (the can of Squeezed Juice orange juice I hold in my hand at this moment).

### 2.2.4 Application-Specific Identification Schemes

Outside the EAN.UCC development, other bar code symbols have been developed, mostly designed to address particular industrial applications. Some of the most widely used schemes are briefly discussed in this section.

*Codabar*, invented in 1972, is a variable length symbology which uses the ten digits plus six additional special characters. It is often used in libraries, medical facilities, photo-finishing, and airline tickets. In particular, the American Blood Commission selected codabar in 1977 as the standard for use in blood banks.

*Code 39*, also invented in 1974, uses both letters and numbers and is widely used internally by vertical industrial sectors. *Code 93* and *Code 128* are updates of Code 39 introduced in 1981 and can represent the 128 ASCII (American Standard Code for Information Interchange) characters. Code 128 in particular represents pairs of numbers in one character symbol to reduce the space required to print numeric data. *UCC/EAN-128* is a special subset of Code 128 reserved for users of the EAN.UCC system and was introduced in 1989 to allow users to provide extra information about products in a single bar code.

*Interleaved Two of Five Code* (ITF) was first developed in the mid-1970s, and in its current form ITF-14 is used widely by companies as part of the EAN.UCC system to mark outer cases. This bar code is well suited to printing on corrugated board because of its simplicity since it uses only two different widths of bars and spaces.

Multi-row or two-dimensional bar codes have been developed in the 1980s and 1990s as a means of reducing the space taken up by conventional linear bar codes. Examples of these include Code 49, Code 16K, Code 1, Codablock, MaxiCode, and PDF 417. In 2002 EAN.UCC published details of new reduced space and composite symbologies which were in development since the late 1990s. These symbols are two-dimensional and are designed to be used alongside the existing EAN.UCC bar codes in specific industrial and retail applications, where either very small bar codes or detailed information is required.

## 2.3 The EAN.UCC System

EAN.UCC is a system for uniquely numbering and automatically identifying products, services, companies, trading locations, logistics units, and assets (for a history of this system refer to Section 2.2). Today, EAN.UCC forms the basis of interoperable solutions for asset tracking, traceability, collaborative planning, order management, and logistics.

The EAN.UCC community currently consists of more than 100 national organizations operating across 133 countries, employing over 1,500 staff. Over a million member companies worldwide use the EAN.UCC system and every day more than five billion transactions are made using EAN.UCC standards. EAN national organizations play a critical role within this community. On the one hand they help their members implement current bar coding systems and business-to-business communications such as Electronic Data Interchange (EDI), and on the other, they represent their corresponding countries in international initiatives for new standards and solutions, including the emerging Electronic Business Extensible Mark-up Language (ebXML) for business communications, reduced space symbology (RSS) bar codes, radio frequency identification (RFID) tags, and the EPCglobal network. In the UK in particular, GS1 UK is the EAN national organization and one of the founder members of EAN International. GS1 is a not-for-profit association and serves more than 17,000 member companies by supporting and further developing the EAN.UCC system in this country.

EAN.UCC standards address three areas: Part I deals with unique identifiers for products, companies, and so forth and data standards for attribute encoding. Part II relates to the encoding of this information into data carriers such as bar codes and RFID tags. Finally, Part III sets data standards for automatic electronic communication through supply chains, including conventional EDI standards that are still mostly employed for business-to-business communications in closed networks as well as the emerging ebXML family of standards for open supply chains based on the Unified Modelling Language (UML) and the Extensible Markup Language (XML).

Overall, the aim of EAN.UCC is to support the efficient operation and management of supply chains and thus create added value for the consumer (cf. Section 8.2 of Chapter 8 for a more detailed discussion of value chain efficiency and the Efficient Consumer Response initiative). EAN.UCC is a complex system in perpetual development. In the following section we will discuss each aspect of this system in turn and show how the different components combine to construct a universal "language" to conduct business.

### 2.3.1 Types of EAN.UCC Unique Identifiers

In addition to the product codes that we have discussed at length in Section 2.2, the EAN.UCC system[6] provides unambiguous numbers to identify goods containers, services, companies, locations, and assets worldwide. These numbers can be represented in bar code symbols or stored in RFID tags and transmitted wirelessly to enable their electronic reading wherever required by business processes. EAN.UCC also provides standard data structures characteristic for different supply chain applications. While an application is free to determine how EAN.UCC numbers are used, it is critical that each number be used in its entirety and not broken into constituent parts. Hence, EAN.UCC data structures guarantee worldwide uniqueness within a particular application area. In this section we will briefly review some of the EAN.UCC identifiers that are relevant to ubiquitous commerce since they provide digital representations to physical objects, locations, and organizations, as well as define corresponding rules of interaction.

An EAN.UCC code is made up of different parts, but it always contains the *company prefix* number. As the name implies, this is a unique number that has been assigned to the manufacturer of a product. Using the company prefix number is a core requirement of all EAN.UCC standards. The *global trade item* number (GTIN) is used for the unique identification of trade items worldwide. A trade item is any item (product or service) upon which there is a need to retrieve pre-defined information and that may be priced, ordered, or invoiced at any point in any supply chain. This includes individual items as well as all their different configurations in different types of packaging.

The *global location* number (GLN) is used to identify any company or physical, functional, or legal location. The *serial shipping container code* (SSCC) is a unique serial number used to identify logistics units individually. The *global returnable asset identifier* (GRAI) is used to identify a reusable entity that is normally used for transport and storage of goods. The *global individual asset identifier* (GIAI) is used to identify individually any entity that is part of the inventory of a given company, and whose lifetime history needs to be recorded. The *global service relation number* (GSRN) is used to identify the recipient of services in the context of a service relationship, for example a customer or patient.

The data structures and data carriers of the EAN.UCC system have been fully considered and approved by ISO. There are too many ISO standards to list here, but all developments have been considered under the aegis of the ISO/IEC JTC 1 Committee (Information Technology) and its sub-committee, SC 31, that is concerned with automatic identification and data capture techniques.

Recently, radio frequency identification (RFID) technology has reached maturity, and passive RFID tags can be produced at relatively low cost. Unlike

---

[6]The full EAN.UCC system standard specifications are freely available and can be found online at: http://www.gs1uk.org/txt_temp.asp?fid=294.

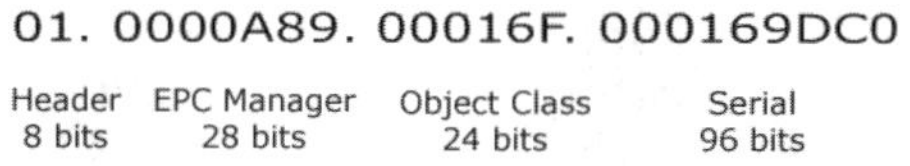

01. 0000A89. 00016F. 000169DC0

| Header<br>8 bits | EPC Manager<br>28 bits | Object Class<br>24 bits | Serial<br>96 bits |

**Fig. 2.2.** An example of the Electronic Product Code.

bar codes, which are still the primary data carriers for EAN.UCC codes, RFID tags do not require line of sight between tag and reader to transmit their content and are more resilient to damage during product transit. This new type of data carrier (discussed in more detailed in Section 3.2) created the need for a new numbering scheme which has become known as the *Electronic Product Code* (EPC).

Due to the higher data capacity of RFID, EPC can carry considerably higher information content across the supply chain. The current EPC Type 1 specification[7] defines a key length of 96 bits and in addition to manufacturer and product type codes incorporates a serial number which identifies unique items. Thus, using EPC it is possible to carry out *item-level tagging*, a capability that far exceeds that of bar codes. It is this aspect of the EPC system and the fact that RFID chips can be read from a distance without any visible effect that has created considerable concern with consumers (cf. Chapters 8 and 12 for a more detailed discussion of the implications of item-level tagging in consumer applications).

Each EPC number is made up of at least four parts (cf. Figure 2.2):

- The *header* (bits 0–7) identifies the length, type, structure, version, and generation of the particular EPC.
- The *manager number* (bits 8–35) identifies the supplier of the product.
- The *object class* (bits 36–59) identifies a product grouping within a particular scheme defined by the manager, and most often it would be a stock keeping unit (SKU) or a lot number.
- The *serial number* (bits 60–95) is the specific instance of the particular product within its object class, and it is exactly this field that allows for item-level tagging.

Additional fields may also be used as part of the EPC, for example to identify the shipping method such as the Shipping Container Code (SCC-14) and the Serial Shipping Container Code (SSCC-18). Application Identifiers (AI) can also be included as well as data used to encode and decode information from different numbering systems into human-readable forms.

---

[7]Complete EPC and other EPCglobal specifications are available on-line via: http://www.epcglobalinc.org/standards_technology/specifications.html and archived at: http://www.epcglobalinc.org/about/AutoID_archive.html.

**Fig. 2.3.** Clockwise from the top left: samples of UCC/EAN-128, EAN-13, EAN-8, ITF 14.

Following the traditional EAN.UCC approach, EPC codes are embedded within Physical Markup Language (PML) structures for transmission across the supply chain. PML is a simple XML-derived language that provides for other attributes of the physical object in addition to the EPC, including date, location, history, and access control credentials. In particular, PML messages are used to communicate with enterprize resource planning (ERP) middleware (cf. Chapter 3) and to query the Object Naming Service (ONS) (cf. Section 3.3).

### 2.3.2 Physical Representation of the EAN.UCC System

Bar code symbols, machine readable symbols printed to well defined specifications, are the primary data carriers used in the EAN.UCC system. Bar codes represent GTINs, the unique identifiers for a particular product line. The bar code itself consists of a rectangle comprising a series of light and dark parallel bars and is normally incorporated as part of the original packaging design or printed onto labels. Figure 2.3 shows four common bar code symbols: UCC/EAN-128, EAN-13, EAN-8, and ITF 14.

The latest developments in the system include new smaller bar codes, especially designed for use when space for bar codes is at a premium, such as on very small packages. These reduced space symbology bar codes are linear symbols, similar to the ones shown above, and can encode the GTIN for a product. A version of this bar code, namely RSS-14 expanded, can represent a GTIN and extra information about the product.

Composite components, which are small two-dimensional bar codes that can encode up to 2,338 data characters, have also been introduced. These will be usable above any of the EAN.UCC bar codes (except ITF-14) to provide extra information such as batch numbers, expiry dates, and so on. The main linear symbol acts as a finder pattern for the 2D element, so that the extra information cannot be decoded without decoding the linear component at the same time. The so-called Data Matrix format has also been defined and is specially designed to be used on healthcare equipment, such as scalpels and other surgical tools.

In the past few years a radically new type of EAN.UCC data carrier has been introduced based on radio frequency identification (RFID) technology, which uses radio waves to communicate EPC information as discussed in Section 3.2. Unlike bar codes, which encode data at optical or infrared wavelengths, RFID carries data programmed into its chip and operates at radio frequencies, typically 125 KHz, 13.56 MHz, 900MHz, and 2.45GHz. Although such chips can also integrate a battery, the most interesting case is that of the so-called passive tags, which use inductance to power up, process requests and transmit their EPC. This approach allows for tags to be independent of a power source and thus cost far less and be used for any period of time.

However, several incompatibilities and other technical problems were identified in the use of these frequencies, and currently work is underway for the so-called Generation 2 Class 1 RFID Interface specification, which operates at the UHF band. One of the principal advantages of the UHF band is that the effects of power absorbtion from the environment and the product itself are far less pronounced. This specification is intended for submission to ISO for acceptance as a standard, but several problems have hindered this process, not the least the existence of patents covering RFID in this frequency, which imply that the cost of the tag would be far higher than what was initially expected.

Similar to bar codes, RFID tags require a corresponding reader. In this case, however, in addition to querying and receiving EPC codes transmitted by the tags, the reader also provides power to the RFID chip. Reader specification and communication protocols have also been defined by EPCglobal. A notable recent addition to this specification has been the inclusion of the so-called "destroy" command which makes the tag incapable of transmitting its EPC (more details of its use and application can be found in Chapter 12). The way in which EAN.UCC-compliant RFID tags can be used in open supply chains is described in the immediately following section.

### 2.3.3 Data Communication on the EAN.UCC System

Defining unique identifiers, their physical representations and corresponding data structures is only the first of the required ingredients to deliver supply chain integration and improve its efficiency. What is also required is a common means to manage, exchange and aggregate this information in ways that promote visibility and thus openness across the supply chain. Several additional data communication components are required to achieve these tasks: messaging vocabularies, languages to describe business processes, electronic catalogues, global data exchanges, and last but not least repositories of global scale that can map codes to specific product items. EAN.UCC standards address all these requirements, and in this section we will discuss each component in turn.

### Electronic Messaging and Closed Supply Chains

Since the early 1960s the United Nations Directories for Electronic Data Interchange for Administration, Commerce and Transport (UN/EDIFACT) has been developing a comprehensive set of electronic messaging standard to promote business. The result has been a particularly complex and overloaded system that is hard to deploy and often leads to unnecessarily irksome implementations. For this reason, over the years several groups have defined subsets that satisfy the particular needs of specific industrial sectors, specific business processes, or specific supply chains. For example, EANCOM is an EDIFACT subset developed within the EAN.UCC system to support cross-border trade and covers the functions required to effect a complete trade transaction.

Another case of EDI vocabulary within a specific market segment of the EAN.UCC system is the Trading Data Communications standard (TRADA-COMS). TRADACOMS was developed in the early 1980s by ANA, the predecessor of the the EAN National organization in the UK, and employs EAN codes for product identification. At the time, several leading companies including Woolworth's, Boots and Tesco were attempting to establish electronic communications with their suppliers but encountered resistance because of different and incompatible message structures and content. Successful implementation of TRADACOMS in trials allowed electronic invoicing to become law, and indeed the system is still widely used in retail applications.

### ebXML and global repositories

EDI was created for closed, proprietary networks and in many ways it is not suitable for use over the Internet. It has been designed primarily as an one-to-one technology and has limited flexibility. Moreover, the requirements for the development and operation of an EDI-based system have proven in practice to be quite significant and hardly affordable by small and medium sized companies. As a result, until recently relatively small businesses have been excluded from participating in electronic data exchanges.

To cater to the new business opportunities opened up by the Internet, the Organization for the Advancement of Structured Information Standards[8] (OASIS) has been developing the electronic business extensible mark-up language (ebXML). Unlike EDI, ebXML assumes that the communications substrate is the Internet and aims to provide a modular rather than a rigid set of specifications for conducting business. An additional benefit is that by being developed on open, well understood Internet standards, expertise on ebXML can be relatively easily developed and supported on the same systems used

---

[8]OASIS web site at: http://www.oasis-open.org

to support consumer electronic commerce. Thus, the cost for business can be considerably reduced.

ebXML is a massive set of specifications which aims to make e-business possible anywhere on the globe, for any company, of any size, in any industry [7]. It is thus impossible to even summarize the different areas it covers in the space of this chapter, but a brief overview of the different areas covered by the specification is in place here:

- **Messaging.** The ebXML messaging functions are a straightforward extension of the EDI functionality and follow the standard envelope-and-message format developed for the Simple Object Access Protocol (SOAP). In ebXML, business data are enclosed in SOAP envelopes and transmitted over the Internet.
- **Business Processes.** ebXML uses standard modelling languages and charting tools, notably the Unified Modelling Language (UML), to systematically capture the flow of business data among trading partners and to represent this business knowledge in a standard format. The systematic definition of specific business processes is then used as the basis for common message sequences across industry boundaries, and several such processes have been recorded in detail.
- **Trading Partner Profiles and Agreements.** In addition to the modelling of specific processes, ebXML also provides systematic representation of company capabilities to conduct e-business in the so-called Collaboration Protocol Profile (CPP). Using the CPP, a company can list the industries, business processes, messages, and data-exchange technologies that it supports. Then, trading partners can use their CPPs to specify Collaborative Protocol Agreements (CPA) that define the business processes, messages, and technologies used to exchange business messages.
- **Registries and Repositories.** ebXML Registries are shared repositories that hold descriptions of industry processes, messages, and vocabularies used to define the transactions exchanged with trading partners in CPP and CPA formats. Such repositories can be queried by other business to retrieve details of e-business capabilities for inspection so as to locate companies with the capabilities desired in forming partnerships.
- **Core Components.** ebXMl Core Components (CC) are standardized XML schemas that represent the core entities involved in ebXML scenarios. CCs are lower level descriptions of the main entities that participate in business transactions and can be viewed as the extension of the traditional EAN.UCC data structures, updates for use on the Internet, and open supply chains operating on the Internet.

The final component required for effective data dissemination in the supply chain according to the EAN.UCC vision has been developed by the Global Commerce Initiative (GCI) working group of EAN, in the form of the Global Data Synchronization (GDS) repository specification [2]. GDS supports master data alignment, that is accurate and synchronized databases for products, prices, promotions, and locations across a supply chain. In practice, the GDS repository forms the basis of a shared electronic catalogue between supply chain partners and plays a critical role in increasing the efficiency of transactions by increasing the quality of information across all supply chain activities. In particular, GDS improves the accuracy of orders, invoices and other business documents; reduces the number of delivery errors; and last but not least, reduces the administrative work related to the maintenance of product and location information.

### 2.3.4 EPCglobal

In Section 1.2 we briefly discuss RFID tags, the most recent data carrier for electronic product information, which allow for the automatic identification of objects without the need for any manual intervention. Yet, although the storage capacity of an RFID chip far exceeds that of a bar code, it is still limited and thus it is hardly feasible to store on it more than simple information, for example the EPC number that corresponds to the product as discussed in Section 3.1. As a result, similar to bar codes, unless product identifiers can be mapped to the physical description and the other product information details, this information is of limited usefulness. Of course, it would be desirable that this mapping would also be carried out automatically between the retailer and manufacturer systems, for example.

This is exactly the purpose of the EPCglobal network,[9] a set of draft specifications that define a network of global scale, overlaid on top of the Internet, that offers directory and information services that link any EPC code to all information available about the product from its manufacturer. In fact, this electronic directory service is closely linked to the Domain Name System (DNS) which maps computer hosts and network names to their IP addresses on the Internet.

EPCglobal has two main components, namely the Object Name Service (ONS) and the EPC Information Service (EPC IS). ONS is in essence a directory service which maps a particular EPC code to a Uniform Resource Identifier (URI), an encoding of the name and address syntax of objects on the Internet defined by the World-Wide-Web Consortium (W3C) – a special case of which is the URL. In fact, because the operation of the ONS is very similar to that of the DNS, EPCglobal envisions that ONS services will be deployed on top of existing DNS infrastructures, a provision detailed in the ONS draft specification. The retrieved URI points to the EPC IS of the product manufacturer (or more generally to the EPC Manager responsible for the particular product item) and may incorporate the access mode of the partic-

---

[9]The operation of the EPCglobal network is illustrated at: http://www.epcglobalus.org/Network/Network.html with more detailed information, including draft specification for the ONS and EPC IS services, available via the Auto-ID Labs web site at: http://www.autoidlabs.org/.

ular server, for example the particular ebXML CC schema that must be used to query the service or any other appropriate protocol.

EPCglobal allows for the whole process of product identification and association with particular data to be completely automated. Indeed, at no stage of this process is it necessary for a human to be involved. Combining the EPCglobal with GDS repositories provides an even more powerful capability: to access full product traceability information, that is to have a complete history of the product from the time it was created until it has reached the consumer. This information can be potentially augmented with additional information, for example regarding environmental conditions during its transversal of the supply chain to prove that storage conditions have been fully observed throughout.

It should be noted that EPCglobal is a work in progress and considerable changes should be expected to its operation. Of particular concern are trust management issues and verification of the quality of the information held in the system, and more work on this will be required in the near future.

## 2.4 The Role of Standardization for Ubiquitous Commerce

One of the lessons of the history of EAN.UCC is that standards are a critical component for business automation. Indeed, this chapter has already discussed many cases when market realities forced fierce competitors to collaborate to establish such standards. This need will only become more pressing with the emergence of ubiquitous and pervasive commerce systems that are fully dependent on machine-to-machine communications to carry out even the simpler transactions.

Given the central role that standardizations plays but also the considerable overhead of this globalized process, EAN International in collaboration with the Uniform Code Council agreed on the Global Standards Management Process (GSMP) to support standards development activity for the EAN.UCC system. The GSMP was developed to maintain standards-based solutions for global trade using EAN.UCC system technologies. The GSMP aims to produce a global consensus process to negotiate supply chain standards that are grounded on business needs and in consultation with users.

Standardization also has a clear business case in that it is the main ingredient for the creation of value networks, thats is combinations of internal and external resources needed to achieve the objectives of the business, that are efficient and adaptable especially to the rapid market changes observed in the modern environment [10]. Indeed, experience has shown that reducing costs, improving productivity, and increasing sales depends on visibility of the supply chain.

## 2.5 Summary

There is clear rationale for businesses to keep the supply chain process simple, standard, speedy, and certain. In the context of the emerging ubiquitous and pervasive computing technologies in particular, it is necessary that all participants in the supply chain exchange information frequently and accurately, that supply chain costs be minimized, and that all goods and services moving through the supply chain be unequivocally identifiable at all times.

Over the last fifty years information and communication technologies have achieved considerable progress towards open, worldwide data standards for globally unique product identifiers and product classification systems, combined with internetworked information services that can be used to track and trace goods and services. Managing this process of global scope is a major challenge and the EAN.UCC systems appears to be the most suitable candidate.

The scope and the effort required to achieve this level of standardization is certainly instructive for the pervasive computing paradigm as a whole, as it highlights the complexities and difficulties that must be overcome to provide truly seamless and indeed ubiquitous services to the end user.

## References

1. S.A. Brown. *Revolution at the Checkout Counter: The Explosion of the Bar Code*. Wertheim Publications in Industrial Relations. Harvard University Press. Cambridge, MA, USA. 1997.
2. Cap Gemini. *Global Data Synchronisation At Work in the Real World: Illustrating the Business Benefits*. Global Commerce Initiative. Whitepaper. March 2005.
3. GS1. *Bar Coding: Getting It Right*. Recommendations for best practice by GS1. Available online at: http://www.gs1uk.org/uploaded/doc_library/Bar%20code%20brochure403.pdf. March 2005.
4. A.L. Haberman. *Twenty-Five Years Behind Bars: The Proceedings of the Twenty-Fifth Anniversary of the U.P.C. at the Smithsonian Institution*. Wertheim Publications in Industrial Relations. Harvard University Press. Cambridge, MA, USA. 2001.
5. G. Ferry. *A Computer Called LEO: Lyons Teashops and the World's First Office Computer*. Fourth Estate. London, UK. 2003.
6. IBM Consulting. *EPC Roadmap*. Global Commerce Initiative. Whitepaper. November 2003.
7. A. Kotok and D.R.R. Webber. *ebXML: The New Global Standard for Doing Business on the Internet*. New Riders Publishing. Indianapolis, IN, USA. 2001.
8. F.F. Land. "LEO, the First Business Computer: A Personal Experience" in R.L. Glass (ed.): *In the Beginning: Recollections of Software Pioneers*: 134–153. IEEE Computer Society. Los Alamitos, CA, USA. 1997.
9. T. McGuffog. *The Virtual Enterprise*. Article Number Association UK. 1998.

10. T. McGuffog and N. Wadsley. "The general principles of value chain management". *Supply Chain Management* 4(5): 218–225. 1999.
11. R.C. Palmer. *The Bar Code Book: Comprehensive Guide to Reading, Printing, Specifying, and Applying Bar Code and Other Machine-Readable Symbols.* Helmers Publishing. Peterborough, NH, USA. 2001.

# 3

## Optimizing Business Processes by Automatic Data Acquisition: RFID Technology and Beyond

Gregor Hackenbroich, Christof Bornhövd, Stephan Haller, and Joachim Schaper

### 3.1 Introduction

Information technology and enterprise software form the backbone of enterprise operations. Enterprise resource planning (ERP) systems automate and control financial and administrative processes. Manufacturing systems structure complex production lines. Inventory and shipping systems help organize the shipment of products to the customer. The enormous success of enterprise software is the result of both business needs such as increasing internal efficiency and customer responsiveness, as well as of advances in computer and software technology.

The first wave of ERP systems took place in the early 1990s [13]. The implementation of such systems forced companies to understand, document, and streamline their internal processes. The benefit was a higher efficiency of the core financial, accounting, and controller functions. In this generation of systems the data for all business programs was integrated in one massive database. This allowed process integration but at the same time led to large ERP installations whose implementation and customization were difficult and expensive.

The 1990s saw the shift from the mainframe architecture to the three-tier client/server model. New applications emerged that could talk to other applications on a network leading to a new level of complexity and flexibility. The modules of enterprise applications grew and became larger components: sales and distribution became Customer Relationship Management (CRM), materials management became Supply Chain Management (SCM), and product development and manufacturing became Product Lifecycle Management (PLM). The functionality of these applications bundled in business suites coordinated the flow of work across departments, divisions, and even companies, thus leading to a high level of information and process integration.

This chapter focuses on the next generation of enterprise applications [2]: in addition to information and process integration it will allow for the automatic identification and tracking of real-world objects, as well as the automatic acquisition of additional data about these objects and their physical environments. The first such technology that currently enters large scale deployment is Radio Frequency Identification (RFID) [7], the contact-less electronic identification of objects through radio waves. RFID tags typically combine a modest storage capacity with a means of wirelessly communicating stored information like an electronic product code (EPC) to an RFID reader. In a supply chain management context, an object to be tagged is usually a pallet, a case or even a single sales item. Passive RFID tags require no on-board battery and can be read from a distance ranging from a few centimeters to a few meters. Active tags, on the other hand, come with an on-board battery which provides larger read ranges and memory sizes but also higher unit cost and size and a limited lifespan of typically 3-5 years.

RFID, however, is not the only emerging technology for object data acquisition: sensor nodes go beyond object identification and measure the status or condition of objects such as the object location, temperature, or acceleration [12]. Sensors equipped with processing and communication capabilities will be able to identify themselves, organize themselves into networks, and collaboratively perform simple business processes [1]. Networked embedded systems comprising even larger processing power as well as sensors and actuators will add intelligence to devices like cars, mining, or manufacturing equipment [10]. They will report the device status to backend systems or download from such systems business rules or software updates.

RFID tags, sensor networks, and networked embedded systems offer a range of devices for product integration; collectively we refer to objects equipped with such devices as *smart items*. The defining property of a smart item is that it can provide data about itself and that it has the ability to communicate this information [9]. Integration of smart items into business information systems can provide businesses with more accurate and timely data about their operations and can help streamline and automate the operations themselves. This leads to cost reduction and additional benefits like increased asset visibility, improved responsiveness, and extended business opportunities. However, bridging the gap between the physical and the digital world requires a flexible and scalable system architecture to integrate automatic data acquisition with existing business processes.

In this chapter, we discuss the kinds of changes that have to be made for enterprise systems to take into account smart items information and also the kinds of business applications that can be built if such information is available. As a specific example, we discuss *SAP's Auto-ID Infrastructure* (AII), which converts object data into business process information by associating it with specified mapping rules and metadata. These mapping rules can feed incoming observation data directly to business processes running on either SAP or non-SAP backend systems, execute predefined business logic, or simply record the data in a persistent store for later analysis.

The remainder of this chapter is organized as follows: in Section 3.2 we describe enterprise software in more detail, focusing on SAP's supply chain management solution [3]. We point out the improvements that Auto-ID technology can bring to SCM. We then address the requirements on Auto-ID systems (Section 3.3) and introduce the architecture of SAP's AII (Section 3.4). Section 5 discusses cases studies that were performed with a research prototype of the AII. Section 3.6 summarizes open research issues. And finally, we summarise our findings in Section 3.7.

## 3.2 Enterprise Software for Supply Chain Management

The adoption of RFID technology by leading retailers has created a large momentum for automatic product identification and ubiquitous technologies in general. To fully unfold the potential of such technologies, object data must be linked to product and asset information kept in business information systems. This involves a number of conceptual and technical challenges that result both from the object identification technology and the business application in question.

This section provides a closer look at the business applications, with a twofold goal: first to impart the reader with basic knowledge of business information systems, and second to introduce a class of business processes that will integrate ubiquitous technologies very soon. An exhaustive discussion of enterprise software applications is beyond the scope of this chapter; therefore we focus on solutions for supply chain management where the business value of Auto-ID technologies is most evident. A discussion of asset management solutions and the benefit that RFID support will bring to them can be found in Chapter 4 by Lampe, Strasser, and Fleisch.

Figure 3.1 depicts the interplay of selected SCM components with ERP systems and ubiquitous devices. For definiteness, we discuss solutions and use the terminology of SAP's enterprise software [8]. The components that reside in backend-systems reside within the top layer; they include the ERP system as well as components for supply chain and data management such as Warehouse Management (WM), Advanced Planner & Optimizer (APO), Supply Chain Event Management (EM), and the Business Information Warehouse (BW) (the functionality of these components will be described below). The business applications exchange data with the Auto-ID Infrastructure that collects and aggregates RFID and sensor data.

The purpose of supply chain support solutions is to provide businesses with all software necessary to analyze, control, operate, and plan its supply chain activities. Within SAP's supply chain management four applications support this task: Supply Chain Networking provides customers, suppliers and partners with a unified view on the activities within the supply chain; Supply Chain Planning synchronizes and optimizes planning activities; Supply Chain Execution deals with all production, procurement and transaction activities; and Supply Chain Coordination helps partners to assess both performance and risks and provides notification upon detection of unexpected

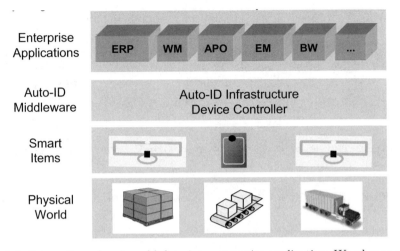

**Fig. 3.1.** Integration of real-world data into enterprise application. Warehouse management (WM), Advanced Planning & Optimizer (APO), and Event Management (EM) are SCM applications.

events. While offering a broad range of functionalities, these applications can still only address particular aspects of the supply chain. To provide a global view on all processes within the supply chain, SCM solutions must also integrate financial and business data; for example, financial data is required for analyzing the costs of supply chain processes. Likewise, Key Performance Indicators (KPIs) obtained from business intelligence systems are crucial for monitoring and controlling the supply chain. As a consequence, SCM solutions must tightly integrate with ERP and Business Warehouse systems.

To select the software components and business processes that gain most value upon integration with ubiquitous technologies, SAP performed an extensive market analysis. That analysis involved customer surveys, workshops, and customer councils. Key business problems that customers need to solve include poor data quality, limited supply chain and inventory visibility, and the substantial amount of manual labor involved in checking and managing incoming and outgoing goods. The components WM, APO, EM, and BW depicted in 3.1 address these problems but can be improved by automatic data acquisition as we show below.

WM deals with all processes relevant within a warehouse, including picking and packing, moving and storing goods, and in/outbound delivery. Warehouse management is facilitated by the integration of mobile devices that workers use to enter and retrieve reliable information about goods stored and moved through warehouse locations. BW may be thought of as a metadatabase. It integrates all databases that an enterprise has in place, guarantees a consistent view on the respective data, and generates from this data Key Performance Indicators. These, in turn, are exploited by the SCM planning system. The

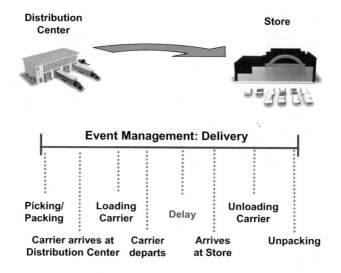

**Fig. 3.2.** Sequence of events in a delivery process. In traditional enterprise systems events must be reported manually. An RFID-enabled solution automatically generates events, thus allowing for automatic real-time supply chain planning and execution. SAP's Auto-ID Infrastructure supports the processes packing/unpacking and loading/unloading.

focus of BW is on the quick integration of huge amounts of data (in the Terabyte-range) from all possible sources within the enterprise. Finally, EM is an application for monitoring, managing, and tracking the progress of supply chain activities. Activities are represented in terms of events like start production/end production, packing/unpacking etc. For each event one can define assessment and execution rules (for example follow-up activities to be executed upon late deliveries). In addition, notification rules specify the persons and systems to be notified, for example in case of alerts, together with the respective communication channels.

To allow for automatic decision making, EM makes use of complex rule engines that take into account correlations along the full supply network including production planning. EM simulates the logistic processes and the correlation of events such as order compliance and replenishment of materials. The system continuously monitors events and detects when they happen outside of predefined tolerances. This allows quick identification of supply chain disturbances so the system can proceed according to the respective exception rules. If, for example, the quality of preliminary products is reported to be outside the allowed tolerance, then planning and scheduling systems get this information and calculate a new plan. A sequence of typical events for a delivery from a distribution center to a store is shown in Figure 3.2.

The sequence of events highlights some of the improvements that smart items technologies can bring to enterprise systems: in traditional enterprise systems events must be reported manually; this is time-consuming, event reporting is not guaranteed, and the process is error-prone. By contrast, RFID-enabled event management ensures accurate, real-time event data that, in turn, improves supply chain execution and optimization. In addition to improving existing processes, smart items technology may generate new processes, e.g., automatic gates can monitor the movement of goods within the store. For example, the system can determine if goods are still in the store back room or already on the shop floor. We discuss this process in one of the case studies below. We note that some of the events shown in Figure 3.2 can be automatically reported using RFID technology and passive tags. In particular this holds for packing/unpacking and loading/unloading, which are already supported by SAP's Auto-ID Infrastructure. Automatic reporting of delays will probably require the use of active tags or sensor nodes.

## 3.3 Auto-ID System Requirements

The existing architecture for our Auto-ID Infrastructure has been developed with the following system requirements in mind:

**Scalability.** Companies like large retailers are assumed to require throughput rates of about 60 billion items per annum [11]. Assuming 100 distribution centers, each with an average of five checking points per item, the system needs to guarantee an average throughput of at least 100 messages per second per distribution center. The size of an observation message can be assumed to be around 200 bytes, and the processing of an incoming observation message usually requires multiple database updates and the execution of business procedures at the backend system.

**Open System Architecture.** In addition to being hardware-agnostic, the architecture should be based on existing communication protocols like TCP/IP and HTTP, as well as syntax and semantics standards like XML, PML [8] and EPC [4]. This will allow the use of sensors from a wide array of hardware providers and will support the deployment of Auto-ID solutions across institutional or even country boundaries.

**Efficient Event Filtering.** The infrastructure needs to provide efficient means to filter out false or redundant readings from RFID or sensor devices. Also, it needs to provide flexible and configurable filtering of events to pass on only relevant information to the appropriate backend processes.

**Event Aggregation.** The infrastructure needs to support the composition of multiple related events to more complex events for further processing. For example, the system must allow the composition of individual object identification events for multiple individual cases and the corresponding pallet to only one complete-pallet-detected event.

**Flexibility.** The infrastructure needs to be adaptable to different business scenarios. Furthermore, the infrastructure needs to provide flexible means at the business logic layer to respond to abnormal situations, like the missing of

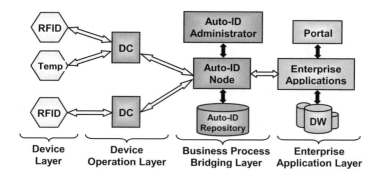

**Fig. 3.3.** System architecture of the SAP Auto-ID Infrastructure.

expected goods or company-internal re-routing of goods. To avoid redundant implementations of the same business rules in different enterprise applications, the infrastructure needs to offer means to deploy and execute them within the Auto-ID Infrastructure.

**Distribution of System Functionality.** A real deployment of an Auto-ID solution can be distributed across sites, across companies, or even across countries. This naturally requires a distributed system architecture. As a first step, we require that the Auto-ID Infrastructure supports the distribution of message pre-processing functionality (for example, filtering and aggregation) and, to some degree, business logic across multiple nodes to better map to existing company and cross-company structures.

**System Administration and Test Support.** The infrastructure must provide support for the testing of individual custom components used in the filtering and aggregation of events, as well as the end-to-end processing of RFID and sensor data. Good administration and testing support is a prerequisite for the deployment of a distributed Auto-ID solution in large-scale applications.

## 3.4 System Overview

The architecture of our Auto-ID Infrastructure (AII) is shown in Figure 3.3. Conceptually, it can be divided into the following four system layers.

At the Device Layer, different types of sensor devices can be supported via a hardware-independent abstraction layer. It consists of the basic operations for reading and writing data and a publish/subscribe interface to report observation events. By implementing this API, different kinds of smart item devices can be deployed within the Auto-ID infrastructure. Besides RFID readers, these devices can include environmental sensors, or PLC devices. The Device Operation Layer coordinates multiple devices. It also provides functionality to filter, condense, aggregate, and adjust received sensor data before passing it on to the next layer. This layer is formed by one or more Device Controllers (DC). The Business Process Bridging Layer associates incoming observation messages with existing business processes. At this layer status and history information of tracked objects is maintained. This information includes object location, aggregation information, and information about the environment of a tagged object. A so-called Auto-ID Node (AIN) realizes this functionality. Finally, the Enterprise Application Layer supports business processes of enterprise applications, such as Supply Chain Management or Asset Management, running on SAP or non-SAP backend systems.

Our Auto-ID Infrastructure provides an infrastructure for realizing a complete Auto-ID solution. Most existing solutions only focus on a portion of such a complete solution. For example, the Auto-ID Savant middleware [5] provide only Device Controller functionality within our reference model. Since Auto-ID solutions can span organizations or even countries, standards for the interfaces between the components are essential. Therefore, the AII is compliant with the standards proposed by the EPCglobal consortium.

As part of the infrastructure, a test and workload generator tool is provided that can simulate messages coming from one or more Device Controllers or backend systems to an Auto-ID Node. Also, a scriptable simulator is available that can simulate multiple RFID readers. These tools allow the testing of an Auto-ID deployment without the installation of physical devices.

The following two subsections will explain the two main building blocks of the AII: the Device Controller and the Auto-ID Node.

### 3.4.1 Device Controller

A Device Controller (DC) is responsible for coordinating multiple smart item devices and reporting incoming observation messages to one or more Auto-ID Nodes. A DC supports two operation modes. In the synchronous mode, the Device Controller receives messages from an Auto-ID Node for direct device operations, such as to read or write a specific data field from/to a tag currently in the range of an RFID reader, or to read the value from a temperature sensor at a given point in time.

In the asynchronous listening mode, the DC waits for incoming messages from the sensor devices. Upon receiving such a message, additional data can be read and event messages can be filtered or aggregated according to the configuration of the DC. Note that when a DC is configured for asynchronous operations, it is still capable of synchronously receiving and executing commands.

Message processing in the DC is based on so-called Data Processors. We distinguish six different types of data processors. (1) Filters filter out certain messages according to specified criteria. For example, they can be used to filter out all event messages coming from case tags, or clean out false reads ("data smoothing"). (2) Enrichers read additional data from a tag's memory or other devices and add this data to the observation message. (3) Aggregators

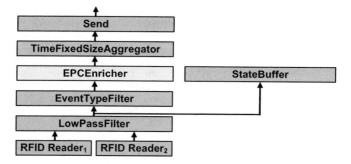

**Fig. 3.4.** Typical Data Processor chain.

can be used to compose multiple incoming events into one higher-level event (for example, mapping data from a temperature sensor to a temperature-increased event), or for batching purposes. (4) Writers are used to write to or change data on a tag or control an actuator. (5) Buffers buffer event messages for later processing and/or keep an inventory of tags currently in the reading scope of an RFID reader. (6) Senders transform the internal data structure of the messages to some output format and send them to registered recipients. Our implementation of the DC currently uses PML Core [8] as the output format. As new standards are developed, they can be incorporated by simply implementing appropriate new Senders.

The core functions of the Device Controller, in particular the message processing described above, are independent of the hardware used. For reading and writing the data on the tags, we use logical field names to abstract from concrete tag implementations. A field map provides the mapping between memory addresses on the tag and logical data fields.

Since all Data Processors implement the same publish/subscribe interface, they can be arranged into processing chains. Powerful message processing and filtering operations can be achieved by chaining together the right, possibly customized, set of simple data processors. This results in a very flexible framework which allows for the distribution of message processing functionality close to the actual sensor devices to reduce message traffic and improve system scalability.

Figure 3.4 shows an example of a typical processor chain used for dock doors in a supply chain scenario. For full coverage dock doors commonly use more than one reader. The main reason for this is national and international regulations that set upper bounds for the emission power in respect to the field strength of RFID systems. Such restrictions limit the range of RFID readers, so frequently more than one devices are required to provide full door coverage.

RFID readers sometimes generate false event messages. For example, because of physical reasons a tag is not seen during a particular read cycle. To filter out these false tag-disappeared messages, a LowPassFilter is applied. Also, every tag that passes the radio field will issue two event messages: a tag-appeared and a tag-disappeared message. Since in the dock door scenario we are only interested in the fact that an item has passed the door, we can safely filter out tag-disappeared messages by using an EventTypeFilter. The EPCEnricher in the example is only needed if non-EPC tags (which are still common today) are used. These tags have a unique ID set by the manufacturer, and the EPC is actually stored in the user memory of the tag. In this case, the EPCEnricher reads the EPC and adds it to the event message. At a dock door, we want to collect all tags that are seen during a certain time window and report them in a single message to the backend system. The TimeFixedSizeAggregator and the Send processor in our example do this. In addition, a StateBuffer keeps track of all tags currently in the reader's scope for auditing and reporting purposes.

### 3.4.2 Auto-ID Node

An Auto-ID Infrastructure can contain multiple Auto-ID Nodes. An AIN is responsible for integrating incoming observation messages from the Device Controllers with the business processes running at the backend systems.

For an AIN, we distinguish between the interactions with Device Controllers (reader events from and control commands to Device Controllers), and interactions with backend enterprise systems (such as receiving master data from a logistics system and returning a confirmation). These interactions with the AIN are treated as either incoming or outgoing messages.

Incoming observation messages are routed to a rule engine which, based on the message type, evaluates a specified list of conditions. The result of the evaluation step is a set of qualifying rules for which one or more actions are executed in a specified order. Such an action can, for example, update the system status of an object in the local repository, communicate with the backend system, or generate and write EPC data to a tag.

Actions of a rule can pass on parameters and can trigger other rules at the Auto-ID Node. Based on the message type, messages can be assigned different processing priorities and can be specified as being persistent in the Auto-ID Node.

An Auto-ID Node provides a local repository which contains information about the current status and history of the objects being processed. This information includes data about the operations that have been applied to an object (e.g, move, pack, or unpack), its movement and current location, and its structure (e.g, packing information). Also, the repository replicates master data from the backend system about products and business partners, or the physical location and type of the RFID readers. The Auto-ID Repository provides the basis for the execution of business logic in the Auto-ID Node.

The use of customizable rules provides a flexible mechanism to specify and execute business logic at the Auto-ID Node. This allows the pre-processing of incoming observation data and the handling of abnormal situations within the Auto-ID Infrastructure, such as discrepancies between a received advanced shipping notification (ASN) and a detected pallet. This, in turn, allows the system to offload processing from the backend systems.

Our work to date has focused mainly on Supply Chain Management scenarios, for which a standard set of rules is in place. The deployment of our Auto-ID Infrastructure in a different context, for example, in asset management or product lifecycle scenarios, simply requires the adoption or extension of the existing rules.

The Auto-ID Administrator provides a graphical tool that supports the reconfiguration of existing or the definition of new rules in an AIN at runtime. In addition, it allows the central configuration and control of the Device Controllers and smart item devices in the system.

## 3.5 Case Studies

The following sub-sections discuss two Auto-ID pilot installations based on a research prototype of the AII: a retail application, and an adaptive planning application. Finally, we summarize the lessons learned from these and other real-world experiences.

### 3.5.1 A Retail Application

The first pilot was conducted at a large retailer in Europe. Here, the Auto-ID Node was used as a kind of "Auto-ID data hub" to feed business event information from several processes to two backend systems: a data warehouse (SAP BW) for analytical purposes, and a tracking system (SAP EM) to track the status of deliveries. On top of this, the SAP Enterprise Portal was used as the user interface to provide both employees and project partners with a unified view of the entire system.

From the perspective of the retailer, the goal of this project was mainly to evaluate if and how RFID technology can be used in practice. While there is a lot of hype about the technology, only by putting it in a real environment can one learn what works and what does not, and possibly how to get around technical difficulties. In addition to technical issues, another question was how customers would accept the technology.

The main process covered by RFID technology was the tracking of deliveries from the distribution center to one dedicated store, as well as the movement of goods from the store's back room to the shop floor. Tagging was done on case and pallet level. There were four read points in this business process:

1. **Packing Station:** At the distribution center, all cases needed to be tagged and assembled into deliveries. An association between the pallet

and the cases loaded onto it was recorded. Once the packing was finished, a message was sent to the Auto-ID Node with information about the pallet and its associated cases.

2. **Goods Issue Gate:** After the deliveries were loaded onto a truck at the distribution center, they passed through a reader that registered what had passed. The reader was mounted in the dock door. The data from the reader was filtered, aggregated and then sent to the Auto-ID Node, which updated its inventory of goods.

3. **Goods Receiving Gate:** Similar to the previous read point, incoming goods were read and recognized as they arrived at the store.

4. **Back Room/Shop Floor Gate:** This represents another automatic gate where goods were scanned when they passed through to determine if goods were in the back room or already on the shop floor. Previously, the retailer was not able to make this distinction.

Bulk reading took place at all read points except at point 1. Depending on the nature of the products (metal cans, bottles with soda water, and so on) in the delivery, it was impossible to always read all tags of inner cases. However, since the pallets were not unpacked until they were on the shop floor, it proved to be unnecessary to achieve a read accuracy of 100%. Since the system provided the information about what was packed together from read point 1 (where the operational process guarantees a 100% read accuracy) in principle it was sufficient to detect only a single tag of the whole delivery at the other read points. The Auto-ID Node was able to deduce the other tags from the packing information.

The Auto-ID Node received observation messages from all read points to update its inventory information in its repository. Information was also sent to the Business Information Warehouse to allow for later analysis. The AIN stored information about the deliveries (actual and expected), so whenever it received a message from one of the first three read points, it inferred the delivery number from the EPCs detected. It could then tell the Event Manager, which was responsible for tracking deliveries overall, about the status change of the delivery, for example, that it had arrived at the shop.

RFID technology was also used on the item level for some distinct goods. For example, processed cheese was tagged in order to track expiration dates using a Smart Shelf. Because of limited space we will not describe these processes in more detail in this paper. This pilot implementation showed that item level tagging is technically feasible, but that the cost of tags themselves, of applying the tags to products, and of the required infrastructure (readers and so on) is currently still too high to make sense economically. Other reasons against tagging at the item level are public concerns regarding privacy.

At the time of the project, EPC tag data standards as now defined by EPCglobal [6] had not been developed. However, user requirements required standard identifiers encoded on the tag. Cases needed to have a GTIN (Global Trade Identification Number) of the product, and pallets either a SSCC (Serial

Shipping Container Code) or a GRAI (Global Returnable Asset Identifier). We therefore had to define our own mapping of these standard identifiers to EPCs, adding a serial number in the case of the GTIN mapping. Our mapping was based on [4].

The main benefit provided by RFID technology in this pilot was increased visibility of the goods, which could be used to make better decisions on when to reorder goods, leading to cost reductions because of lower inventory levels and increased sales because of increased on-shelf availability.

The software worked reliably. Because of the size of the pilot, scalability was not an issue and a single Auto-ID Node was sufficient. More daunting were the challenges regarding the hardware, like positioning and tuning the reader antennas to achieve good read accuracy while conforming to regulatory requirements in Europe, tag placement, cabling, and availability of tags, just to name a few. Workplace safety regulations added additional constraints.

### 3.5.2 A Real-Time Adaptive Planning Application

The second pilot involved a large retailer and a manufacturer in North America. In this pilot, SAP provided the same components as in the pilot described in Section 3.5.1, plus the supply chain planning component SAP APO. This pilot included three sites: a distribution center of the manufacturer, a distribution center of the retailer, and a retail shop. The main operational process consisted of three steps.

First, in the distribution center of the manufacturer, items were packed into cases and shipped to the distribution center of the retailer based on shipment orders. In the second step, the distribution center of the retailer verified the shipment on the case level and then sent a case to the retail shop. Finally, in the retail shop, the case was first placed in the backroom and then moved to the shop floor. The items contained in the case were put on a smart shelf in the shop. The following read points were defined:

1. **Pack Station at the Manufacturer:** After packing a case, a message with all the EPCs of the case and the contained items was sent to the Auto-ID Node. The Auto-ID Node forwarded the EPC of the case and associated shipment order to the tracking system (SAP EM), where an Event Handler was created with the expected shipment time, a tolerance for the shipping time and rules for exception handling — that is, what to do when a shipment did not arrive in time.
2. **Goods Receiving Gates at the Retailer:** There were similar gates both at the distribution center and at the shop. When these gates detected a case tag, messages with the detected case tags were sent to the Auto-ID Node. After updating the status of the associated locations and the physical objects, the Auto-ID Node sent a message to the tracking system to update the status of the corresponding Event Handler.

3. **Back Room / Shop Floor Gate:** These read points were similar to the read points at the receiving gates of the retailer.
4. **Smart Shelves in the Shop:** When items were added or removed from the smart shelf, messages containing the EPC of the moved objects were sent to the Auto-ID Node with the logical reader ID and the timestamp of when the objects were scanned. The AIN then forwarded the observation message for the first item from a case that appeared on the smart shelf to the tracking system to indicate that the contents of a case had been put onto the shelf and that the tracking process for that case was completed.

In this pilot, a shipment was associated with a single case as only one case was sent from the manufacturer to the retailer at a time. The Auto-ID Node maintained the status and also the history of the objects, including cases, items, and shipments. The tracking system was used to track all shipments. Therefore, only messages on the case level were sent to the tracking system, which monitored the delivery of shipments and handled possible exceptions in almost real-time.

Through the Auto-ID Node, the manufacturer could get inventory information about its products in the retail shop. Based on the history of sale records, the Auto-ID Node maintained a local prediction model. This model could be used to trigger a request to the SAP Advanced Planning and Optimization to adjust the shipment planning.

SAP Business Information Warehouse was used for analytical operations and reporting, in a similar way as in the pilot discussed in the previous section.

### 3.5.3 Evaluation

Our experiences with the pilots described in the previous sections as well as with the first months of Auto-ID ramp-up phase can be summarized by the following lessons learned.

**End-to-end Solutions.** Many customers request end-to-end solutions from the tags to the business applications. To offer such solutions, hardware providers, business software providers, and system integrators must join competencies. Solutions on the device and business process layers must support interoperability with different providers to facilitate partnerships.

**Cross-Organizational Collaboration.** The pilots contained multiple sites, and in the case of the second pilot even multiple companies. The full potential of smart items technology can only be unlocked through collaboration and data sharing across sites and organizations. A basis for such collaborations could be flexible risk sharing strategies that help increase profits for all partners along the supply chain. The hope is that the potential business improvements offered by Auto-ID technology can bring companies to overcome their current reluctance to collaborate in the near future. This reluctance, as well as technical integration challenges, are the main reasons why EDI has not been implemented to the extent initially expected.

**Standards.** One of the key issues is the use of common standards. To avoid integration nightmares, standards on the hardware layer (readers, tags), the communication layer (HTTP, XML), and also on the syntax and semantics layer (PML, EPC) should be used or must be developed. Deployment of components from different providers becomes feasible at a reasonable cost of ownership only with the right standards in place. We are actively involved in ongoing standardization efforts at EPCglobal and the W3C. Standardization has been largely focused on RFID, and is much less advanced for other smart items technologies such as wireless sensor networks and networked embedded systems.

**Automatic Identification Is Not Just RFID.** The main use case of smart items today is the universal unique identification of items. RFID is not the only technology that allows this; for example, barcodes can be used as well. Different technologies have different advantages and use cases. Thus, all of these must be easily integratable into one system. Furthermore, in a real environment RFID readers sometimes need to work with other devices such as traffic lights and light beam sensors. These heterogeneities are the rule, not the exception.

**100% RFID Reading Accuracy Cannot Be Expected.** For physical reasons, one cannot expect to have a 100% tag reading accuracy. One way to work around this problem is the proper selection of RFID frequency and hardware. A second strategy is to keep information about how objects are assembled and have the Auto-ID Infrastructure infer the missing information. For example, detecting the movement of a pallet known in the system will allow the system to infer the movement of all associated cases. We expect the reading accuracy problem to diminish when the hardware technology matures (but not to vanish for the physical reasons mentioned earlier).

**Need to Support Out of Sequence Messages.** To an Auto-ID Node, the connected Device Controllers form a distributed environment. In a real-world installation, network latency, different system clocks at the readers, and message batch processing all can cause the order in which observation messages arrive to be different from the order in which the corresponding events took place in the physical world. Therefore, the Auto-ID Infrastructure needs to be able to reorder incoming event messages based on knowledge about the physical structure and the business processes of a given site.

**Business Logic at the Point of Action.** Distributing data and functionality among a hierarchy of device controller(s) and AIN(s) allows for efficient event filtering and event aggregation. However, distribution poses new challenges for error detection: it happens that errors can only be detected at higher layers and that error handling commands must be passed downwards to take proper action. As an example, consider a wrong pallet that arrives at a retailer's receiving gate. The discrepancy between this pallet and the expected pallets according to the advanced shipping information will only be detected by the AIN. The AIN, in turn, could send a command to the device controller, and a red warning light could flash up at the receiving gate. In this case, error detection creates additional network traffic as compared with local handling directly at the point of action. However, the huge reduction of traffic by filtering and aggregation clearly overcompensates for that effect, indicating the advantage of our distributed system architecture.

**Device Administration and Management.** The deployment of an Auto-ID solution usually includes a large number of RFID and sensor devices. Centralized administration tools to visualize, plan (capacity planning), deploy, configure, test, monitor, and upgrade remote devices is a prerequisite for the operation of large, highly distributed Auto-ID solutions. Our existing tools are a good a starting point but more powerful tools are needed.

**Deploying an Auto-ID Solution Is a Long-Term Task.** The deployment of an Auto-ID solution will change the IT infrastructure, the business processes, and the operational processes of an organization. These fundamental changes cannot be done in a few weeks and may result in significant costs up front. It is essential for a company to have a long term migration plan addressing the required changes in the organization. Therefore, it is a good idea to start with a small pilot installation to learn about the required changes in an existing business environment before rolling out an Auto-ID solution on a large scale.

## 3.6 Open Issues

Based on our experiences with the existing prototype, we would like to point out the following open issues for future research in the area of smart items technology.

**Different Qualities of Service.** Different smart items applications require different qualities of service regarding event processing. For example, for high data quality, an Auto-ID infrastructure may have to provide end-to-end transaction support to guarantee that each observation message is only processed exactly once. That is, the system needs to guarantee that a predefined reaction to an event is executed exactly once - even in the case of a system or power failure. There is obviously a trade-off between higher degrees of reliability on the one hand and performance on the other. Accordingly, different qualities of service need to be defined and provided for different application classes.

**Distributed Smart Items Infrastructure.** The nature of smart items applications as well as scalability requirements may force a distributed system architecture. Although our existing Auto-ID Infrastructure allows the distribution of functionality between Device Controllers, Auto-ID Nodes, and backend systems, a full-fledged solution to the distribution problem needs to support the distribution and replication of functionality and data, requiring the sharing and synchronization of data across multiple nodes. The evaluation and adaptation of distribution and replication strategies developed in distributed database systems, database caching, distributed event-based systems, and peer-to-peer systems could be a good starting point.

**Seamless Integration of Environmental Sensors.** Currently, most work in the area of smart items has focused on RFID and Supply Chain Management. To support application scenarios like product life-cycle management (PLM) or transportation, we need to seamlessly integrate other sensors like environmental sensors with RFID technology. From the application perspective, RFID readers and environmental sensors like temperature or light sensors simply provide event sources. From the perspective of the infrastructure, however, they are different. RFID readers are aperiodic event sources, whereas environmental sensors provide a stream of periodic events, that is, discrete readings of the corresponding environmental conditions. Conceptually such a sensor provides a current value for each point in time. The seamless integration of RFID and environmental sensors requires means to represent and resolve this mismatch.

**Networked Embedded Systems.** Smart items provide small embedded systems capable of independently collecting information from their environment, processing data, and communicating over wireless networks. With advances in memory capacity and processing power, these devices allow the execution of business logic at the periphery of a smart items infrastructure rather than in the middle layers or in a central backend system. Smart items can form entire networks of collaborating devices, thereby increasing reliability (through replication), efficiency, and flexibility. In addition to the question for new appropriate system architectures, efficient ways are required to model, generate, deploy, and manage business functions at the devices. Here approaches developed in the area of grid and peer-to-peer computing could be a good starting point for further research.

**Privacy.** The use of RFID technology, especially in retail, has raised a lot of discussion regarding privacy. The main concerns here are the possible profiling of customer behavior and the potential to track people. Although this discussion is not a purely technical one, on the technical side mechanisms are required that enable the efficient encoding of tag and sensor information, ensure data security, and allow the disabling of tags at predefined stages in a retail chain. The resulting technology needs to be an integral part of a sophisticated smart items infrastructure. To promote an open and transparent dialogue on RFID technology, SAP is hosting an open community, enabling customers, partners, vendors, and other stakeholders to share information on RFID-related topics. This community provides an open, Web-based platform divided into the areas technology, applications, data security, and privacy. Further discussion of privacy issues related to RFID is provided Chapter 11 by Garfinkel.

## 3.7 Summary

We have described our Auto-ID Infrastructure which was architected with scalability, flexibility, and usability in mind. Device Controllers allow the processing of event messages close to the periphery of the system; Auto-ID Nodes enable the execution of business logic in the infrastructure and integrate incoming observation messages with backend business processes. We have discussed our practical experiences with different pilot projects and the early ramp-up phase of the SAP Auto-ID component and summarized the main lessons learned. Smart item technology is very likely to change current business and operational processes, which will require changes in the IT infrastructure of many companies. Challenging issues remain that make this area an interesting topic for both hardware and software research.

## References

1. I.F. Akyildiz, W. Su, Y. Sankarasubramaniam and E. Cayirci. "A Survey on Sensor Networks". *Computer Networks*, 38: 393–422. 2002.
2. K. Alexander, T. Gillian, K. Gramling, M. Kindy, D. Moogimane, M. Schultz and M. Woods. *IBM Business Consulting Services - Focus on the Supply Chain: Applying Auto-ID within the Distribution Center*, Auto-ID Center. White Paper IBM-AUTOID-BC-002. 2003.
3. C. Bornhövd, T. Lin, S. Haller and J. Schaper. Integrating Automatic Data Acquisition with Business Processes - Experiences with SAP's Auto-ID Infrastructure. *Proc. of the 30th Conference on Very Large Data Bases (VLDB)*. Toronto, Canada. 2004.
4. D.L. Brock. *Integrating the Electronic Product Code (EPC) and the Global Trade Number (GTIN)*, Auto-ID Center. White Paper MIT-AUTOID-WH-004. 2001.
5. S. Clark, K. Traub, D. Anarkat and T. Osinski. *Auto-ID Savant Specification 1.0*. Auto-ID Center. White Paper MIT-AUTOID-TM-003. 2003.
6. EPC Global. *EPC Tag Data Standards Version 1.1 Rev. 1.24*. EPCGlobal Standard Specification. 2004.
7. K. Finkenzeller. *RFID Handbook: Fundamentals and Applications in Contactless Smart Cards and Identification*. 2nd Edition. John Wiley & Sons, London. 2003.
8. C. Floerkemeier, D. Anarkat, T. Osinski and M. Harrison. *PML Core Specification 1.0*, Auto-ID Center Recommendation. 2003.
9. S. Haller and S. Hodges. *The Need for a Universal Smart Sensor Network*. Auto-ID Center. White Paper CAM-AUTOID-WH-007. 2002.
10. U. Hansmann, L. Merk, M.S. Nicklous and T. Stober. *Pervasive Computing: The Mobile World*. 2nd Edition. Springer SMB. Berlin, Heidelberg. 2003.
11. S. Miles, D.L. Brock and D. Engels. *Web Services WAN SIG: Proposals for Engineering the 'Silk Road of the Internet'*. Auto-ID Center. White Paper MIT-AUTOID-WH-04. 2003.

12. A. Thede, C. Schmidt, C. Merz. Integration of Goods Delivery Supervision into E-Commerce Supply Chains. *Second International Workshop on Electronic Commerce (WELCOM'01)*. Heidelberg, Germany. 2001.
13. H. Österle, E. Fleisch and R. Alt. *Business Networking*, 2nd Edition. Springer SMB. Berlin, Heidelberg. 2001.
14. D. Woodsand and J. Word. *SAP NetWeaver for Dummies*. John Wiley & Sons, London. 2004.

# RFID in Movable Asset Management

Matthias Lampe, Martin Strassner, and Elgar Fleisch

## 4.1 Introduction

The management of movable assets such as vehicles, containers, or tools in an industrial environment is still a major challenge, since today's asset management systems lack fine-grained status, location, and usage information on individual assets. They only manage aggregated asset information like the number of assets in stock but not individual assets, and they are not designed to store large amounts of related data such as usage or status information. Another problem is the accuracy of the stored information, since most of the data is captured manually, which is expensive and error-prone. As a consequence, employees waste a lot of time searching for assets, which results in increased process costs. For example, misplaced tools in an aircraft might lead to a delivery delay or in the worst case to an accident, or missing transport containers for special parts could lead to assembly delays.

Radio Frequency Identification (RFID) technology, as one of the major technologies that is frequently discussed in the area of ubiquitous computing, could play a major role in solving these problems. The automatic identification (Auto-ID) of assets provided by RFID makes it possible to bridge the gap between the physical world of assets and the digital world of IT systems and eliminates the task of manual data capture. Several market research institutions predict that the RFID market will grow by 20% per annum in the next few years [17, 16] and that supply chain management will be the application that drives this development. Such predictions stem from the fact that retail giants like Wal-Mart and Metro are planning to introduce RFID in their supply chains at pallet and case level as from 2005. However, some analysts are skeptical about these plans as the prices for RFID tags will need to come down in order to arrive at positive business cases in such open loop applications [23].

The situation is different in the case of asset management, which usually involves closed loop applications where RFID tags can be reused. Pilot projects have shown that quick benefits are possible in this area (see Section

4.3). For example, TrenStar uses RFID to manage beer kegs [18], and Nortel Networks uses it to track their equipment [6]. For these companies, the main reasons for using RFID are better utilization of the assets, prevention of shrinkage, avoidance of the manual handling required for stocktaking and searching, and the avoidance of errors as a consequence of incorrect usage of an asset.

Existing standard business software such as ERP systems shows an increasing trend toward asset management support. However, the following criteria for good asset management are often not met. Asset management systems should be able to

- manage assets individually,
- allow the location of the right assets,
- provide information about the current physical status (quality) of an asset,
- permit the definition of triggers based on certain conditions of assets, and
- keep an information history for an asset.

In this chapter we show that RFID technology has the potential to appropriately support these tasks. The fact that RFID can be used as a means to directly link movable assets to IT systems is identified as the prime reason for this potential (see Section 4.2). Three case studies demonstrate how RFID-enhanced asset management leads to improved process efficiency and helps to avoid errors (see Section 4.3). In Sections 4.4 and 4.5 we present the status quo of adoption as well as existing hurdles and suggest how companies can proceed to overcome these hurdles. Section 4.6 closes with a summary of our findings and provides a perspective on how the impact of ubiquitous computing technology on movable asset management may develop in the future.

## 4.2 RFID-Enhanced Asset Management

Miniaturization and cost reduction in computer technology as well as advances in mobile communications rank among the drivers of ubiquitous computing. More and more objects use information technology to become "smart objects" [14]. This smartness is achieved amongst others through Auto-ID technologies such as RFID that integrate the digital and the physical world by seamlessly connecting objects in the physical world with their representations in information systems, such as ERP or e-Business systems [22]. Data about every product such as its history or product-related information can be made available through a standardized infrastructure.

### 4.2.1 RFID Primer

The main components of an RFID system infrastructure are the RFID tags (also called smart tags), the readers and the RFID middleware (cf. Figure 4.1).

The RFID tag is attached to objects that need to be identified. It is comprised of an antenna that is used to communicate with the reader and a microchip that contains the unique identification number of the RFID tag. The readers communicate wirelessly with the RFID tags using alternating electromagnetic fields. A reader contains the radio frequency interface to the tags, internal storage, processing power and an interface to a host computer system in order to transfer the sensed data. The RFID middleware manages and filters the data while it is collected, and supplies it to business software systems such as ERP-systems in real time or makes it accessible via the Internet.

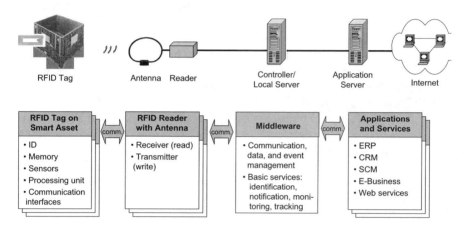

**Fig. 4.1.** RFID system architecture.

RFID systems can be distinguished by different criteria such as the type of power supply for the RFID tags, the operating frequency, the reader-to-tag coupling, the amount of memory on the tag, and the anti-collision algorithm [3]. There are two main types of power supply for RFID tags: active and passive systems. Passive RFID systems use the emitted field of the reader to power the microchip, whereas active systems include a battery. Typical operating frequencies of RFID systems that are defined by governmental bodies and that have their own radiation power and bandwidth regulations are 135 kHz (LF), 13.56 MHz (HF), 915 MHz in the US, and 868 MHz in Europe (UHF), plus 2.45 GHz (MW). The two common types of reader-to-tag coupling are inductive coupling (similar to loosely coupled transformers) and backscatter coupling (similar to RADAR). The memory on RFID tags can vary from a few bits to hundreds of bytes. Usually, the memory contains a unique ID that is read-only, and more complex tags have additional read-write memory. The anti-collision algorithm is a method for controlling access to the shared radio channel to avoid interference in the case of tags that respond simultaneously to a request from the reader.

Depending on the particular choice of technical characteristics, RFID systems can have different performance profiles, such as maximum read range, data transfer rate between reader and tag, speed at which tags can be identified, susceptibility to various error sources, and cost. This means that the characteristics have to be chosen in such a way that the resulting properties fulfill the requirements set by the application.

### 4.2.2 Benefits of RFID

Compared to traditional Auto-ID technologies like the barcode, RFID further reduces the media break in data acquisition to a level where no human intervention is required (see Figure 4.2). This has the potential to improve the efficiency of business processes through automation and leads to reduced cost since less expensive manual effort is required, human errors are eliminated, and laborious manual data gathering is avoided. More efficient processes that can even be fully automated and new services will be the result [21].

RFID can turn physical assets into "smart assets." According to the definition of smart objects [10], smart assets have a unique ID, may use sensors, have a memory, and are able to communicate. Using these features, they are able to meet the requirements for good asset management systems that were stated in the previous section. An attached RFID tag makes it possible to identify and manage smart assets individually. With an infrastructure of readers in place, assets can be identified, tracked, and located. Sensor-enhanced RFID tags enable them to monitor their physical context such as temperature or moisture, and thus making them aware. The memory of smart assets can be used to store history information (for example about usage) or messages that need to be attached to the asset (for example shipping labels) and can be requested at any time from the asset. As a result, most tasks in asset management such as identification, data acquisition, tracking, and monitoring can be performed automatically.

Compared to other Auto-ID technologies such as the barcode, the two main advantages of RFID which have a positive impact on a business case for asset management applications are increased handling efficiency and its support for higher data granularity (see Table 4.1).

**Table 4.1.** Benefits of RFID Compared to Traditional Auto-ID Technologies

| Handling Efficiency | Data Granularity |
| --- | --- |
| - No line of sight required | - Bulk reading capabilities |
| - Rewriting of tag information | - Unique and reliable identification |
| - Accurate product-related data | - Real-time information |

The reasons for increased handling efficiency are automatic identification without line of sight, the capability for bulk reading, and the possibility

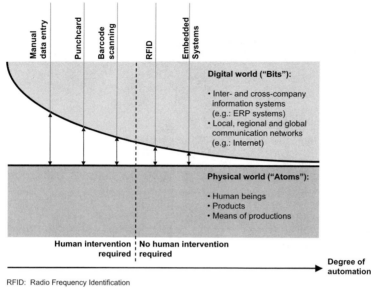

Manual data entry | Punchcard | Barcode scanning | RFID | Embedded Systems

**Digital world ("Bits"):**

• Inter- and cross-company information systems (e.g.: ERP systems)
• Local, regional and global communication networks (e.g.: Internet)

**Physical world ("Atoms"):**

• Human beings
• Products
• Means of productions

Human intervention required | No human intervention required

Degree of automation

RFID: Radio Frequency Identification
ERP:  Enterprise Resource Planning

**Fig. 4.2.** The Media Break between the Physical and the Digital World (image from [4]).

for rewriting the information on a tag which helps, for example, to avoid frequent relabeling. These advantages are rather small in the case of well guided processes, such as those employed in modern warehouses where existing barcode systems work well. However, in some industries asset management still includes many manual processes since traditional Auto-ID systems fail in unguided processes where flexibility is needed. Higher data granularity is achieved by unique identification, additional product-related data, and real-time availability of accurate data in the IT systems. For this reason, high potentials of RFID technology exist in cases where accurate and granular data is required, such as customization, quality and security checks, and tracking and tracing.

## 4.3 Case Studies on Smart Asset Management Solutions

The following case studies[1] demonstrate how the integration of physical assets with IT systems using RFID technology provides the benefits that were described above. The case studies (see also Table 4.2) present a first step in achieving smart asset management since they are "island solutions" within a

---

[1]The authors were involved in these case studies within the scope of several research projects.

**Table 4.2.** Overview of Case Studies

|  | Case Study A: Cool Chain Management at Migros | Case Study B: Special Bin Tracking at Volkswagen | Case Study C: Tool Management in Aircraft Maintenance |
|---|---|---|---|
| **Status** | Operative | Pilot project | Project concept, demonstrators |
| **RFID Technology** | Active UHF | Active UHF | Passive HF |
| **Middleware** | ObjectControl | VisuM | Ubiquitous computing infrastructure |
| **Applications** | Fleet management, cool chain management | Container management | Smart toolbox, Smart tool inventory |
| **Benefits** | Process efficiency, avoidance of error-related costs, value-added service | Process efficiency, avoidance of error-related costs | Process efficiency, avoidance of error-related costs |
| **Amortization** | 1 year | 1.1 years | 1 year[2] |

single company. A path toward a broader approach where a chain or network of companies participates is presented in Sections 4.4 and 4.5.

---

[2]Based on calculations for the smart toolbox and tool inventory application.

### 4.3.1 Case Study A: Cool Chain Management at Migros

The Swiss retailer Migros (www.migros.ch) is piloting the use of RFID technology to track deliveries of frozen goods at one of their warehouses. The system provides the retailer with real-time information on arriving and departing trucks and temperature conditions during transport in order to make the process safer and more efficient.

Delayed processes and spoiled deliveries were the problem that was solved by introducing an RFID system. As the warehouse staff did not receive information about arriving trucks in advance, the truck drivers frequently had to wait until they were able to unload the trucks. Data for the existing fleet management system that was used for optimizing routes was entered manually. The consequence was that, after unloading, the truck driver had to wait again until the fleet management system assigned a new tour. A second problem was unreliable information regarding the temperature conditions during transport. The temperature loggers that were used had to be checked manually, which was not always done with due care in some cases. In addition, process analysis showed that a common reason for spoiled deliveries was not a malfunction of the cooling unit but the problem that workers simply did not switch it on.

The RFID system that Migros uses today is based on active RFID tags with temperature sensors that are mounted inside a truck. Each RFID tag stores a unique ID that is linked to a specific truck. The readers are mounted at the entry and exit of the warehouse as well as at the loading platforms. The readers are connected via the Auto-ID middleware ObjectControl[3] with Migros' fleet management system (cf. Figure 4.3). The improved process using RFID comprises the following steps:

- Upon entry or exit of a truck, the reader at the gate reads the truck ID and transmits it to the ObjectControl middleware.
- ObjectControl calculates the direction (entry or exit) and transmits the ID, direction, and time to the fleet management system.
- If a truck enters the warehouse, it is directed to a loading platform where a reader acquires the truck ID and the temperature log that has been stored on the RFID tag during transport. The data is transferred to the fleet management system that signals an alert if the temperature has deviated outside the permitted range. Otherwise it provides the truck driver with a new tour.
- While a truck is being loaded with frozen goods, a reader at the platform checks the temperature data from the RFID tag inside the truck. If the temperature is too high, the system alerts the driver to interrupt loading and check the cooling unit.

---

[3]ObjectControl was developed by the system integrator Intellion based in St. Gallen, Switzerland (www.intellion.com).

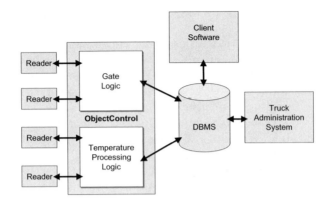

**Fig. 4.3.** RFID Solution architecture for cool chain management at Migros.

The benefits that were derived from this solution are more efficient use of the fleet as a consequence of avoiding delays in unloading and assigning routes, savings in manual labor through the automatic transmission of truck arrival and temperature data, historical data that is used for process optimization and improved planning, and reliable and documented temperature data that ensures product quality and prevents customer complaints. Migros made a cost-benefit calculation for the project which yielded an amortization time of one year for the investment.

### 4.3.2 Case Study B: Special Rack Tracking at Volkswagen

The car manufacturer Volkswagen (www.volkswagen.de) uses special racks for internal factory transport of car body parts from its press machine to the car assembly line. The special racks are customized for each car model and cost approximately USD 500 per unit. If racks are missing at the press machine, the body parts cannot be transported to the assembly line, workers and have to search for empty racks and sometimes even need to stop the press machine.

Volkswagen uses internally developed software called LISON[4] for container management, but the data it provides is not accurate since employees often forget to return empty racks to the rack pool or fail to manually update the system. As a consequence, Volkswagen faces inefficient rack use and machine downtime. In addition, they detected shrinkage of 5% during annual stocktaking of the racks.

To explore a solution to the problem, Volkswagen performed an RFID pilot project in which they tagged 600 racks and installed reader gates at shop floor entrances and exits. They used active RFID transponders in the

---

[4]Ladungstrger-Informations-System Online (Container Information System Online)

ultra-high frequency (UHF) band and reader devices from Identec Solutions (www.identecsolutions.com). The reader gates transmit the data relating to detected RFID transponders in the racks to the middleware known as VISUM (Visualization and Map Matching). VISUM is connected to LISON and maps the IDs that it receives from the reading gates to the racks that are managed in LISON (cf. Figure 4.4). It automatically provides accurate data about racks that enter or leave the shop floor. VISUM also provides interfaces to other applications that manage finished cars and company cars. To summarize, VISUM provides the following functionality:

- Monitoring of location and time of the racks, and the battery status of the active transponders.
- History management.
- Visualization of rack data.
- Mapping of tag IDs that are stored on the RFID transponders and object IDs that are stored in the application.

Based on the results of the pilot, Volkswagen carried out a cost–benefit analysis for a possible solution rollout including approximately 600,000 special racks used at its factory in Wolfsburg. The benefits that are considered to have resulted in an amortization time of 14 months are potential savings in manual efforts related to searching for containers and stocktaking, error costs as a consequence of machine downtime, and the required express deliveries as well as investments for containers as a consequence of slow circulation and shrinkage.

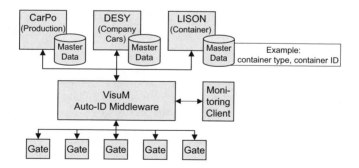

**Fig. 4.4.** RFID solution architecture of special rack tracking at Volkswagen.

As a first step, Volkswagen decided to roll out the solution to 13,000 special racks to prove the expected benefits of the system. Once an infrastructure of reading gates is in place, the investments required to incorporate additional racks into the tracking system are reduced to the costs of equipping them with RFID transponders. In order to avoid the development of incompatible island systems, Volkswagen has set the RFID system of the pilot project as a standard for the company.

### 4.3.3 Case Study C: Tool Management in Aircraft Maintenance

In aircraft maintenance, strict regulations define requirements in respect to quality, safety, and documentation of maintenance, repair and overhaul (MRO) tasks. MRO costs correspond to 12% of the total operating costs of an aircraft. Consequently, a commercial aircraft undergoing maintenance will mean high opportunity costs for the owner. For example, the costs of having planes idle during unplanned maintenance are estimated at USD 23,000 per hour [2]. The problem analysis and solution concept for a ubiquitous computing-supported MRO process including smart tool management was performed in cooperation with the maintenance department of an aircraft company and the system integrator SAP-SI (www.sap-si.com). In the following description, we concentrate on the RFID solution for tool management.

All MRO tasks are carried out in an aircraft hangar where several mechanics work together on one airplane. Each mechanic has his personal toolbox including a set of typically used tools. Additional tools can be checked out from a central tool inventory. Since regulations state the period after which a tool has to be exchanged or maintained, all tools must be uniquely identifiable. Major weaknesses have been identified that can delay delivery or have an impact on the quality of the result: it is estimated that mechanics spend 15-20% of their time searching for tools or documentation [15]. In addition, each mechanic has to check the completeness and correctness of his toolbox including weekly cross-checks with a colleague that can take several hours. In the tool inventory, the checkout and return tasks are performed manually, and tools are handed out to a mechanic in exchange for a metal token with the personal ID number of the mechanic inscribed on it to enforce checkout limits.

The weaknesses in these tasks relate to missing documentation of checkouts and human errors. This means searching for tools that are checked out, misplaced tokens, exchanged tools, and forgotten completeness and correctness checks. If searching for a missing tool after MRO delays the delivery of the aircraft, this may result in costly penalties. In addition, as no data is available about tool usage, tool maintenance can only be performed on the basis of manual inspection. Sometimes problems are only discovered during usage, causing safety risks and delays. Costly safety stocks are kept to ensure that enough tools are available.

The RFID solution that is envisioned for the MRO scenario is based on two tool management applications, that is the smart toolbox and the smart tool inventory (cf. Figure 4.5). The smart toolbox [7, 13] is designed to automate the required completeness and correctness checks for the tools using RFID, and to notify the mechanic if tools are missing or if wrong tools are located in the toolbox. All tools are marked with RFID tags and the toolbox is equipped with readers, which allows the tools to be uniquely identified. While the smart toolbox mainly operates autonomously, it uses wireless communication with the ubiquitous computing Infrastructure to send reports of checks and tool usage to the ERP system. Since the handling of tools and toolboxes does not change, the smart toolbox seamlessly integrates into the MRO process in a way that the mechanic is used to. A demonstrator was implemented using a simplified toolbox to illustrate the concept. A real world implementation of the smart toolbox would need to use RFID technology that is specially designed to operate in metal environments since most of the tools and the toolbox are made out of metal.

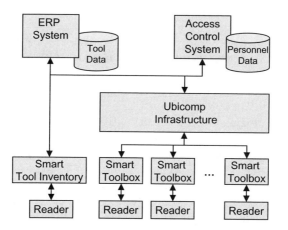

**Fig. 4.5.** RFID solution architecture for tool management.

The smart tool inventory [13] automates the checkout and return processes and enables mechanics to perform self-checkout and return of special tools from the tool inventory. As with the smart toolbox, all tools are uniquely identified using RFID tags, and a reader is incorporated in the checkout counter. In addition, a mechanic is identified using his RFID security badge and the existing infrastructure of the access control system. The smart tool inventory was implemented as a prototype that consists of two parts: (a) an RFID client that handles the identification of tools and mechanics, and manages the checkout and return via a connection to the ERP system (in this case an SAP R/3 system), and (b) the web application that allows access to information about the checkout status of tools and notifies a mechanic if a tool has to be returned. Since the tools trigger all processes, no explicit user interaction with the system is necessary on the part of the service operator, which makes the checkout and return processes straightforward. In addition to the current status of a tool, the history of checkout and return processes is stored.

The smart tool inventory was an implementation using a low-frequency RFID system (125 kHz) to ensure operation since many tools are made out of metal.

The overall benefits of the RFID solution for tool management are the improved MRO process efficiency and the avoidance of error-related costs. Delays caused by search operations for tools or broken tools are avoided thanks to automated tool management, which also leads to higher quality and security since the chance of tools being left in the aircraft is minimized. In addition, stocks of tools in the toolboxes and the tool inventory can be reduced on the basis of detailed statistics relating to tool usage and optimized checkout times. Based on the expected benefits of the solution concept, a cost-benefit estimate for implementing the smart toolbox and smart tool inventory applications yielded an amortization time of one year.

## 4.4 Critical Success Factors for RFID Adoption

Current RFID activities show that the broad-scale adoption of RFID technology is in its infancy. Many companies carry out pilot projects in order to test the technology, gain experience with RFID and acquire data for the calculation of business cases. As there is no "out-of-the-box" solution available, each company defines interfaces and develops a middleware solution on its own initiative. The following section gives an aggregated view of current activities and challenges based on a survey that Booz Allen & Hamilton (www.boozallen.com) and the M-Lab (www.m-lab.ch) conducted with 24 European companies encompassing the automotive industry and logistics service providers [8, 9]. Based on these results and potential benefits that have been described above, we suggest ways in which companies can proceed in adopting RFID.

### 4.4.1 Status of RFID Projects in Industry

The interviewees who took part in the study see improving operational efficiency as the most important driver for RFID adoption. Having this goal in mind, the automotive industry has been using RFID systems in production control such as work-in-progress tracking for more than a decade. However, RFID solutions for the management of high-value logistical assets, such as, forklifts, trailers, and special racks, have only recently been explored.

The evaluation of the interviews indicates that many companies in the industry have experience with RFID technology: 58% of the companies interviewed run at least one operational application, 67% are undertaking pilot projects, and 63% have developed concepts for RFID applications that are yet to be piloted or become operational (cf. Figure 4.6). The applications range from work-in-progress tracking of vehicles in production and vehicle identification in distribution to the tracking of deliveries in the supply chain.

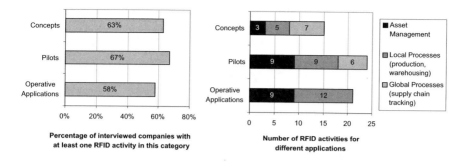

**Fig. 4.6.** Status of RFID activities.

Most operational applications and pilots are to be found in the area of local processes, including production control and warehousing (21 applications). There are also 18 operational applications and pilot projects for asset management such as container tracking. Only 13 pilots or concepts are related to global supply chain processes. In general, the concept of implementing RFID over the whole supply chain does not play as important a role for the automotive industry as it does for the retail industry.

However, the total number of operational RFID applications (21 applications) is low. This indicates that RFID solutions still have an exceptional character and are not used as a company-wide standard solution. The majority of the applications are closed loop applications, which means the tagged objects do not leave the company and the RFID tags can be reused. Open loop applications play a minor role. There are few companies that have concrete plans to build global process applications since there are several challenges that have to be overcome in this context.

### 4.4.2 Challenges in RFID Adoption

The RFID applications presented in the case studies (cf. Section 4.3) do not show the potential that is typically associated with RFID in supply chain management. They are mainly independent island solutions. Even within one company, several types of RFID systems are used, which might lead to a certain amount of migration effort in the future if a company decides to use a standard infrastructure.

The interviewees in the study see a number of risks that need to be addressed before they start further RFID activities. *Missing business cases* are stated as the most important risk for RFID projects. Either current costs for hardware do not justify the rollout of the majority of existing concepts or pilot projects, or there is no significant advantage over a solution using barcode. However, business cases are largely dependent on the type of application. For certain applications where tags can be reused such as asset management,

RFID already pays off or approaches a critical price for large-scale rollouts. For supply chain applications, there is a lack of *cost–benefit sharing models* that not only focus on local benefits but also on a collaborative approach. For example, the costs for equipping products with RFID tags arise at the level of production. Partners in the supply chain who follow suit only have to make investments in infrastructure to benefit from RFID.

Collaborative IT systems like supply chain management systems need RFID standards for communication between RFID tags and readers, or more-over a common IT infrastructure that supports data sharing between enter-prises. For example, if RFID is applied to the special rack tracking and the racks are used by different trading partners, they will need a common RFID standard for the RFID air protocol, the data that is stored on the tag, and the data that is exchanged in the infrastructure. Non-existent or inadequate stan-dards are a major reason for companies to delay RFID projects. EPCglobal (www.epcglobalinc.org) and the Auto-ID (www.autoidlabs.org) labs are currently developing a concept for a ubiquitous Auto-ID infrastructure based on the Electronic Product Code (EPC) as a global standard for RFID-enabled asset identification.

Many RFID pilots using passive RFID systems fail as a result of tech-nological problems. The interviewees complained about *short reading ranges* (especially if there is metal or water in the environment), *inadequate maturity of the technology, high integration efforts* and *deficient bulk reading capabil-ities*. These problems are partly due to the physics of RFID and partly to incorrect setup of RFID systems, such as, incorrect antenna setup or tuning. More experience in RFID technology and the usage of standard solutions can help to avoid such problems. While today's users are required to develop their own middleware for system integration, technology providers are developing middleware solutions such as SAP's Auto-ID Infrastructure [19] and Infineon's YOU-RTUBEs Architecture [11] that can be used to integrate RFID technol-ogy with standard software systems.

From the outside perspective, a major roadblock for the broad applica-tion of RFID beyond island solutions is the lack of central management and roadmap definition for RFID at corporate level. At the moment, projects are mainly driven by operational management at the production plant level, which means that each factory decides independently on the implementation of RFID to improve local processes. This is about to change in several com-panies that have set up umbrella programs for better coordination of RFID activities.

The *privacy concerns* that have been raised [1], especially for RFID appli-cations where customers are affected such as in retail stores, are at present less critical for industrial applications. However, smart assets also have the potential for employee surveillance, and in this respect may affect the privacy of employees. For example, on the basis of the information provided by a fork-lift that monitors its usage (and thus who is using it and when) the company could derive how many breaks the operator takes or the operator's efficiency.

Companies that plan to adopt RFID should take these fears into account, respect privacy guidelines and make the kind of personal data that a smart asset records transparent.

## 4.5 Recommendations for a Pathway to RFID Adoption

The adoption of RFID to support smart things continues a trend in business computing toward greater integration range and integration depth (cf. Figure 4.7). In the last decade, companies have on the one hand implemented IT systems to increase integration range. They started by networking functional units using ERP systems and proceeded with e-Business systems to support collaboration with other companies. On the other hand, the trend went from mainframes and client/server solutions to the use of mobile computers to support integration depth with the aim of improved coordination of operational resources [5]. Integration depth complements integration range. For example, companies that are able to manage their own assets and make their supply chains more reliable will be a preferred partner in collaborative business networks. Another example is applications that are supported by e-Business systems like Vendor Managed Inventories (VMIs), which require reliable data on inventory stocks to achieve an efficiency gain over manual ordering.

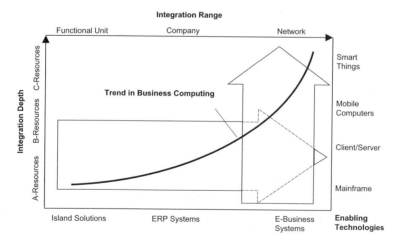

**Fig. 4.7.** Dimensions of integration in information processing [5].

Whether a company uses mobile computers to integrate a specific resource will depend on its specific cost-benefit ratio for this application. Today, companies are already using mobile computers for the integration of high-value assets that are critical for operation (A-resources) with ERP systems [12]. For example, shipping companies use GPS systems to support route planning and increase the efficiency of their fleet. In this case the benefit of increased availability and better control of the vehicles exceeds the additional IT costs caused by the mobile system. Further decreases in prices for mobile computers will make the integration of assets that are less critical for operations like containers (B-resources) or even single products (C-resources) profitable. RFID is an enabling technology to continue the trend toward greater integration depth. As a low-cost computing technology, RFID might be well suited to enhancing ordinary assets with a permanent link to companies' ERP systems, which means that they become smart assets.

Closed loop applications with a focus on local processes and high-value assets such as production control and fleet management are a starting point for RFID adoption. While the investment risk for such applications is small, companies can acquire experience in how to cope with the technical challenges and in possible use cases. The benefits could be increased by adding more and more types of assets to the RFID solution, which means a greater integration depth. For example, a next step in the Migros case might be to tag the bins that are used to transport the goods inside the warehouse. This would provide more data on the supply chain and would make it possible to track the goods not only from the supplier to the warehouse entrance but also inside the warehouse. Item tagging enables a further step in integration depth. In the Migros, case it would mean tagging each product which supports tracking from the supplier to the point of sale and possibly beyond. The aircraft maintenance case is an example of an item tagging application since the tools and not just the toolboxes are tagged.

For all RFID solutions, companies must always look at the business case, irrespective of whether the additional degree of integration will be profitable. A closed loop application for the management of high-value assets may provide quick benefits. Typical benefits for such scenarios are the more efficient use of assets, savings in the manual effort required to use the assets, and the avoidance of errors. Costs and benefits are local and associated with only one company, as shown in the case studies.

The overall benefit of using a smart asset is increased if all companies in a chain or network that deal with the smart asset are able to derive benefits from its smartness. For example, a smart container that is frequently used to move goods through the supply chain and is able to store a shipping label on its RFID tag can save a large amount of manual handling over its lifetime. However, this scenario requires RFID standards and models for cost-benefit sharing that are yet to be established.

To prepare themselves for open loop RFID applications, companies could use local closed loop applications as a starting point for building an RFID infrastructure and gaining experience in using RFID. As mentioned above, companies should determine the kind of assets from which they stand to benefit the most if the assets are integrated with their IT systems. The benefits for a specific asset will depend on the following criteria: high manual effort for identification and data acquisition, high costs caused by shrinkage or spoilage, improper use or wrong identification, or by nonavailability, and benefits from accurate status information. Companies should prioritize their movable assets according to these criteria and start with their top priorities. That way, companies start building up RFID infrastructures that will reduce the costs for including further assets and increase their integration depth step by step (cf. Table 4.3).

**Table 4.3.** Expansion of RFID Systems and Impact on Integration

| | | Closed Loop System | Open Loop System |
|---|---|---|---|
| Integration Depth ↑ | Item | Production control, tool management, e.g. aircraft maintenance case (C) | Supply chain tracking from supplier to customer, e.g. spare parts |
| | Container | Management of containers on a predefined route, e.g. Volkswagen case (B) | Management of containers that are used on different routes, e.g. sea containers |
| | Vehicle | Local fleet management, e.g. Migros case (A) | Global fleet management, e.g. vehicles of international shippers |
| | | Closed Loop System | Open Loop System |

Integration Range ⟶

It is important to consider RFID and data standards in order to derive benefits from connecting island solutions and to prepare for open loop systems. Eventually, the growing maturity of the technology and the dynamic of the market will favor the expansion of RFID. The process of technology maturity is supported by an increasing number of RFID systems, since technology providers will learn to create solutions that will be better suited to customers' needs. The dynamic of the market is supported by a decrease in costs for hardware and integration, which will lead to more positive business cases. Once a critical mass of RFID infrastructures in place will be reached, companies will be able to use their RFID systems for collaborative applications such as the shared use of assets as a consequence of the increased integration range of RFID (cf. Table 3).

## 4.6 Conclusions

We have shown that RFID technology has a high potential to improve movable asset management in several ways based on automatic and unique identification. The benefits such as identifying the right assets, locating assets, monitoring the quality or status of assets, and keeping the history of assets are the result of avoiding media breaks by automating or reducing manual tasks.

There are still several challenges to overcome when using RFID to enable smart assets. First, the technology is still immature. Leading-edge engineering and IT know-how is needed for setting up an RFID system since there are no plug&play solutions available and traditional ERP systems still lack the capability to manage such large numbers of individual assets. Second, there is a lack of established standards for RFID. However, this is likely to change with the forthcoming standards of EPCglobal. Third, as a consequence of the small number of RFID applications in operation, there is an absence of proven business cases, deterring many companies from using RFID.

In the light of current prices for RFID and the maturity level of the technology, applications for critical assets like high-value or frequently misplaced assets are good starting points. Such applications offer quick benefits but also support the expansion of an RFID infrastructure that reduces the costs for including further assets and supports the increase in integration depth.

In addition to local RFID systems, collaborative RFID systems provide integration through the use of a common infrastructure that supports the emergence of further services, such as the outsourcing of asset management to logistics service providers, pay-per-use models, and real-time information about status and location. However, the pace of the shift from closed loop to open loop applications will be primarily dependent on the benefits of such services. In this field, further research is needed on collaborative application scenarios that are based on the shared use of smart assets.

# References

1. J. Bohn, V. Coroama, M. Langheinrich, F. Mattern and M. Rohs. "Living in a World of Smart Everyday Objects — Social, Economic, and Ethical Implications". *Journal of Human and Ecological Risk Assessment* 10(5). 2004.
2. P. Brown. Companies get creative in their Inventory Management Solution. *Aviation Now*. Archived at: www.aviationnow.com. 2003.
3. K. Finkenzeller. *RFID-Handbuch: Grundlagen und praktische Anwendungen induktiver Funkanlagen, Transponder und kontaktloser Chipkarten. 3., aktualisierte und erweiterte Auflage.* Carl Hanser Verlag. Mnchen, Wien. 2002.
4. E. Fleisch and M. Dierkes. *Ubiquitous Computing: Why Auto-ID is the Logical Next Step in Enterprise Automation.* MIT Auto-ID Center White Paper. Massachusetts, USA. Archived at: www.autoidlabs.org/whitepapers/STG-AUTOID-WH004.pdf. 2003.
5. E. Fleisch. Betriebswirtschaftliche Perspektiven des Ubiquitous Computing. In H. U. Buhl; A. Huther; B. Reitwiesner (eds) *Information Age Economy*:177–191. Physica-Verlag, Heidelberg. 2001.
6. Frontline Solutions. *Test and Development Lab Tracks High-Value Assets Throughout Multi-Story Facility With 3D-iD.* Archived at: www.frontlinemagazine.com/rfidonline/whitppr.htm. 2000.

7. C. Floerkemeier, M. Lampe and T. Schoch. The Smart Box Concept for Ubiquitous Computing Environments. *Proceedings of Smart Objects Conference.* Grenoble, France. May 15-17, 2003.
8. E. Fleisch, J. Ringbeck, S. Stroh, C. Plenge, L. Dittmannand M. Strassner. *RFID - The Opportunity for Logistics Service Providers.* M-Lab Working Paper No. 23. St. Gallen/Zurich, Switzerland. 2004.
9. E. Fleisch, J. Ringbeck, S. Stroh, C. Plenge and M. Strassner. *From Operations to Strategy: The Potential of RFID for the Automotive Industry.* M-Lab Working Paper No. 24. St.Gallen/Zurich, Switzerland. 2004.
10. H.-W. Gellersen, A. Schmidt and M. Beigl. Adding Some Smartness to Devices and Everyday Things. *IEEE Workshop on Mobile Computing Systems and Applications.* Monterrey, CA, USA. December 7-8. 2000.
11. F. Gillert. Infineon Technologies AG - mit "Ident Solutions" als Generalunternehmer fr RFID-Systemlsungen am Markt aktiv. *Ident Jahrbuch 2004.* Archived at: `www.ident.de/uploads/media/Jahrbuch_04_Firmenprofil_Infineon.pdf`. 2004.
12. K. Kurbel, F. Teuteberg and J. Hilker. Mobile-Business-Anwendungen im Enterprise Resource Planning. *Industrie Management* 1:72–75. 2003.
13. M. Lampe, M. Strassner and E. Fleisch. A Ubiquitous Computing Environment for Aircraft Maintenance. *Symposium on Applied Computing.* Nicosia, Cyprus. 2004.
14. F. Mattern. "The Vision and Technical Foundations of Ubiquitous Computing". *Upgrade* 2:2–6. 2001.
15. M. Mecham. "Software Solutions Making MRO 'Smarter'". *Aviation Week & Space Technology* 151(9):44–45. 2003.
16. Venture Development Cooperation. *The Global Market and Applications for Radio Frequency Identification and Contactless Smartcard Systems.* 4th Edition. Archived at `www.vdc-corp.com/autoid/white/03/03rfid.pdf`. 2003.
17. RFID Journal. *ABI: RFID Market Poised for Growth.* Archived at: `www.rfidjournal.com/article/view/506`. July 18. 2003.
18. G.D.N. Miller. *Advanced RFID Systems in Practical Use.* SACO. Archived at: `www.saco.co.za/appinst.html`. 1999.
19. SAP AG. *SAP Auto-ID Infrastructure, Integrating and Leveraging Sensing and Identification Technology.* Archived at: `www.sap.com/solutions/netweaver/autoidinfrastructure.asp`. 2004.
20. S. Sarma. *Towards the 5c Tag.* MIT Auto-ID Center White Paper. Cambridge, MA, USA. Archived at: `www.autoidcenter.org/publishedresearch/MIT-AUTOID-WH-006.pdf`. 2001.
21. M. Strassner and T. Schoch. Today's Impact of Ubiquitous Computing on Business Processes. *First International Conference on Pervasive Computing,* Short Paper Proceedings: 62–74. ugust 26-28. Zurich, Switzerland. A2002.
22. R. Want, K.O. Fishkin, A. Gujar, and B.L. Harrison. Bridging physical and virtual worlds with electronic tags. *Proceedings of the ACM SIGCHI Conference.* May 15-20. Pittsburgh, PI, USA. 1999.
23. J. Woods. *Prepare for Disillusionment with RFID.* Gartner Research Note. Archived at: `www.gartner.com`. 2004.

# Part II

# Business

# Ubiquitous Services: Extending Customer Relationship Management

Anatole Gershman and Andrew Fano

Western economies are already service economies. In fact, according to the World Bank, almost two-thirds of the gross domestic product of high-income countries comes from services that range from the physical performance of mundane tasks to the delivery of high-level intellectual content. But technological advances are about to improve our ability to deliver services and broaden the concept of what a service can be.

In particular, two classes of emerging technologies are creating the new infrastructure for service delivery. These are ubiquitous computing and web services. Ubiquitous computing makes everyday objects smart and connected. Web services provide a common language and a common architecture for building applications based on smart objects.

## 5.1 Ubiquitous Devices as a Service Channel

Mobile and embedded devices represent a new, constantly present, personal service channel. This is a relatively new phenomenon. We are only beginning to see connections that are "always on" such as NTT DoCoMo's i-mode[1], GPRS the General Packet Radio Service,[2] and third generation (3G) mobile services [3]. At home, only a minority of Internet users currently have a high-speed (DSL or cable modem) connection. When these "always on" connections become ubiquitous, businesses that provide services will be challenged to be "always on," ready to respond to their customers whenever customers might need them. For example, if we see some products we like – whether in a store or on the sidewalk – we should be able to pull out our mobile devices and get information on that product, order it, as well as invoke a variety of supporting services, from training to insurance to financing, to name a few. Some of these

---

[1]http://www.nttdocomo.com/i/

[2]http://www.gsmworld.com/technology/gprs.html

[3]http://www.3gnewsroom.com/

services can be implemented with today's technologies. When we walk into a wine store we see hundreds of wines, each of which is excellent according to the store owner. If we do not want to rely entirely on the shop owner's advice, we should be able to pick up any bottle and punch the number under the barcode on the back label into our cell phone (or better yet to scan the barcode with our camera phone) and for a small fee get a review of the wine by a wine critic.

While the new connections certainly open up a new marketing channel for existing services, more interesting are the new kinds of services that will become possible. Once an always present, always-on channel becomes a reality, access to customers will cease being a constraint on commerce. Not only will you, the user, be able to get services anywhere, anytime — services, in effect, will be able to casually tap you on your shoulder and whisper in your ear. But what should these new services whisper? And how will this newfound access be managed across competing interests?

## 5.2 Ubiquitous Devices as Sensors

Until recently, most mobile devices were essentially deaf, dumb, and blind. Service providers depended upon users to enter all necessary information. Consequently, services available today are essentially those that can be delivered despite these rather drastic limitations. Over time, however, ever more powerful mobile and embedded devices will become equipped with a variety of sensors:

- *Geo-positioning* capabilities such as the Global Positioning System (GPS) will inform devices of their location.
- *Biometrics* such as fingerprint or retina scanners will identify the user.
- *Tagging and tracking technologies* such as radio frequency identification (RFID) tags will identify the objects around them.
- *Temperature, humidity, and other environmental sensors* will capture the physical characteristics of the surrounding environment.
- *Chemical and radiation sensors* will alert us to potential hazards.
- *Cameras and microphones* will capture and communicate what we or smart objects can see or hear.

In short, ubiquitous devices will begin to open their eyes to the world around them, and as a result we will begin to see services that don't depend solely upon the user's explicit input to establish, interpret, and communicate their present situation.

One simple example of a sensor that can add value to a mobile device is a bar code scanner. There are already several personal digital assistants (PDAs) on the market equipped with a bar code scanner. These devices are widely used in inventory control and warehousing applications. Other miniature sensors such as GPS, cameras, microphones, thermometers, fingerprint scanners, and even chemical analyzers are becoming commercially available as well. The problem is that if we integrate all of these in a single mobile device it will become rather unwieldy and unusable. Fortunately, Bluetooth can solve this problem. It creates a wireless extension bus for portable devices and will enable users to mix and match the exact combination of sensors that is necessary for the task at hand. We can have a wireless camera on our lapels, a wireless earphone for our 3G phone, a PDA in our pocket, along with perhaps a video player — all working together.

Devices for ubiquitous commerce will not be limited to mobile phones and PDAs with various accessories. Most electronic devices will have these capabilities. No one device will do everything, and while some of the capabilities will overlap, others will complement each other. There are already digital cameras on the market equipped with communications capabilities. At first, they will be used by professionals (journalists, insurance adjusters) to send their pictures back to their offices. As prices come down, it is not unreasonable to envision people sharing their vacation experiences in real time or getting a 10 minute photography lesson as a Web service delivered right through the viewfinder of your camera. All your camera will need is a Bluetooth connection to your 3G mobile phone.

Camera phones are the latest ubiquitous gadgets rapidly growing in popularity in Japan and Korea, where they represent over 80% of all new cell phones sales. IDC estimates there will be 300 million camera phones worldwide by 2007. Users can instantly and inexpensively send and receive snapshots taken with these cameras. We believe that these are not isolated gadgets but an important component of the new emerging infrastructure with significant consequences for many business processes. Later in this chapter, we examine its impact on customer interaction, customer service, and more specifically how it will affect call centers and the roles of call center agents

## 5.3 Ubiquitous Devices as Effectors

The ubiquitous commerce trend is not just about personal devices but about the technology that infuses our physical environments. Just as millions of people are acquiring mobile phones, millions of objects of various kinds — kiosks, displays, cars, kitchen appliances — are now acquiring wireless capabilities of their own. In other words, the mobile user is increasingly surrounded by smart appliances and infrastructure of all kinds. Mobile services delivered through portable devices should be aware of what is available in the environment and be able to use it. For example, PDAs that receive TV listings should also be able to control our TVs and video recorders. A customer in a store interacting with a customer service through a mobile phone should be able to switch to a nearby kiosk that has a far better screen than their phone. In fact, the mobile device, by virtue of its presence on one's person, has the chance to be the user interface for the myriad of intelligent objects we find around us. Today we can point a phone at a soda machine and buy a Coke. Soon we will be able to point to a far larger array of objects and receive supporting services. In effect, the mobile device becomes a remote control to the world.

Most of today's mobile services consider only the mobile device and make few, if any assumptions about technology in the physical vicinity. Ultimately, however, it is a mistake to overlook the amenities offered by the physical environments we find ourselves in. Consider the automobile. Once the automobile became an accepted technology and universally used, we did not just add features onto automobiles, we adapted our environments. We control traffic not with devices in cars, but with traffic lights. We have parking lots and gas stations. New services have been offered that assume cars such as drive through banks and restaurants and drive-in movies. Similarly, as we consider mobile services we need to consider the overall environment in which services will be delivered, not just a user's mobile device.

## 5.4 Web Services as a Common Language

This seamless integration of services relies on the widespread adoption of web services. The idea behind web services isn't new. Application-to-application communication has been technically feasible for years, although it has been limited by its reliance on proprietary languages. The compelling change today is the emergence of open standard network and application protocols, which are beginning to make communication transparent across a variety of systems and platforms. Offering a common language equally available to everyone, these protocols can vastly enhance the usefulness of a particular service by lowering the cost, broadening the reach, and increasing the number and variety of participants.

Web services really aren't services but layers of standards that are emerging in stages. The most basic layer is already in place. Extensible markup language (XML) is the common language that underpins web services, describing how data is structured. Simple object access protocol (SOAP) defines how applications communicate information. These standards enable applications based on different technologies (including legacy systems) to communicate. The next layer enables service providers to describe what their services actually do using the web services description language (WSDL). Universal description, discovery, and integration (UDDI) is the set of specification for the creation of service directories — the Yellow Pages for applications. Other standards for security, user profiles, industry-specific nomenclatures, etc are still emerging. From a business point of view, the details of the protocols are not as important as the potential for web services to redefine the way business is conducted.

Look at what needs to happen for a service — nearly any service — to be provided today. Each transaction has five basic steps the provider and user have to find each other, connect, and communicate what one party desires and the other offers. The service itself then has to be rendered and, finally, paid for.

With web services, each of those five steps can be done differently. The finding, linking, communicating, and paying can all happen automatically. When applications speak the same "language" based on common standards, any number of service providers can market themselves via the Internet to any potential user. The consumer of the service can use applications that will review and select a provider, engage the appropriate service to complete a task, and handle the payment process. Even the service itself can be rendered differently: sensing technology and mobile devices can act as the service provider's eyes and ears.

The ability of technology to change how a service is provided should come as no surprise — look at the history of manufacturing in the United States. Until the 1800s most products were made in small shops and consumed locally. Then the railroad came, and goods, many now made in factories, could be shipped cross-country. The telegraph enabled long-distance communication, so people could place orders from almost anywhere. And the advent of standardized parts made it possible for any number of goods to be assembled from pre-selected components manufactured in remote locations. Manufacturing achieved cost efficiency and national, then global, scope.

Like the railroad and the telegraph, the Internet expands the geographic possibilities, making it feasible for services to be solicited and delivered from almost anywhere. Web services add another dimension, as applications rather than individuals find and engage services. The interaction no longer needs to be local — and no longer even needs to be performed by a human.

Just as standardized parts enabled products to be more easily assembled from components, web services are standardizing the components of service. Beyond technical standards that enable systems to communicate, web services require a common language for describing what will be offered and how. In the auto industry, for example, all participants need to agree in advance on the specific nature of various parts so that they can be bought and sold in the open marketplace.

As with manufacturing, services can be delivered at greater volume and efficiency. By automating and improving the transaction process, web service providers can reduce costs and therefore stimulate demand.

## 5.5 Re-thinking Business Functions

We believe that these capabilities of the new ubiquitous devices — a service channel, a sensor, and an effector combined with the web services platform — will change the way we think about many business functions. For example, today Customer Relationship Management (CRM) is mainly concerned with identifying and targeting the right customers and with handling customer contacts. Ubiquitous computing will greatly expand and transform this function by providing real-time responses to user needs, improving customer satisfaction and strengthening relationships. Take package delivery, for example. Each business day, express shippers deliver more than 13 million packages worldwide. Missed deliveries cost money and cause frustration all around. But suppose package delivery were shifted from being address-centric to being user-centric so that the package is delivered efficiently at a time and place convenient to the user.

Accenture Technology Labs has developed a Dynamic Delivery prototype, which enables the shipping company to locate recipients in real time and send a delivery alert to the device of their choice — cell phone, pager or PDA. Recipients could then "sign" electronically using identification such as a thumbprint, or they could choose to route the delivery to another address or schedule another delivery time. Alternatively, recipients could preauthorize access to a personal calendar, allowing the shipping company to find and pick a convenient time and place for delivery.

## 5.6 Re-thinking Business Location

Ubiquitous commerce will also redefine conventional wisdom about business locations. Today your customers have to come to your store, office or Web site to conduct business with you. Tomorrow, you will be able to conduct your business at your competitor's location — in effect the location of your customer will become the location of your business. One of the early prototypes called Pocket Bargain Finder [1] created at Accenture Technology Labs demonstrated how this could be done. We equipped a cell phone with a bar code scanner and took it to a bookstore. We were able to use the store's resources to browse through the books and select those we wanted to buy. Using our modified cell phone we were able to scan the bar codes on the back cover and instantly shop for the same books in online stores. What was a clunky experiment a few years ago will become well within the capabilities of the new generation of camera phones. As your business follows your customers, your customer services will have to follow them as well, or someone else's will.

**Fig. 5.1.** Pocket bargain finder.

Today, stores have a monopoly on customer services while customers are on their premises. As the above example shows, this is likely to change. Tomorrow's customers will arrive at a store armed with mobile devices that could connect them to any number of customer services (including the store's own). Consider the purchase of any sophisticated or expensive object — say, buying a printer in an electronics store. Soon, the buyer may be able to point a mobile device at the printer and instantly access information that includes product reviews, recommendations, warranty details, and payment options. The manufacturer would be offering value-added service or a third-party provider might do so for a fee. This will not necessarily diminish the role of the store or take away their business. At Accenture Technology Labs we developed a demonstration of how a store can work together with manufacturers and third party service providers to improve customer experience and help close the sale [2].

In the situation depicted in Figure 5.2, the customer points his PDA or mobile phone at a printer of interest and connects to his favorite customer service provider. The provider takes over the nearest big screen in the store and re-directs the interaction to that screen, which is a much more ergonomic venue than the customer's own tiny device. The salesperson on the store's floor is alerted to the customer's needs and preferences and is prepared to close the sale. In this scenario, it makes sense for the store and to the third-party services to cooperate. Even if the customer decides to buy the item from an on-line retailer or directly from the manufacturer, the store will get its commission.

**Fig. 5.2.** Mobile valet.

Today, RFID tags are beginning to be used to track products through supply chain. However, as discussed in Chapter 6 in this volume, the value of pervasive technologies comes from the new services that take advantage of the unique capabilities offered by these technologies, rather than from simply re-implementing old applications with new technologies. Merely replacing bar codes with RFID tags is of very limited value. Their framework provides a perspective on how to value new services, such as those described here. Assuming that the privacy issues are resolved, tomorrow's products, equipped with RFID labels, will continue to communicate with their manufacturers after they are sold. Manufacturers will know where they are and how they are performing. That also will become part of customer service. Tomorrow, we will expect the manufacturer of our jacket to let us know when we need a pair of pants that actually match our jacket. Your products will be your best sales representatives. If you sell clothing, each garment might have an RFID label using technologies such as Hitachi's mu-chip, which is only 0.4mm2 in size. A teenager wearing this garment might let his friends scan the label using their mobile phones with RFID readers. At this point, your additional sales should be only one click away. In a demonstration called Real World Show Room [1] shown in Figure 5.3, a sweater is being scanned by an online PDA equipped with an RFID reader. The merchant who sold the sweater to the first individual will now have a chance to sell it to the second while giving a small commission to the first. This kind of service is increasingly feasible due, in part, to the development of AutoID standards, discussed by Roussos in Chapter 2 of this volume.

**Fig. 5.3.** Real-world showroom.

## 5.7 Smart Appliances and Intelligent Agents

Smart objects are not limited to mobile devices. Many common appliances and even furniture will become conduits for services. One of the early examples of such an appliance is the Online Medicine Cabinet [8], a situated portal to online health information embedded in a medicine cabinet. One door of the cabinet contains a traditional mirror, while the other door houses a flat screen that displays a personalized selection of health care information. The Online Medicine Cabinet also has a camera (for face recognition capabilities), a microphone and speakers (for speech-based interaction), a computer with an internet connection, and a variety of devices related to health maintenance. This on-line medicine cabinet also knows something about your health. For example, if you have allergies, it monitors on-line resources that measure the local pollen count and warns you to take your medicine. If you suffer from hypertension, the cabinet reminds you to take a blood pressure reading and automatically communicates the results to the doctor's office. Through the use of sensors and smart labels on pill containers, the cabinet also knows what medicines are inside and which one has been taken out, warning you if you pick up the wrong one. It can establish real-time connections to your doctor, pharmacist and other providers of health care related services when the situation calls for it. A working prototype of the Magic Medicine Cabinet is depicted in Figure 5.4.

**Fig. 5.4.** Online medicine cabinet.

With the proliferation of RFID tags, ordinary wardrobes and closets could become online service terminals. Figure 5.5 shows Online Wardrobe, a research prototype of what we call smart furniture [9].

The wardrobe has a built-in RFID tag reader and an LCD screen. It can detect the clothing articles being put into the wardrobe or taken out. The key feature of the wardrobe is not yet another way of surfing the Internet from your home. Rather, it provides a new kind of interface — physical interface — to the online marketplace and customer services. You can use it to shop from online stores using what is in the wardrobe as the shopping context. For example, while shopping for a dress shirt, the service provider behind the wardrobe might suggest the color and the style that go well with your existing pants and jackets. When you bring home a new tie, the wardrobe recognizes the new arrival and suggests the best combinations. When you look at your current collection and complain that "you have nothing to wear," the wardrobe (or rather the service behind it) is happy to suggest suitable additions available in the affiliated online stores.

Online Wardrobe and Online Medicine Cabinet raise several important issues about the future of customer service. They illustrate how technology

**Fig. 5.5.** Online wardrobe.

gives businesses the means for very frequent, almost continuous contact with their customers. Are today's businesses ready for such "customer intimacy?" Are they ready to provide almost continuous attention to their customers? Clearly, today, most businesses are not ready. They do not have the personnel and the systems to support the intensity of customer interactions that would be required. Imagine a dedicated person remotely interacting with us through our wardrobe. In addition to knowing what we have in our wardrobes, such an assistant would need to know a great deal about our habits, preferences, and life styles. Moreover, the assistant will need to know about our current goals, needs, and even moods. The assistant will also have to be very savvy choosing the right moments to talk to us and what to say. While this already seems like a formidable challenge for an experienced human being, we will need to provide such a service automatically if we want to make it economical on a mass scale. Fortunately, we have the technologies that make possible the creation of an intelligent agent capable of providing many elements of ubiquitous customer service.

Using Machine Learning techniques, we can create an agent which learns about styles and purposes of our clothing. At Accenture Technology Labs we built a prototype of such an agent called Product Profiler [5, 6]. Our agent will not win the best dresser contest, but it does a reasonably good job filtering items from on-line stores that roughly match the style and the purpose of the clothing we are looking for. For example, if we are looking at a pair of casual pants for a teenager, it will show us corresponding shirts, belts, and shoes. How does the agent know what to look for? After all, even if it can read the RFID tag on the garment and find the corresponding entry in the merchant's data base, all it will learn is the SKU number of that article. In fact, today, most retailers' transactional data bases can only tell us that a particular customer

**Table 5.1.** Features Extracted from Every Product Description

| Feature Name | Possible Values | Description |
|---|---|---|
| Age Group | Juniors, Teens, GenX, Mature, All Ages | For what ages is this item most appropriate? |
| Functionality | Loungewear, Sportswear, Evening-wear, Business Casual, Business Formal | How will the item be used? |
| Formality | Informal , Somewhat Formal, Very Formal | |
| Conservative | 1(gray suits) to 5 (Loud, flashy clothes) | Conservative vs. flashy? |
| Sportiness | 1 to 5 | |
| Trendiness | 1 (Timeless Classic) to 5 (Current favorite) | Popular now but likely to go out of style vs. timeless? |
| Brand Appeal | 1(Brand makes the product unappealing) to 5 (high) | Is the brand known and appealing to a sizable group? |

bought so many SKUs from which a data mining program might conclude that customers like to buy a lot of SKUs right before Christmas. To get more meaningful information about products, we had to scrape retailers' web sites. There, they have short marketing descriptions of the garments they sell. These descriptions are crafted by professionals who are trying to convey the style, the purpose, and other attributes of the garment that influence customers' buying decisions. Here is an example of such a description:

DKNY Jeans Ruched Side-Tie Tee
Get back to basics with a fresh new look this season. The Ruched Side-Tie Tee has a drawstring tie at left hip with shirred detail down the side. Stretch provides a flattering, shapely fit. V-neck.

These descriptions enabled us to rate each article along 7 dimensions or features shown in Table 5.1.

We collected several hundred descriptions from various web sites of online retailers and then asked a dozen or so experienced shoppers to manually extract the above features from these descriptions. From this training set, our intelligent agent learned how to extract these features automatically. Now, our agent was ready to watch our shopping behavior and to provide recommendations.

The ability to capture salient features of customers' behavior and to provide recommendations is necessary but is far from sufficient for an intelligent customer service assistant. If we want intelligent agents to initiate interactions with us, we need to develop acceptable "social" rules for such interactions. These rules will be based on the agents' ability to detect situations such as: "the customer is in danger," "the customer is in a hurry," "the customer is unhappy," and many others. Technologies that will enable intelligent agents to perform these tasks are still in a research stage but will become increasingly important.

## 5.8 Microservices on Tap

Not all ubiquitous services will be focused on selling new products. Already on the horizon is a new category of services that could come in granular bits, on demand. Many services consist essentially of information, advice or hands-on assistance, which ideally would be provided when and where needed. Web services could make it feasible and cost-effective to dynamically bring together the provider and the user, while ubiquitous sensors and devices would enable the service to be provided virtually.

**Fig. 5.6.** Virtual home improvement services.

Picture a homeowner having trouble installing a light fixture. What to do? Reread the instructions? They weren't clear the first time. Hire a handyman? That's expensive — and it's Saturday night. Now imagine this: still up on the ladder, the homeowner pulls a device containing a wireless microphone out of a pocket and describes the project and the problem. This prompts a computer to search for service providers and choose one who is available, qualified, and affordable. The homeowner then turns on a wireless camera. The service provider and homeowner look at the problem, and then the homeowner follows step-by-step, real-time instructions. The charge is billed electronically. The feasibility of this approach was demonstrated at Accenture Technology Labs by the Virtual Home Improvement Services prototype [10] depicted in Figure 5.6.

The prototype has two stations: an online workbench with an overhead camera and an ordinary-looking flashlight with a built-in wireless mobile camera. Using these appliances, the customer can actually show his problem to the service provider rather than describe it in words only. The service provider sees not only the customer's problem but also the customer's history, appliances and their service records, and other relevant information. The service provider's screen of the prototype is shown on Figure 5.7. We believe that the same approach would work wherever a real-time personal coach could help — cooking, shopping, gardening, auto repair, first aid, fitness training and more.

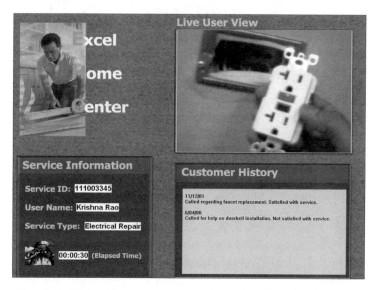

**Fig. 5.7.** Virtual home improvement services: Provider's screen.

Smart objects will not be limited to personal devices and appliances. Public infrastructure is becoming increasingly permeated with sensors. The most common public sensor today is the surveillance video camera. There are tens of thousands of them in every big city and dozens in and around every office building, and increasingly these cameras are IP-based. Our prototype of Personal Security Services [11] demonstrates how on-demand micro-services can dynamically bind to the web services provided by the public surveillance infrastructure.

Here is how it works. Picture a woman walking through a parking garage late at night. Uneasy, she takes out a device with a global positioning satellite receiver and a microphone and asks for protective assistance. Instantly, an application finds, screens, and connects her to a service. Now a security representative can access a nearby camera to watch her, scan the surrounding area, talk to her through her microphone, and call for any help she might need. Once in her car, the woman signs off and is automatically billed. Variations of this service could be used to watch over the elderly or ill, children or pets, or a home or office during an extended absence.

These applications make business sense for users and providers. Users are able to purchase otherwise expensive services in affordable increments as needed. And providers may be able to extend the services they can offer. For example, the elderly or ill may be able to have in-home monitoring and

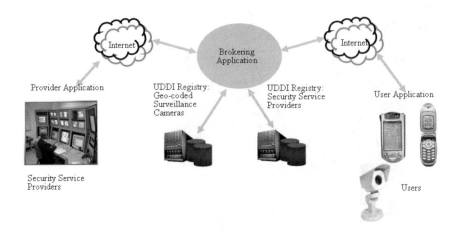

**Fig. 5.8.** Components of the virtual personal security service.

companionship, helping them to remain independent longer. That would be a benefit for their families — and a new business opportunity for health care.

Providers may even be able to offer these services by leveraging existing resources. Skilled healthcare staff and in-house experts almost always have some downtime during which they could log on and offer virtual services. Ubiquitous computing and web services, by removing the constraints of cost, time and geography, make it feasible for them to find and serve customers during those intervals.

## 5.9 Camera Phones — the New Element of Ubiquitous Services Infrastructure

Mobile phone is currently the most ubiquitous wearable device in the world. Over a billion people use it to communicate among themselves, with businesses, and with governments. Most of the new mobile phones sold in developed countries are equipped with simple cameras that can capture and send still pictures and even short videos. These cameras are rapidly improving in quality and capabilities. Camera phones are becoming an integral part of the communication infrastructure and, like every new infrastructure, camera phones will force businesses to adapt their strategies and business processes to the new capabilities. Those who adapt faster and better will gain significant competitive advantages. Call centers are a prime example of businesses having to adapt their processes to accommodate the adoption of a new technological infrastructure. The introduction of automatic telephone switches made call centers possible. In 1956, Pan Am introduced one of the first 24/7 call centers, giving customers a local phone number in every market. In 1967, AT&T's introduction of toll-free "800" numbers opened a flood gate for phone-based customer services. Today over 70% of customer interactions are handled by telecommunications channels. Call centers have become standard practice as an effective business tool and as a convenience expected by consumers.

Until now, in a typical interaction with a call center, people used the telephone to say something to a business. As people grow accustomed to using camera phones to show things to each other, inevitably they will want to use them to show something to a business. It is also likely that they will expect businesses to show things to them [4]. We believe that this change is momentous — in a very real sense, businesses through their call centers will gain millions of eyes into the world of their customers, but they will also need much greater intelligence to provide intelligent responses to vastly increased amounts of information they will be receiving.

This is already beginning to happen in public services. Citizens use their camera phones to take snap shots of non-working parking meters, car accidents, potholes, damaged property, crime suspects, etc., and try to send them to their local police departments. Unfortunately, most police departments today have no systems to deal with this type of information. To explore the likely transformation of call centers, at Accenture Technology Labs we developed a demonstration of a multi-media response center. Imagine a citizen on a train platform in Chicago witnessing a mugging. He pulls out his camera phone, takes a picture of the fleeing suspect and calls the emergency number. The screen of the emergency operator might look similar to the one shown on Figure 5.9.

The operator receives the picture and asks the caller the necessary questions. He can also see the caller's location and all the security surveillance cameras nearby. He can add their captured output to the new multimedia incident report. The operator can also send an alert and a picture of the suspect to the mobile phones within a specified distance of the crime location, thus tapping into potentially dozens of "smart sensors" — people who can use their judgment when they take pictures or notice something suspicious. As the new calls related to the original incident come in, they are attached to the report which is also immediately accessible to the responding police officer.

As citizen- and surveillance-generated media starts flooding emergency response centers, their operators' role will start changing from dispatchers to "producers" of multimedia incident reports actively soliciting and collecting real-time information from people and sensors. Investigators will become heavy users of multimedia, which will require extensive media storage, indexing and searching. Eventually, businesses will have to follow as well and re-design their call centers. And all this because of the little cameras that were at first considered mere toys.

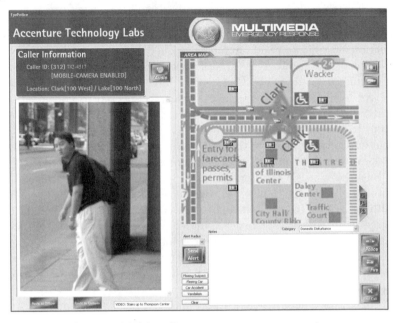

**Fig. 5.9.** Multimedia emergency response center.

## 5.10 Conclusions

Ultimately ubiquitous computing is a set of claims about the applications and services possible given changes in the infrastructure — the technical capabilities that can be assumed to exist by a service provider or application developer. These capabilities will not all arrive overnight, but rather tend to come in waves as individual classes of new devices are adopted. These devices include mobile phones, camera phones, short-range wireless, displays, etc. The camera phone is likely to become the next device to achieve ubiquity, and as we argue in this chapter, it presents both interesting opportunities and formidable challenges to businesses. It is an opportunity because it creates a media-rich channel of communication between companies and their customers. It is a formidable challenge because this channel does not simply reduce the cost of doing today's business. It demands new ways of interacting with one's customers and will require a substantial redesign of customer service processes and systems [3]. Examples used in this chapter illustrate some of the key differences between current and future customer relationship services:

**Location of your customer becomes the location of your business**. Ubiquitous devices will enable you (and your competitors) to conduct business with your customers at their location, not necessarily yours. Businesses will need points of presence where their customers are, either through wearable devices such as cell phones or through kiosks and appliances.

**Your products become channels for your services**. Pervasive networks will enable businesses to communicate with their products after they have been sold. This is already true with many software products that automatically update themselves and provide integrated online help. In the near future we expect the whole range of physical products from cars to refrigerators to be connected through the Internet to their manufacturers and other service providers.

**Service providers will compete for the best use of local contextual information provided by sensors**. Mobile devices and appliances will become the eyes and ears of service providers. This means that service providers will have to use sophisticated real-time data analysis techniques to determine the immediate needs of their customers and the best ways to interact with them.

These conclusions can be summarized as the following three "always" commandments for businesses wishing to compete in the world of ubiquitous services:

- To be always on and connected to their customers.
- To be always aware of their customers' real-time context (where the customers are, what they are doing, what is around them).
- To be always pro-active, taking advantage of the real-time opportunities to satisfy customer needs.

# References

1. A. B. Brody and E. J. Gottsman. Pocket "BargainFinder: A Handheld Device for Augmented Commerce". *Proceedings of the International Symposium on Handheld and Ubiquitous Computing HUC 99.* September 27–29. Karlsruhe, Germany. 1999.
2. A. E. Fano. "Mobile Valet: Enabling Collaboration between Remote Services, Mobile Users, and Task Location". *Proceedings of 2001 AAAI Fall Symposium on Intent Inference.* November 2–4. North Falmouth MA, USA. 2001.
3. A. E. Fano and A. Gershman. "The Future of Business Services". *Communications of the ACM*, 35(12):83–87. 2002.
4. A. Gershman and A. E. Fano. "Customer Service with Eyes". *Proceedings of Workshop on Ubiquitous Commerce at Ubicomp 2003.* October 12–15. Seattle WA, USA. 2003.
5. R. Ghani and A. E. Fano. "Building recommender systems using a knowledge base of product semantics". *Proceedings of the Workshop on Recommendation and Personalization in E-Commerce at the 2nd International Conference on Adaptive Hypermedia and Adaptive Web based Systems.* May 28. Malaga, Spain. 2002.
6. R. Ghani and A. E. Fano. "Using Text Mining to Infer Semantic Attributes for Retail Data Mining". *Proceedings of IEEE International Conference on Data Mining.* December 9–12. Maebashi, Japan. 2002.

7. R. Ghani and A. E. Fano. "Building recommender systems using a knowledge base of product semantics". *Proceedings of the Workshop on Recommendation and Personalization in ECommerce at the 2nd International Conference on Adaptive Hypermedia and Adaptive Web based Systems*. May 28. Malaga, Spain. 2002.

8. D. Wan. "Magic Medicine Cabinet: A Situated Portal for Healthcare". *Proceedings of the International Symposium on Handheld and Ubiquitous Computing*. September 27–29. Karlsruhe, Germany. 1999.

9. D. Wan. M"agic Wardrobe: Situated Shopping from Your Own Bedroom". *Proceedings of the Second International Symposium on Handheld and Ubiquitous Computing*, September 25–27. Bristol, UK. 2000.

10. D. Wan. "Virtual Handyman: Supporting Micro Services on Tap through Situated Sensing and Web Services". *Supplemental Proceedings of ACM 2002 Conference on Computer Supported Cooperative Work CSCW 02*, November 16–20. New Orleans, Louisiana, USA. 2002.

11. D. Wan and A. Gershman. "Protecting People on the Move through Virtual Personal Security". *International Workshop on Ubiquitous Computing IWUC 04 at the 6th International Conference on Enterprise Information Systems ICEIS*, April 13–14. Porto, Portugal. 2004.

12. D. Wan. "Personalized Ubiquitous Commerce: An Application Perspective". In C. Karat, J. Blom and J. Karat (Eds.) *Designing Personalized User Experiences for e-Commerce*. Kluwer Academic Publishers. 2004.

# 6

# The Business Value of Ubiquitous Computing Technologies

Elgar Fleisch and Christian Tellkamp

## 6.1 Introduction

Although there is no widely accepted definition of ubiquitous computing to date, one can probably say that applications based on ubiquitous computing technologies involve large numbers of non-traditional networked computing devices that are often mobile and/or equipped with sensors to collect data [15]. Ubiquitous computing technologies include automatic identification technologies (for example Radio Frequency Identification or RFID), sensors for location (for example Global Positioning System or GPS), temperature, acceleration and other environmental parameters, as well as wireless communication technologies (for example Global Standard for Mobile Communication or GSM). One of the main factors that underly the recent emergence of ubiquitous computing is the trend towards further miniaturisation of electronic components. Indeed, sensors, processors, and other computing elements are becoming smaller and cheaper and can now be integrated into various products in our everyday lives.

Ubiquitous computing technologies also offer companies the opportunity to improve processes (cf. Chapter 3), to enhance products by making them smart, and to develop new services. Current research in this area often focuses on consumer applications. Researchers have, for example, examined how ubiquitous computing will change the relationship between companies and their customers (cf. Chapter 5) by helping companies to get to know their customer needs better and to achieve more direct access to them. These new capabilities create both opportunities and challenges and require companies to redefine their service offering [14].

The fact that ubiquitous computing can also be used to improve intra-organisational as well as inter-organisational processes is often overlooked. This chapter focuses on these business applications of ubiquitous computing. One of the main capabilities of ubiquitous computing technologies in the context of business applications is their potential to reduce media breaks between the physical world and information systems [15]. This provides the opportunity for a more accurate, timely, and detailed integration of the real and the virtual world.

As ubiquitous computing technologies become mature [25], commercial applications gradually become feasible [15]. There are a number of ubiquitous computing business applications which are either in pilot phases or already available on the market. However, so far little is known about the impact of ubiquitous computing technologies on business processes and how applications based on these technologies can create value for companies. Some authors mention economic concerns as one of the inhibitors to deploying ubiquitous systems [10].

We believe there is no general answer to the question of which ubiquitous computing applications are value-creating. Companies wishing to invest need to determine the value of a ubiquitous computing application on a case-by-case basis. If they find it difficult to identify promising applications, this can delay adoption.

This chapter discusses how companies can benefit from ubiquitous computing applications. The first part argues that ubiquitous computing improves integration of the real and the virtual world, and thereby addresses common problems of companies that involve physical assets. Investing in ubiquitous computing applications only makes sense if the benefits exceed the cost. This leads to the question of how companies can identify value-creating ubiquitous computing applications. This is no easy task, as the second part of this chapter shows. We propose a framework which suggests a number of challenges that companies face and provide examples for each of the challenges. This is followed by a description of how the retail industry is addressing these challenges for RFID technology. The final part concludes that companies have to choose between a proactive or reactive approach towards ubiquitous computing.

The examples used in this chapter stem from our research on business applications of ubiquitous computing technologies. Most of the research was conducted in a research project called the Mobile and Ubiquitous Computing Lab (M-Lab), a joint initiative of the University of St. Gallen (HSG) and ETH Zurich, Switzerland. M-Lab's corporate partners include SAP, Infineon, Swissccom Mobile and Migros. Further insights, especially on RFID applications, came from a number of bilateral projects, including companies involved in the Metro Group Future Store Initiative [26], and from our activities as one of the Auto-ID Labs.

## 6.2 Ubiquitous Computing: Integration of the Real and the Virtual Worlds

### 6.2.1 Lack of Integration in Today's Information Systems

Despite heavy investment in integrated information systems, many business problems still prevail due to a lack of integration between the real and virtual world. These problems include product availability, shrinkage, counterfeiting, inventory accuracy, recalls, and recycling. Low data quality currently limits enterprise computing. Better data quality and digital management control loops can help to solve (or at least reduce) these problems. Ubiquitous computing technologies, including automatic identification, are the technological enabler towards improved data quality.

Existing information systems already solve many integration problems. However, the vision of the real-time company will not be achieved for some time to come. Businesses continue to suffer from a lack of useful data, which causes inefficiencies. For example, consumer goods and retail companies are currently unable to effectively deal with their out-of-stock, shelf lifetime, cool-chain, theft, and counterfeit problems. If a retail company knew exactly which products were on the shelf and which were in the backroom of the store, it could considerably increase product availability [19, 20]. Why cannot retail chains simply collect the corresponding data or derive it from their barcode-based check-out systems? The answer to this question is straightforward and comes back to the integration problem: based on today's technology, full data collection, which can be regarded as the integration of information systems with the physical world, is expensive.

Thus, companies have developed data gathering and processing methods for which low data quality is sufficient. For instance, since collecting reliable inventory information is time-consuming and expensive, companies conduct inventory counts only once or twice a year. Similarly, because it is too costly to check the accuracy of each incoming and outgoing delivery, companies rely on random checks. The current high cost of integrating the real with the virtual world results in decisions which are based on low-quality information. Managers rely heavily on statistics based on historical data.

## 6.2.2 Data Quality Improvements with Ubiquitous Computing Technologies

With the declining price of sensors and actuators, conventional data entry and data leveraging methods are being replaced by ubiquitous computing technologies. In addition to this substitution effect, an elasticity effect can be observed: additional sensors and actuators are employed where companies can create value from higher data quality, that is where the benefits from higher data quality exceed the cost.

Data quality can be described in four dimensions. The first dimension is the timeliness of data. Timeliness is low when, as in the example of inventory counting, data capture is so time-consuming and expensive that it only allows an occasional reality check. Timeliness is high if the sensor technology's marginal cost is so low that it justifies ongoing checks with the physical environment (cf. Figure 6.1). Information systems with such a high data timeliness do not rely on statistics based on historical data – they always employ

up-to-date information. In principle, they can collect a complete history of a
physical instance and detect real-world events in real time.

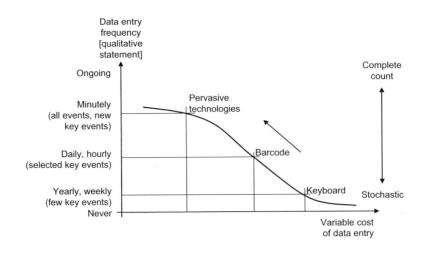

**Fig. 6.1.** Ubiquitous computing increases data timeliness.

The next two data quality dimensions deal with the physical objects that
are to be integrated. One dimension describes the type of object. With the
advent of ubiquitous computing technologies, business cases for integrating
smaller and less valuable objects are starting to become viable. Today, there is
often justification for tagging reusable transport containers [1]. With the roll-
out plans of Wal-Mart, the U.S. Department of Defense, and Metro [31, 11, 27],
the tagging of pallets and cartons is likely to reach a critical mass for writing
a sound business case. In some industries, for example in the textile industry,
which deals with high-value and highly individual products, even item tagging
is starting to pay off [23].

The third data quality dimension describes how many physical objects of
a class (for example boxes) are integrated. As it becomes less expensive to
integrate physical objects with the digital world, more objects (instances of
boxes) within one object class (all boxes) will be equipped with ubiquitous
computing technology. As a consequence, the number of integrated objects
per class rises. Integrating 100% of objects is not necessarily a requirement.
For instance, if a mail order company equips 5% of its video camera boxes
with RFID tags to trace them through the supply chain, object granularity
is still rather low. However, when the company can use this information to
detect where high-value shipments are typically delayed, lost or stolen, such
a low level of granularity may be sufficient.

The fourth dimension of data quality likely to be affected by ubiquitous
computing technologies is the variety of data that is automatically collected.

As a minimum, the integration of physical objects requires a unique identifier for each object class or object instance. Three decades ago, EAN/UCC started to provide the retail industry with a unique class identifier. In 2003, the Auto-ID Center proposed the electronic product code, a unique identifier at instance level [3]. Advanced ubiquitous computing applications, for example in the automotive and high-tech industries, already collect additional object-related data such as quality management data, subsequent production stages, customer name, or target configuration. Adding new sensors allows for the integration of data from the immediate environment of the objects (cf. Figure 6.2).

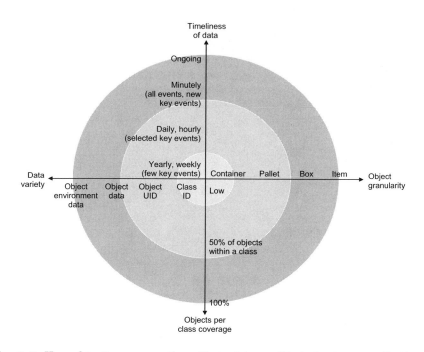

**Fig. 6.2.** How ubiquitous computing affects data quality in business applications.

### 6.2.3 Digital Management Control Loops

Ubiquitous computing reduces the marginal cost of integrating the real with the virtual world. It thus enables information systems to collect more detailed data at the point of creation (POC) and eventually allows managers and machines at the point of action (POA) to implement decisions based on high quality, real-time information. Ubiquitous computing technologies, particularly automatic identification, sensor and actuator technology, are the technical foundation for the digitisation and automation of POC and POA.

They are essential prerequisites for creating digital management control loops (cf. Figure 6.3).

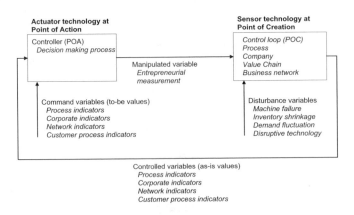

**Fig. 6.3.** Digital management control loop.

Ubiquitous computing technologies will primarily be used in control-intensive processes that require high data quality. Auto-ID technologies, embedded systems, and sensor networks will not be implemented if existing statistical methods work cost-effectively and provide sufficient data quality. There has to be a positive business case for closing the digital management control loop.

### 6.2.4 Incremental Versus Radical Change

The change in control-intensive processes can be divided into two classes. Class 1 contains existing processes which are control-intensive by nature or by law. Class 1 processes such as quality assurance need to be tightly controlled, irrespective of whether ubiquitous computing technologies are employed. New technology only makes those processes faster, more accurate, reliable, and cost-effective. It creates incremental rather than substantial change. Most of the current RFID projects deal with Class 1 process changes: RFID reduces failure rates, shrinkage and operating stock, and enhances on-time delivery, shipment quality, and so forth [16]. Overall, Class 1 process changes provide value by modifying the way in which companies manage their resources ("how"), but do not change companies' business models ("what").

Class 2 changes deal with new business models that become feasible with the advent of high data quality. In the case of Class 2 changes, companies do not question how they could improve their current processes with ubiquitous computing technology. Instead, they investigate which new products and services could be offered to customers, given that control-intensive processes can be managed at reasonably low cost. Whereas Class 1 changes seek incremental improvements that, in the short term, typically affect only a company's efficiency, Class 2 changes strive for more radical innovations which affect customer relations, services, and revenue models [37].

## 6.3 Identifying Value-Creating Ubiquitous Computing Applications

### 6.3.1 Improved Processes, Enhanced Products, and New Services

Many business scenarios based on ubiquitous computing technologies that are currently being discussed or implemented focus on Class 1 changes that are aimed at automating quality checks. In a typical supply chain, for instance, quality checks are performed before, during, and/or after critical process steps, such as change of ownership or events with the potential to create and destroy value. These quality checks often require manual work and are time-consuming, costly, and error-prone. With ubiquitous computing-based quality checks, not only is the number of checks likely to rise and thus the supply chain quality; also, under certain conditions (high failure cost that declines with higher data quality; strong increase in cost for manual quality checks with increasing levels of data quality), the sum of checking and failure costs will decline.

Once a company knows which events drive or destroy value and is able to collect these events cost-effectively, it can initiate Class 2 changes. One possible route is to change the company's business model from selling services at a fixed price to usage-based billing. Vendor and customer would negotiate a price that is not based on the average cost over all customers, but on the individual cost of the customer in question. Using GPS sensors and mobile technologies, for example, a car insurance company could collect the driving patterns of its customers and calculate premiums based on whether the driver is driving by night or day, on a motorway or in town, in a good or bad neighbourhood or weather conditions, and so forth. Initial pilot tests on usage-based car insurance are underway [24]. Product companies may become service companies that do not sell products, for example drilling machines, any longer. Instead, they may use ubiquitous computing technologies as the enabler to sell services, such as drilling holes or managing the entire machinery fleet at a construction site.

Data from ubiquitous computing applications can also provide evidence of accountability. A constant log of highly granular data could answer questions such as: Who gave the patient the wrong medicine? Who replaced the bumper with the counterfeit product of minor value that led to a mass collision on a motorway? Who let the frozen oysters warm up, causing food poisoning? Ultimately, this raises questions such as: Who is accountable for value added or value lost? Who has to pay for the consequences? Such detailed and objective high-quality data might enable and force companies to change contracts with customers and suppliers in order to take this new level of accountability into account.

Product companies that offer product-related services earn on average more than companies which only sell products [17]. The service business is appealing from a financial, marketing, and strategic perspective: services can generate additional sales, promise higher margins, are a relatively stable source of revenue, and are more difficult to imitate than products. Ubiquitous computing offers an opportunity for manufacturing companies to augment their products with services [16]. They may, for example, engineer printers, lighting systems, video projectors, and so forth that "order" cartridges and spare parts automatically at the right time and thereby help to reduce total cost of ownership.

### 6.3.2 Valuation: A Difficult Task

It is not always easy to determine whether the benefits of an investment, such as an upgrade of process equipment, or the development of a new product or service portfolio are sufficient to make the investment pay off. Authors often distinguish between tangible and intangible benefits. Whereas tangible benefits can easily be transferred into monetary values, intangible benefits are harder to grasp. Benefits can be seen as intangible, for example, (a) if there is a complex causal chain between the functionality the system provides and the monetary value derived from the functionality, or (b) if the benefits only materialise in a medium- to long-term future that is hard to predict. The extent to which tangible or intangible benefits are prevalent varies with the type of information system. Systems aiming at internal efficiency (which are similar to Class 1 changes) are likely to have a high proportion of tangible benefits, whereas investments in IT infrastructure and strategic systems (which are similar to Class 2 changes) are likely to have a high proportion of intangible benefits [38].

Currently, many companies require a formal "business case" before starting a project. Projects that cannot demonstrate a positive value are unlikely to be approved. This is a reasonable strategy as companies should only invest in projects that have a positive return; otherwise, they destroy value. There are a variety of techniques for estimating the pay-off from an investment: companies can, for example, use discounted cash flow or real option approaches.

For many applications, however, a financial valuation of this kind is a difficult task. In some instances, intangible benefits need to be included in the valuation process in order to justify the investment. The project team then faces the difficult job of quantifying intangible benefits (for example, better customer service, higher flexibility, shorter lead times) in monetary terms as well as they can. In other words, they need to make these benefits tangible.

Companies need to find a balance between focusing solely on "hard" (or tangible) benefits on the one hand and making decisions entirely based on "soft" (or intangible) benefits on the other. Short-term orientation and an inability to proceed with potentially valuable projects is sometimes attributed to a failure to capture intangible benefits [38, 36]. It is highly likely that the results of the valuation process will only provide a rough approximation of the value. However, bearing this in mind, Kaplan states that managers need not follow accountants who "prefer being precisely wrong to being vaguely right" [22, p. 92].

### 6.3.3 A Framework of Challenges for Identifying Value-Creating Applications

The identification of ubiquitous computing applications that create value for a company is a difficult task. Integrating intangible benefits into the valuation process is one of the challenges, but not the only one. The framework in Figure 6.4 contains four challenges which complicate the identification of value-creating ubiquitous computing applications: the network challenge, the constraints challenge, the implementation challenge, and the valuation challenge.

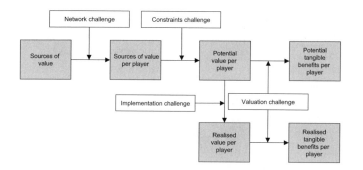

**Fig. 6.4.** From sources of value to tangible benefits per player: challenges in identifying value-creating ubiquitous computing applications.

The framework proposed here uses ideas taken from the model presented by Chircu and Kauffman [9], although its intention is different. Our focus is on the challenges of identifying value-creating applications, both *ex ante* and *ex post*, whereas Chircu and Kauffman focus on the barriers that prevent the sources of value from being fully realised, without considering whether such barriers are visible.

### 6.3.4 Network Challenges

Ubiquitous computing applications often involve more than one company. Network challenges deal with the issue that, in general, companies will not invest in an application unless they see a positive value for themselves. An analysis at the network level may indicate high sources of value. However, this is only a necessary but not an adequate criterion. What is relevant is the balance between cost and benefits at the level of the individual company.

The relevance of the network challenge is illustrated by the introduction of RFID technology in retail supply chains. Retailers such as Wal-Mart expect to benefit from the use of RFID tags to track pallets and cases and are working on introducing the technology [31]. They are implicitly expecting their suppliers to bear — at least a large part of — the cost of the RFID tags. For some manufacturers, the cost of the RFID tags is likely to exceed the gains from the investment [4, 6]. These suppliers may initially not be willing to introduce RFID technology. A solution needs to be found so that every player in the supply chain can agree to use RFID.

### 6.3.5 Constraints Challenges

Constraints challenges are issues which inhibit realisation of the entire sources of value. Major constraints include existing systems and processes. Specifically for ubiquitous computing applications, Davies and Gellersen [20] mention technical challenges as well as social and legal issues (cf. Chapter 9). Social acceptance will be low, for example, if customers have the impression that printers order new cartridges too early in order to create additional profit for the manufacturer at the expense of higher maintenance cost, or that their freedom of choice is limited due to strong technology-based lock-in. Legal issues include accountability, privacy (cf. Chapter 11), and data security. The effect of these challenges is that a player can only reap a certain part of the value sources, referred to as the potential value.

A project on smart vending machines can illustrate some constraints challenges. Today, a lot of vending machines already contain sensors that monitor inventory levels and other operating parameters. However, this information is often only available locally. In the project, the data is transferred via the GSM network. The project's aims include improving product availability and decreasing maintenance cost by allowing timely and event-based refill and maintenance processes.

As we discovered, current processes and cost considerations prevent some of the value sources from being realisable. Although in theory the data could improve product availability, the company involved in the project currently finds it difficult to establish a positive business case: first, the current inventory management system is already quite sophisticated. There is a system in place for managing product availability. Sales data for each slot in a vending machine is registered, and refill intervals and levels are defined on the basis of this information. The system already takes seasonal demand patterns into account. The value of real-time information is therefore limited. Real-time inventory data would only help the company to detect unexpected fluctuations in demand that can lead to out-of-stock situations. Second, there is no system in place that allows dynamic routes to be defined based on product availability in certain vending machines and the personnel cost for refilling these machines. The company has defined fixed routes that specify which vending machines are refilled on what dates. A major issue in defining a tour is minimising the time an employee needs to get from one vending machine to the next. Any additional travel time for the company's employees could easily consume the additional margins from higher sales. A dynamic routing system would have to take information into account from roughly ten thousand vending machines that are serviced by about 30 employees.

### 6.3.6 Implementation Challenges

As the term already indicates, implementation challenges become relevant when a company wants to realise an application. Limited resources and knowledge prior to and during the implementation or low actual use of the system can diminish the potential value. Delays in the project can reduce the potential value as (a) cash flows are delayed in time and (b) an initial competitive advantage may be lost. The following example illustrates how implementation challenges can affect potentially valuable projects.

For a car manufacturer, we analysed whether RFID tags attached to spare parts could improve the efficiency of handling incoming and outgoing deliveries and increase delivery and inventory accuracy in the company's spare parts business. Although the potentials of RFID technology look promising, the company has not yet implemented the solution. Making the technology work would have required the company to invest significant resources, for example in conjunction with the selection of appropriate tags, positioning of antennas, and integration into legacy systems. At that point in time, the project was competing for scarce financial and human resources with other projects. Given that it would take several years before the system became fully operational, the company decided to postpone the project.

### 6.3.7 Valuation Challenges

Valuation challenges refer to the problem of determining the tangible benefits from a project. Valuation challenges are present at two distinct points in time: *ex ante*, before a decision is made to go ahead with an investment, and *ex post*, after the solution has been implemented.

For a pharmaceutical company, we examined a solution that monitors the compliance of patients with chronic illnesses in taking their prescribed medication. By increasing the compliance of these patients, pharmaceutical companies hope to increase sales, for example by reducing the churn rate. The solution uses Bluetooth and GSM technology for data communication. To illustrate the concept, a demonstrator was built as part of the project. The system would have required the co-operation of doctors, pharmacists, and patients. Their willingness to co-operate was hard to judge, and we were not able to determine *ex ante* with reasonable accuracy (a) whether a monitoring solution would be able to increase compliance and (b) to what extent the pharmaceutical company would benefit from this. The potential benefits of the application thus remained intangible.

It can also be difficult to assess the value of an application *ex post*. A common approach is to conduct a pilot project to see whether the potential benefits are achievable in a real world setting. While it is often quite easy to measure efficiency gains, for example the effect of lower cost for data capture, it can be difficult to determine the effect of higher data quality on performance.

A large European retailer is testing different technologies in one of its supermarkets, among them RFID technology. In this test, RFID tags are used to track the movement of cases and pallets from the distribution centre to the store and from the backroom of the store to the shop floor. Furthermore, a number of products are tagged at item level. This allows the company to monitor product availability on the retail shelf. However, processes in a pilot are frequently unable to fully reflect the real thing. In the pilot, for example, cases are manually tagged in the distribution centre before they are shipped to the store, and the data gathered from RFID is not yet used extensively to drive store and replenishment processes. It is therefore difficult to measure whether labour productivity in the store has increased. A factor which is even harder to assess is the impact of RFID on data accuracy and product availability.

# 6.4 Overcoming the Challenges: RFID in the Retail Industry

### 6.4.1 The Adoption of RFID in the Retail Industry

Despite the heavy use of data capturing (barcode) and data transmission technologies (EDI), data quality in the supply chain is still far from perfect. This is one of the reasons why leading retailers, including Wal-Mart and Target in the USA, Tesco in the UK and Metro in Germany, have announced that they are to roll out RFID in their supply chains at case and pallet level within the next two to three years. In keeping with our general description of the impact of ubiquitous computing on business applications, these companies are introducing RFID to reduce the cost of data acquisition and to improve data quality. The anticipated benefits from RFID include increased product availability, improved warehousing operations, and reduced shrinkage.

Wal-Mart, Tesco, Metro, and other retailers as well as several large consumer packaged goods manufacturers, including Coca-Cola, Nestlé, Procter & Gamble, and Unilever, support the standards developed by EPCglobal. They use low-cost, passive RFID tags that contain only a unique identifier, the electronic product code (EPC). Passive RFID tags use the electromagnetic field of the reader for their energy supply.

RFID technology offers automatic identification of products and can be regarded as a first step towards better integration of the real and the virtual world. In the retail industry, RFID as described above effectively "competes" with the barcode and to a lesser extent with manual data capturing methods as well. Using RFID has the advantage that the tags can be read without human intervention and without line of sight, which allows bulk readings.

The effort to introduce EPCs stored on RFID tags in the retail industry started in 1999 when the Auto-ID Center at the Massachusetts Institute of Technology (MIT) was founded. Among the early sponsors were retailers such as Wal-Mart and CPG manufacturers such as Procter & Gamble and Gillette. In 2003, EPCglobal took over the standardisation activities for the EPC Network. The parent organisations of EPCglobal, EAN International and the Uniform Code Council (UCC), create, develop and manage, among others, the barcode standards that consumers find on the vast majority of products sold in supermarkets (cf. Chapter 2). The Auto-ID Labs at MIT, University of Cambridge (UK), University of Adelaide (Australia), Keio University (Japan), Fudan University (China), and University of St. Gallen (Switzerland) that formed the Auto-ID Center are part of EPCglobal and focus on research issues.

The previous section of this chapter contained several examples of the use of RFID in the retail industry. We now describe below how the retail industry tackles the challenge of identifying which applications of RFID can create value. The focus is on activities related to the Auto-ID Center/EPCglobal and companies that support these standards.

## 6.4.2 Addressing the Network Challenges

Right from the beginning, the sponsors of the Auto-ID Center were interested in an assessment of the overall return on investment for RFID in the retail industry. As part of the Auto-ID Center, the Business Case Action Group was responsible for establishing the business case for RFID in the retail industry. The group consisted of representatives from several retailers and manufacturers, Auto-ID staff, as well as two large consultancies. The results of their work were published in a series of white papers and suggest that the retail industry as a whole can benefit from RFID. Frequently mentioned benefits of RFID include reduction in out-of-stocks, receiving and shipping efficiency and accuracy, picking efficiency and accuracy, reduction in shrinkage and unsaleables, and check-out efficiency. The benefits and costs differ, depending on whether RFID tags are applied at the pallet, case or item level. Whereas pallet and case level tagging can already pay off today, the cost of item tagging every product sold in supermarkets is still prohibitive (see for example [21]). At the item level, RFID tags are likely to be used first on products with high shrinkage rates (for example Gillette razor blades) or in product categories such as apparel. These results can be interpreted as one of the reasons why retailers such as Wal-Mart and Metro are initially introducing RFID on pallets and cases.

With the business case established for the retail industry (at least in theory), there is the question of how cost and benefits are distributed. This network challenge for RFID in the retail industry has already been described above: there might be an imbalance between the cost and benefits for manufacturers and retailers, with the manufacturer carrying the major part of the cost [4, 6]. Retailers such as Wal-Mart have reacted to these claims at an early stage and have encouraged their suppliers to identify the value of RFID in their operations [31]. All retailers are working closely with a number of key suppliers. Metro has opened an RFID Innovation Center at one of its distribution centres where suppliers can test their hardware and software in order to prepare for the RFID roll-out [28]. However, some suppliers find it difficult to justify an investment in RFID [18]. In order to ensure compliance, retailers may ultimately use their purchasing power and make the use of RFID mandatory for their suppliers. (Whether this will ultimately happen is still unclear. Retailers such as Wal-Mart are known for their commitment to collaboration and their emphasis on good relationships with suppliers [18].) Non-compliance may then simply not be an option for most manufacturers. In this case, the decision to adopt RFID can be seen as value-creating for suppliers as this is a prerequisite for staying in business.

### 6.4.3 Addressing the Constraints Challenges

The activities of the Business Case Action Group and other industry participants have helped to determine the "size of the pie" that is attainable in principle by each player. However, there are a number of constraints that companies need to take into account. Existing systems and processes, technical challenges, and social and legal issues can limit the value that companies can derive from RFID.

If companies use RFID merely to achieve a higher level of automatic data capture than is possible with the barcode and to reduce errors in current processes (Class 1 changes), our research indicates that RFID is of limited value. Companies need to find and implement new processes and change their IT systems so that they can make full use of RFID (Class 2 changes). Companies can, for instance, use RFID to track and trace individual products through their supply chain, not just classes of products as is the case today. This would largely extend the amount of data to be processed and stored. Current enterprise resource planning applications in the retail industry are generally not able to track individual products.

Gathering this data only makes sense if companies can generate value from the data. This requires new applications which contain additional business logic. Truth Software is one of the companies that intends to develop these applications. The start-up is aimed at integrating the additional data gathered from RFID systems into forecasting models in order to reduce the out-of-stock problem [32].

One technical challenge is the read rates of RFID tags. In order to test RFID technology in real world environments, the Auto-ID Center started a field test in early 2001. Independently of this test, several companies also conducted RFID trials. In general, the Auto-ID Center field test has demonstrated that RFID technology works. The pilot test has also shown that read rates of 100% for bulk reading cannot be achieved with current technology [2]. At the moment this constrains the benefits of RFID in the supply chain. For example, companies may find it hard to conduct automatic quantity checks at the receiving dock doors for products that contain water and metal. Nevertheless, the Auto-ID Center Field Test had a significant impact in the community: it has helped to establish confidence that the technology works, but also clearly highlighted the areas in which further development is needed.

One of the main social and legal issues is privacy. This is especially relevant for item level tagging. Although the companies do not mention it officially, protests from consumer activists were one of the factors contributing towards Wal-Mart's and Tesco's decision to stop tests with "smart shelves" in 2003. The Auto-ID Center has already addressed the issue of privacy before consumer activists started their protests: in 2002, the Auto-ID Center commissioned several studies with consumer groups in order to understand their attitude towards RFID. The initial reaction from participants was slightly negative. Consumers were concerned about abuse, privacy invasion, potential health risks, and did not see much benefit for themselves. The report concludes that such concerns can be overcome by offering consumers a choice, installing proper governance, gathering more information (for example on health issues), and communicating responsibly and proactively [12]. The Auto-ID Center and subsequently EPCglobal have drawn up privacy guidelines, and both Wal-Mart and Metro have issued individual policies. In general, the positions of EPCglobal and the consumer activists do not seem to be that far apart from one another (see EPCglobal's "Guidelines on EPC for Consumer Products" [13] and the "RFID Position Statement of Consumer Privacy and Civil Liberties Organisations," issued by several consumer activist groups [8]). There is, however, one potentially important difference: the EPCglobal guidelines do not envisage consumers being informed each time an RFID tag is read. So far, it is too early to determine what role privacy will play in the longer run. In the near future, there will hardly be any readers on a supermarket's shop floor.

Although the industry has addressed privacy aspects early, the current discussion indicates that the industry has failed to reach consumers in good time. Consumers have not received the message that they can benefit from RFID through higher product availability and lower prices due to efficiency gains in the supply chain. As a result of privacy concerns, companies such as Gillette or the apparel industry that are at the forefront of RFID at the item level might find it difficult to introduce RFID in the short term. This will therefore restrict the benefit that can be achieved with RFID.

### 6.4.4 Addressing the Implementation Challenges

Companies that want to roll out RFID currently face a number of implementation challenges: for example, it will be well into 2005 before RFID tags and readers based on the new ultra high frequency (UHF) reader interface protocol become widely available [33]. Furthermore, technology components, including readers and middleware software, are not yet "plug and play." Some articles have also claimed that, at least in the short term, there is a shortage of skilled labour [30]. Another implementation challenge that can limit the value of an RFID system is the adoption rate: if only a few suppliers implement RFID, the benefits will be limited as there will be a need for retailers to run two distinct processes, one RFID-based, the other one barcode-based.

At the moment, companies that want to deploy RFID need to factor in these aspects in their roll-out plans. Clear communication is one of the main approaches to addressing the challenges. This includes forums such as the European Adoption Program (EAP), a group within EPCglobal where European retailers and CPG manufacturers meet regularly to share information on the status quo and to discuss the next steps.

In order to avoid a situation where only selected suppliers tag their deliveries (which would drastically reduce the benefit of RFID for retailers), the retailers have issued a very detailed timeline for the roll-out. The retail industry also needs to communicate the relevant information (for example, on timelines and business requirements) to the technology providers. This is one of the tasks of the Business Action Group within EPCglobal. In addition, the individual companies that are driving the adoption process need to state their plans. If, for example, they publish their expected demand for RFID tags over the next few years, they will give chip and label producers the opportunity to plan their production capacity adequately. This will reduce the risk for producers and is likely to encourage competition, which will drive down prices.

### 6.4.5 Addressing the Valuation Challenges

Valuation challenges refer to the problem of estimating *ex ante* and measuring *ex post* the benefits of an investment. Experience with the introduction of the barcode in the retail industry showed that an investment needed to be justified by "hard" benefits alone and that "soft" benefits were widely disregarded [5].

Before investing in RFID, every company has to determine what it expects to gain from RFID in its own specific set of circumstances. This can take some time. Building a business case for RFID is far from easy [18]. The most advanced retailers and manufacturers have been working on their business cases for years. Manufacturers that find it hard to justify RFID in their operations are faced with the difficult task of determining how to deal with the retailers' RFID mandates. They have to weigh the cost and benefit of different options. On the one hand, they can aggressively move forward with RFID in the hope of gaining additional market share. On the other hand, they can not comply (or comply with a time delay) in order to save the cost of RFID tags, with the risk of damaging their customer relationships and losing business in the future. Initially at least, a number of suppliers may follow a simple "slap and ship" approach, as some industry observers (for example, Forrester Research [34]) recommend.

As already described, it is very hard to measure the actual benefits of RFID at the moment as roll-out is still at a very early stage. Close collaboration between a retailer and a few key suppliers, for example during pilot tests, is one way forward. As part of a broader pilot, the partners can then specifically focus on processes and the business impact of RFID. One example is Metro, which has worked with Procter & Gamble in order to establish a business case for RFID [29].

## 6.5 Conclusions

Ubiquitous computing technologies improve the integration of the real and the virtual world. They allow companies to improve data quality and realise digital management control loops. However, identifying value-creating ubiquitous computing applications is far from easy. Companies need to take several challenges into account when trying to determine whether an investment in a business application based on ubiquitous computing technologies can pay off. This chapter focused on the network, the constraints, the implementation, and the valuation challenge. These challenges are not unique to ubiquitous computing applications. However, some of the challenges — the network challenge, the constraints challenge, and the ex-post valuation challenge — could well be of specific relevance to ubiquitous computing applications.

The network challenge occurs when more than one company is involved in an application. This is frequently the case with business applications of ubiquitous computing technologies. The question of appropriate business models is far from being solved for a lot of scenarios [20]. Further examples of complex scenarios involving ubiquitous computing technologies where the business model might not be obvious can be found for example in Fano and Gershman [14], and Tarasewich and Warkentin [35].

The constraints challenge deals with the limitations in achieving the value sources due, for example, to compatibility issues with existing processes or systems. One of the main challenges for ubiquitous computing applications is putting the information that can be gathered into use. New kinds of application logic may be needed in order to benefit from the additional data. Moreover, the proliferation of technology in our everyday lives raises questions about privacy, along with other social and legal issues that companies need to consider.

**Table 6.1.** Addressing the Challenges: The Example of RFID/EPC in the Retail Industry

| Challenges | Description | Activities |
|---|---|---|
| Network Challenges | For the adoption of applications based on a new technology, it is often not sufficient for the total value to be positive; each player must expect to profit | Engage in industry initiatives and establish high-level business case for the industry |
| | | Collaborate closely with key suppliers and customers |
| | | Share experiences and learnings from field trials |
| | | Seek win-win with partners and force adoption only as a measure of last resort |
| Constraints Challenges | Existing processes and systems, technological limitations, as well as social and legal issues can limit the potential value | Determine implications for processes and systems and develop concepts on how these can be changed |
| | | Conduct extensive technology tests |
| | | Identify potentially critical social and legal issues early and address them within industry |
| | | Communicate proactively with the public and stress benefits for consumers |
| Implementation Challenges | Limited resources, availability of technology, or low actual use can reduce the realised value | Define key technology requirements within industry |
| | | Clearly communicate requirements to industry partners and technology providers |
| | | Establish a timeline and set specific milestones |
| Valuation Challenges | Ex-ante assessment and ex-post measurement of tangible benefits are often difficult | Start early with the development of a business case for your company |
| | | Try to identify tangible benefits and "make intangible benefits tangible" whenever possible |
| | | Set up pilots that allow business case assumptions to be tested |

The ex-post valuation challenge refers to the problem of measuring the value that is supposed to be created by an application. Even when benefits are tangible *ex ante* and can be demonstrated in theory (for example, increased product availability due to higher inventory accuracy), they can be difficult to observe and may only show in the long run. For such applications, it might take some time to prove that tangible results are delivered.

The fact that it is challenging to identify value-creating ubiquitous computing applications has certain implications for the adoption of ubiquitous computing applications. Previous comments might suggest that companies should follow a rather reactive, low-risk strategy of "follow, don't lead" [7, p. 48]. And if a company decides to lead, it might focus on Class 1 applications that deliver incremental improvements and quick wins. These are likely to be applications which involve only a limited number of players, rely on proven technology, do not require extensive changes to existing systems, and are consistent with existing processes. Furthermore, companies may select applications with tangible benefits that can easily be observed after implementation. However, there might be an alternative to this strategy. To a certain degree, a company may be able to improve its evaluation process and thereby reduce the risk of failure when attempting Class 2 changes. Only companies that follow this proactive approach are likely to develop applications that provide an — at least temporary — competitive advantage. There is a rationale for starting early: in the long term, many applications are likely to become a strategic necessity, rather than a source of competitive advantage. The experience with RFID shows that the few retailers and CPG manufacturers that rank among the leaders have followed this strategy. Table 6.1 summarises how these leading companies in the retail industry have addressed the individual challenges. A good understanding of the challenges can lead to a higher probability of correctly identifying value-creating applications of ubiquitous computing technologies that are fundamental in nature. Knowledge seems to play an important role if this strategy is to work. Companies wishing to pursue this strategy are advised to engage in industry initiatives, collaborate with other companies, develop internal resources, conduct extensive pilots, and seek close contact with academic institutions.

# References

1. Aberdeen Group. *RFID-Enabled Logistics Asset Management: Improving Capital Utilization, Increasing Availability, and Lowering Total Operational Costs.* Report. 2004.
2. S. Albano. Auto-ID Field Test: Lessons Learned in the Real World. Presentation at *EPC Symposium.* Chicago, USA. September 16, 2003.
3. K. Asthon and S. Sarma. "Introducing the EPC Network". *Presentation at EPC Symposium.* Chicago, USA. September 16, 2003.
4. A.T. Kearney Consulting. *Meeting the RFID retail mandate: A discussion of the issues facing CPG companies.* Report. A.T. Kearney Consulting. 2003.

5. S.A. Brown. *Revolution at the Checkout Counter: The Explosion of the Bar Code.* Harvard University Press. Cambridge and London. 1997.

6. J. Byrnes. Who Will Profit From Auto-ID? *Harvard Business School Working Knowledge.* Archived at: `hbsworkingknowledge.hbs.edu/item.jhtml?id=3651&t=dispatch`. September 1, 2003.

7. N.G. Carr. IT Doesn't Matter. *Harvard Business Review* 41:41–49. 2003.

8. CASPIAN. *RFID Position Statement of Consumer Privacy and Civil Liberties Organizations.* Archived at: `www.privacyrights.org/ar/rfidposition.htm`. November 20, 2003.

9. A.M. Chircu and R.J. Kauffman. Limits to Value in Electronic Commerce-Related IT Investments. *Journal of Management Information Systems* 14:59–80. 2000.

10. N. Davies and H-W. Gellersen. Beyond Prototypes: Challenges in Deploying Ubiquitous Systems. *IEEE Pervasive Computing* 1:26–35. 2002.

11. Department of Defense. *DoD Announces Radio Frequency Identification Policy.* Available at: `www.defenselink.mil/releases/2003/nr20031023-0568.html`. October 23. 2003.

12. H. Duce. *Public Policy: Understanding Public Opinion.* Executive Briefing. Auto-ID Center. 2003.

13. EPCglobal. *Guidelines on EPC for Consumer Products.* Archived at: `www.epcglobalinc.org/public_policy/public_policy_guidelines.html`. 2004.

14. A. Fano and A. Gershman. The Future of Business Services in the Age of Ubiquitous Computing. *Communications of the ACM* 45:83–87. 2002.

15. E. Fleisch. *Business Perspectives on Ubiquitous Computing.* M-Lab Working Paper No. 4. University of St. Gallen. St. Gallen, Switzerland. 2001.

16. E. Fleisch and M. Dierkes. *Ubiquitous Computing: Why Auto-ID is the Logical Next Step in Enterprise Automation.* White Paper. Auto-ID Center. 2003.

17. T. Friedli and H. Gebauer. Behavioral Implications of the Transition Process from Products to Services. *Journal of Business and Industrial Marketing.* Forthcoming. 2005.

18. Gartner Research. *Prepare for Disillusionment with RFID.* June 29, 2004.

19. T.W. Gruen, D.S. Corsten and S. Bharadwaj. *Retail Out-of-Stocks: A Worldwide Examination of Extent, Causes and Consumer Responses.* Report. Grocery Manufacturers of America, the Food Marketing Institute and CIES — the Food Business Forum. 2002.

20. IBM Business Consulting Services. *Focus on Retail: Applying Auto-ID to Improve Product Availability at the Retail Shelf.* White Paper. Auto-ID Center. 2002.

21. IBM Business Consulting Services. *Applying Auto-ID to Reduce Losses Associated with Shrink.* White Paper. Auto-ID Center. 2002.

22. R. Kaplan. Must CIM be justified by faith alone? *Harvard Business Review* 64:87–95. 1986.

23. Kaufhof Warenhaus AG. *Session I: RFID-Roll-Out bei Kaufhof.* Presentation at RFID-Fachkongress für Partner der METRO Group. Cologne, Germany. May 14, 2004.

24. T.A. Litman. *Implementing Pay-As-You-Drive Vehicle Insurance: Policy Options.* The Institute of Public Policy Research. Technical Report. 2002.

25. F. Mattern. The Vision and Technical Foundations of Ubiquitous Computing. *Upgrade* 2:2–6. 2001.

26. METRO Group. *RFID - Uncovering the Value: Applying RFID within the Retail and Consumer Package Goods Value Chain.* Report. Metro Group Future Store Initiative. 2004.

27. METRO Group. *METRO Group to Introduce RFID Across the Company.* Archived at: `www.future-store.org/servlet/PB/show/1002083/04-01-09_Pressemeldung_engl.pdf`. January 9, 2004.

28. METRO Group. *Background: The METRO Group RFID Innovation Center in Neuss.* Archived at: `www.future-store.org/servlet/PB/-s/16tprrchhqfp9ltz87xvd1xus182q6y9/show/1003392/RFIDnet-IC-Factsheet-engl-04-07-06.pdf`. July 7, 2004.

29. METRO Group and Procter & Gamble. Session III: RFID in der Logistik am Beispiel von METRO Group und Procter & Gamble. Presentation at *RFID-Fachkongress für Partner der METRO Group.* Cologne, Germany. May 14, 2004.

30. RFID Journal. *Labor Pains.* Archived at `www.rfidjournal.com/article/view/515`. June 28, 2003.

31. RFID Journal. *Wal-Mart lays out RFID roadmap.* Archived at: `www.rfidjournal.com/article/articleview/647/1/22`. November 10, 2003.

32. RFID Journal. *Solving the Out-of-Stock Problem.* Archived at: `www.rfidjournal.com/article/view/997`. June 23, 2004.

33. RFID Journal. *Will Users Be Stuck for RFID Labels?* Archived at: `www.rfidjournal.com/article/view/1005`. June 28. 2004.

34. RFID Journal. *Suppliers Must 'Slap and Ship'.* Archived at: `www.rfidjournal.com/article/view/855`. April 2, 2004.

35. P. Tarasewich and M. Warkentin. Information Everywhere. *Information Systems Management* 19:8–13. 2002.

36. K. Toraskar and P. Joglekar. Applying Cost-Benefit Analysis (CBA) Methodology for Information Technology Investment Decisions. In R. Banker, R. Kauffman and M. Mahmood (Eds) *Strategic Information Management: Perspectives on Organizational Growth and Competitive Advantage* 119–142. Idea Group. Harrisburg, USA. 1993.

37. N. Venkatraman. IT-Enabled Business Transformation: From Automation to Business Scope Redefinition. *Sloan Management Review* 35:73–87. 1994.

38. R. Whiting, J. Davies and M. Knul. Investment appraisal for IT systems. In L. Willcocks (Ed) *Investing in Information Systems: Evaluation and Management* 37–57. Chapman & Hall. London. 1996.

# 7

# Ubiquitous Computing, Customer Tracking, and Price Discrimination

Alessandro Acquisti

## 7.1 Introduction

The availability and cost-efficiency of modern information and communication technology have made "interactive marketing" and individual customer addressability not only possible but economical. In 1991, Blattberg and Deighton [5] defined the new frontiers for marketing opened by interactive computer technologies as the "age of addressability." Today, ubiquitous computer systems make it possible for consumers and providers of services and goods to engage in repeated, seamless interactions regardless of their respective physical locations.

Ubiquitous computing refers to methods of enhancing computer use by making networks of sensors and computers available and embedded in the physical environment [31]. The technologies on which ubiquitous computing applications are based span automatic identification (Auto-ID), such as Radio Frequency Identification (RFID); (wireless) communication systems, such as Global Standard for Mobile Communication (GSM); positioning services, such as Global Positioning System (GPS); and sensor networks. Together, these technologies are making new or improved business models, services, and products possible, and attention in the academic literature is naturally growing towards the business opportunities of ubiquitous computing. The volume of ubiquitous commerce, in particular ("any transaction with a monetary value that is conducted using ubiquitous computing technology" [21]) is expected to increase significantly in the coming years as e-commerce and wireless technologies continue to expand (the m-commerce or mobile commerce market alone is expected to be worth over \$50bn by 2009 [7]). Ubiquitous commerce involves transactions as diverse as mobile phone based purchases, "intelligent" shopping carts, context-aware wallets, and other applications that have only started being explored. In commerce scenarios, ubiquitous computing devices will act as channels for sellers' services, as sensors of environmental and customers' conditions, and as "effectors" mediating between the customer's needs and the provider's services (see also [14] and Chapter 6 of this volume).

Advancements in information and communication technologies give companies better tools to study their customers, perfect their marketing strategies, and dynamically change their value propositions based on the information collected. In ubiquitous computing environments, customers may be uniquely identified and recognized by ubiquitous computing sensors because of the devices they are carrying. Based on the analysis of individual data, sellers in industries adopting these technologies may offer to each individual a different service — depending on factors such as previous purchase history, location, or other personal or environmental traits. Customers may receive "on the spot" personalized promotions, discounts, as well as targeted products, differentiated content, and individualized information — on their own mobile computing devices, based on the information they are revealing through their presence in a network of sensors.

These scenarios open new revenue opportunities for technologically savvy sellers but also raise new trade-offs for buyers.

On the seller's side, of particular interest to this chapter's analysis is the possibility of combining context, historical, location, and other personal data to dynamically alter the price of a product for each consumer — a form of price discrimination also known as dynamic pricing. On the Internet there have been accounts of attempts at dynamic pricing in the past (see [25] and [26]). Pervasive computing environments, because of their ubiquitousness and invisibility, offer sellers new powerful tools to quietly implement such pricing strategies.

On the consumer's side, ubiquitous computing technologies offer promises and opportunities and also some risks — notably, privacy invasions and, in fact, price discrimination [1]. Nobody likes to pay more for the same product than the other person spent. Faced by intrusive information policies and price discriminating strategies, however, consumers can decide to bypass the seller's tracking attempts through privacy enhancing and anonymizing technologies, or to avoid the seller altogether.

In prior work on intertemporal price discrimination [4], we addressed some of the pricing issues associated with generic tracking technologies. We used models of repeated interactions between sellers and their customers in which sellers use various information technologies to track customers over time (such as Internet "cookies" in online shopping), and customers use strategies (such as delaying purchases, selecting a different vendor, or adopting anonymizing or privacy technologies) to avoid being tracked. The models highlighted the conditions under which sellers find it optimal to use tracking data about their customers for price discrimination, and the conditions under which customers find it optimal to reveal or hide their identities.

In this chapter we apply and extend that analysis to ubiquitous computing scenarios, in which sellers may use customer personal, history, or context data for price discrimination. To this goal, we first discuss the features of ubiquitous computing technologies of interest to commerce (Section 7.2). We then focus on the application of ubiquitous computing technologies for customer tracking and price discrimination, and we investigate the consequences for buyers and sellers of the application of these technologies. We first summarize the single good model presented in [4] for the dynamic pricing case, and we show how it can be applied to ubiquitous computing environments (Section 7.3). We then extend the model to consider various cost specifications, multiple goods, and additional marketing strategies that may be natural applications in ubiquitous computing environments (Section 7.4). Finally, we summarize the implications of our model in the context of ubiquitous computing commerce (Section 7.5).

In addition to the literature on ubiquitous computing commerce that we discuss in the next sections, our analysis naturally touches different areas of the economic and marketing literature: the literature on intertemporal price discrimination (in particular [24], [23], [19], [15], [29], and [30]); the literature on consumer addressability (in particular [5], [18], [20], [27, 28], [9], and [8]); and the literature on economic aspects of personal privacy (in particular [6] and [26]). In what follows, we will only discuss related articles when relevant to the model. For a more complete review of the literature we refer the reader to [4].

## 7.2 Ubiquitous Computing and Commerce

Ubiquitous computing applications rely on networks of computing, sensing, and communicating devices that are often mobile, wireless, and embedded in the environment. Since Mark Weiser's [31] seminal work, research on those applications has steadily increased, but only recently the literature has focused on their commercial and business aspects: see [11], [14], [16], [10], [12], [17], and also Chapter 6 of this volume.

According to Christ, Fleisch, and Mattern [10], ubiquitous computing "is the basic technology behind the next innovation thrust to follow e-Business." The combination of automatic identification technologies, (wireless) communication technologies, positioning services, and sensor network technologies should lead to new business processes in areas as diverse as supply chain management, customer relationship management, and retailing.

Christ, Fleisch, and Mattern [10] believe that sensor networks may recognize or cause modifications in environmental conditions and allow decision making based on real time environmental data, leading to cost savings and quality improvements. Ubiquitous computing may integrate businesses' information systems with the actual operational environment of the firm, thereby closing the "gap between information system and reality" [10]. One significant contribution of ubiquitous computing technologies may be the reduction of the marginal cost of the integration of the real and the virtual world, enabling "information systems to collect more detailed data at the point of creation (POC) and eventually [allowing] managers and machines at the point of action (POA) to implement decisions based on high quality, real-time information" (cf. Chapter 6). These improvements may lead to better information systems integration, data quality improvements, and digital management control loops.

In addition to optimization of business processes, other researchers believe that ubiquitous computing may make new sources of revenue possible through novel services and enhanced products. Of particular interest here are the consequences of ubiquitous technologies on commerce and retailing. In Chapter 5, Anatole Gershman and Andrew Fano noted that commerce will be affected by the ability of ubiquitous computing technologies to provide service channels from the provider to the user, to inform users about those services, and to act as "effectors" of the user's needs to affect the environment. For example, Christ, Fleisch, and Mattern [10] note that ubiquitous computing could be used to track inventory and decrease the costs associated with out of stock or dead stock material, as well as to increase customer confidence in the quality of a product and trust in the seller. Kourouthanassis and Roussos [16] propose that context aware ubiquitous computing applications could provide shoppers with personalized services, promotional information, and offers based on the recognition and tracking of their identities, current choices, and other characteristics (such as location). For example, Gillette's collaboration with Wal-Mart and Tesco focuses on "smart shelves" applications that increase availability of Gillette products and attempt to reduce theft [10]. Prada New York store uses RFID tags on clothing items to display information about them on a screen [10]. MyGrocer, an ubiquitous computing application for the grocery sector, focuses on home replenishment schema and service quality enhancement in smart-home and in-store scenarios [16, 17]. In the in-store scenarios, "RF tags uniquely identify each product and are constantly transmitting the presence of the product to RF-receivers, effectively positioned on the shopping cart. When the consumer enters the supermarket she logs in MyGrocer through her cart. The system identifies the user and displays her shopping list (missing products) to the shopping carts display screen" [16]. This project found [17] that such shopping features made possible by ubiquitous computing technologies "provide a more entertaining and stress-free shopping trip compared to conventional shopping, and thus transform a utilitarian activity into an opportunity for entertainment."

However in Chapter 6 of this volume, Fleisch and Tellkamp warn that identifying the value-creating applications is not trivial. They suggest, for example, changing a company's business model from selling services at a fixed price to usage-based billing. But aggressive pricing strategies may end up alienating customers. In this chapter we study the incentives for sellers to use ubiquitous computing tracking technologies to enforce price discrimination, and the possible reactions by their customers. Thanks to modern information and communication technologies, companies can gather massive amounts of data about consumers, infer from that data trends in consumer behavior, and then attempt to use their analysis to increase their profits. This may certainly involve the ability to discern the customer's reservation price for a certain good, and thereafter the ability to dynamically change prices of the same product for each individual customer based on that information. However, standard micro-economics analysis can be used to show that these forms of price discrimination *per se* are not optimal: a seller facing strategic customers (whose taste it does not know in advance) cannot do better than committing to optimal single period contracts (see for example [15], and below). Why and how exactly should sellers use ubiquitous computing technologies to track customer information and use it dynamically to maximize their profit, without alienating buyers with aggressive price discriminative policies?

In the rest of this chapter we use tools from micro economic theory to examine the conditions under which sellers will find it optimal to engage in price discrimination when consumers can adopt strategies to protect their privacy, and whether a balance can be found between sellers' and buyers' different needs.

## 7.3 Tracking and Price Discrimination

By tracking and analyzing individual consumer data, sellers can implement interactive marketing strategies and present to each individual a personalized offer. In particular, sellers can use consumer information (combining context, historical, location, and personal data) for price discrimination.

An intriguing result in the micro-economic literature, however, shows that price discrimination is not an optimal strategy when the seller can commit to prices and consumers have stationary valuations for the good: intertemporal price discrimination cannot do better than fixed prices strategies (see [24], [23] and [19]).

Acquisti and Varian [4] show that the same result applies when customers can be *individually* tracked through information technology. They use a simple model of dynamic pricing that can be applied to the ubiquitous computing tracking scenario, with a single profit-maximizing seller of a good that can be provided at zero marginal cost. The seller has some mechanism for recognizing, tracking, and recording purchase histories of customers (in the ubiquitous computing case, for example, the mechanism could be a network of RFID sensors and other mobile devices in a supermarket that detect and react to Auto-ID devices used or carried by the consumer and associated with her identity — for example, an RFID tag on her shopping cart). We can refer to this mechanism simply as an automatic "ID" (the so-called Auto-ID infrastructures are discussed in some detail in Chapter 2 and Chapter 4 in terms of standardization and software systems). Consumers may sometimes have mechanisms to avoid being tracked (for example, the RFID "killer" tag that disrupts the radio communication between the tag and the sensors discussed in more detail in Chapter 12). We will loosely refer to such mechanisms simply as "anonymizing technologies."

Imagine that customers are rational and forward looking (they know that their current behavior will affect the vendor's future choices). We limit our analysis to two shopping opportunities, or "visits." In other words, we assume that consumers visit the store (the ubiquitous computing commerce environment) at most twice. When they visit the seller for the first time, their personal information or ID is sensed and registered, and a price for the good of interest to the consumer is presented (for example on her mobile computing device or through other ubiquitous computing tools: [10] observe: "[c]hanging the price labels is no longer necessary as all the shelves [may be] equipped with labels made from electronic paper which immediately show the modified price."). The consumer's decision about whether to purchase at that price is observed and recorded by the seller. The second time the consumer comes into the same ubiquitous computing environment for another purchase, the price she is offered can be conditioned on her earlier behavior (recorded by the system and associated to the consumer ID).

Imagine that there exist two consumer types — one type values the good $v_H$, more than the other type, $v_L$ — and that a fraction $\pi$ of the population has the higher willingness to pay for one unit of the good. The seller could set a flat price at each period (either pricing at the lower valuation, getting all customers; or at the higher valuation, getting only the high valuation customers). Or, the seller may change prices dynamically across the two shopping opportunities, "conditioning" them on the reaction of customers to the prices in the first period. Since high-value forward looking consumers will realize that purchasing at a high price may guarantee that they will face a high price in the future, they may adopt some anonymizing technology to avoid establishing a purchase history or they may just delay purchase (by refusing an offer at a certain price in the first purchasing experience).

For this model, [4] prove that there is one undominated discriminatory pricing policy for the seller, which leads to the high value consumer type purchasing in both periods, and the low valuation type purchasing only once. It also turns out, however, that the profit from the discriminatory policy never exceeds the profit from flat pricing.[1] When selling to high-value customers is more profitable than selling to every consumer at the lower price, the seller will prefer to sell only to high-value consumers at the high price (rather than providing discounts to also attract the low valuation type). In other words, it appears that using tracking data for price discrimination may not lead to higher profits for the seller.

## 7.4 Interactive Marketing and Optimal Profit

If simple price discrimination based on customer tracking is not optimal with rational consumers, in what ways can merchants use tracking data and interactive marketing to enhance their profits? How can they optimally use

---

[1]See [4] for the mathematical details.

personal information such as purchase history, ubiquitous computing context data, and revealed preferences?

### 7.4.1 Making It Costly to Hide Previous Behavior

First of all, the merchant may make it costly for the customer to hide previous behavior in a ubiquitous computing environment (for example, her purchase history).

While sophisticated consumers may always delay purchases at little or no cost, they may face costs when trying to hide their purchase history through anonymizing technologies (for example, their previous high evaluation and purchase of a certain product). The merchant could structure the ubiquitous computing environment precisely in a way that it makes the adoption of privacy enhancing, anonymizing strategies or technologies costly (for example, by requiring customers in a supermarket to carry and pay only through personally identifiable wireless devices). The consumer may still bypass these efforts, but at a cost.

We can model the cost of using a generic form of anonymizing technology. Imagine that $f$ denotes the cost of a technology that allows the buyer to present herself as a "first time customer" in the model discussed in Section 7.3 even after repeated purchases. This means that when the seller sees a customer with "no ID," it cannot be sure whether that is really a new customer, or an old one who deleted her ID. Assume that if consumers have no ID information indicating a prior visit, they are charged a price $p_0$; if they have an ID indicating that they bought on a prior visit, they are charged $p_b$; if they have an ID indicating that they did not buy on their earlier visit, they are charged $p_n$.

The relevant parameter values for $f$ are therefore those where

$$2(v_H - v_L) > f > 0.$$

We are interested in studying the price discriminatory strategy for the seller in which the high-value type consumes both periods and the low-value type consumes only in the first period. This leads to a simple mechanism design problem [13] with the following incentive compatible and individual rationality constraints:

$$2v_H - p_0 - p_b \geq 2v_H - 2p_0 - f, \tag{7.1}$$
$$2v_H - p_0 - p_b \geq 0, \tag{7.2}$$
$$v_L - p_0 \geq 2v_L - 2p_0 - f, \tag{7.3}$$
$$v_L - p_0 \geq 0. \tag{7.4}$$

The first inequality says that the high-value consumer must prefer to purchase at $p_0$, have her ID information recorded, and pay price $p_b$, rather than remove the ID information and incur the cost $f$. The second inequality says that the high-value consumer must get non negative utility from buying twice at the given prices. The third and fourth inequalities make similar statements for the low-value consumer.

The solution to these inequalities is

$$p_0 = v_L, \tag{7.5}$$
$$p_b = v_L + f, \tag{7.6}$$

which leads to profit of $v_L + \pi(v_L + f)$. For example, the seller can charge $v_L$ the first time a customer comes around, and then $v_l + f$ the second time around. Note that this is almost the same as flat pricing at $v_L$, at least for small values of $f$.

When is this profit larger than the profit resulting from charging a flat price of $v_L$? One needs

$$v_L + \pi(v_L + f) > 2v_L,$$

which reduces to

$$f > \frac{1 - \pi}{\pi} v_L. \tag{7.7}$$

When is this profit larger than flat pricing at the high price? When

$$v_L + \pi(v_L + f) > 2\pi v_H,$$

which reduces to

$$f > 2v_H - \frac{1 + \pi}{\pi} v_L. \tag{7.8}$$

Equations (7.7) and (7.8) describe a set of relationships among the parameters that determine the optimality of the conditioning solution when there is a cost to avoid being identified by ubiquitous computing (or any other tracking) technologies. When the costs of concealing information (i.e., anonymizing) are high, price conditioning based on a "low price first, then high price" strategy can become profitable even with sophisticated consumers, who will just let sellers track them over repeated transactions rather than going through the hassle of using an anonymizing technology.

This is not surprising: if anonymizing technologies are deemed too expensive, consumers simply will not use them. But then, perhaps more interestingly, how expensive are these technologies?

The cost $f$ of an anonymizing technology is not only its monetary price, but also the inconvenience (such as usage costs, learning curves, and other hassles) that customers have to incur to use it. Even when small, these costs might be enough to turn customers away from these technologies. On the other side, one can also interpret the $f$ parameter as representing the perceived risk of losses of privacy (in which case the expected losses enter $f$ with a negative sign). In other words, the costs of privacy-related decisions depend on two factors: short-term monetary costs or hassles of protective technologies or strategies, and the longer-term expected value that each customer forecasts she will obtain from using an anonymizing technology. This value may be expressed in negative terms when it represents the avoidance of the expected future random shocks due to the loss of privacy. If customers are not aware of the risks they incur when they do not protect their privacy, they will not consider the negative part of $f$, which means that even relatively cheap privacy technologies will not be adopted. Hence, they will choose not to protect their privacy (see [3], where privacy issues other than those associated with price discrimination are also discussed).

## 7.4.2 Offering Enhanced Services

In IT-rich environments (and in particular in ubiquitous computing environments) the merchant can, however, offer something back to customers in exchange for using their information for dynamic pricing. For example, the merchant could make additional purchases by the same customer more efficient or pleasant through "enhanced services" of some form, enabled by the information the customer has revealed during the first purchase, and made possible by a system of sensor networks and mobile devices that channel the merchant information to the consumer and the consumer's decision to the merchant. Practical applications could be  targeted recommendations, personalized service or content, one-click shopping, or a variety of other enhanced services discussed in [4]. For example, in a grocery application, the system may identify the user and provide information through the shopping cart display about missing items on the shopping list [16].

Acquisti and Varian [4] study the scenario in which sellers can make the second unit of consumption more valuable than the first unit of consumption and whether this can lead to increased profits. They find out that conditioning prices can maximize profits if the high-value purchaser values the enhanced services relatively more than the low-value user: for example, automated check-out through smart wireless wallets may be more valuable to consumers who shop more frequently or with higher values of time, which may be positively correlated with their valuation for the good itself.

The analysis holds for marginal costs of offering enhanced services that are lower than the customers' evaluations of those services. After the investment in information technology to track customer purchases and provide enhanced services is made, the marginal costs associated with each additional transaction are generally very low. One of the economic features of information technology is, often, the reduction of the marginal costs associated with certain repeated transactions and interactive marketing. Therefore it is reasonable to expect that after large initial investments to set up systems with enhanced services, the marginal costs of direct marketing and customer care for IT- and ubiquitous computing- focused sellers may be low. Large investments in IT might pay off in terms of the subsequent ability for the seller to offer particular services that competitors cannot provide, offering both a barrier to entry and benefits from price discrimination. In this respect, value-creating uses of ubiquitous computing technologies (see also Chapter 6) may be those associated with low marginal cost offers based on previous investments in information technology.

### 7.4.3 Making the Second Visit More Valuable

In Section 7.4.2 we refer to the case in which the second unit of *consumption* has a different value than the first. However, it may be that even if the consumer chooses not to purchase on the first visit to a seller, the second *visit* to the same merchant may generate higher value for the consumer. For example, registration, even without purchase, may lead to benefits such as automated checkout or personalized information. Certain stores, enhanced by ubiquitous computing technologies, may ask their visitors to create accounts before they can see products and prices and make any purchase. Hence the enhanced features considered in Section 7.4.2 might be offered to all *returning* customers whether or not they have purchased on their first visit. How does this affect the analysis?

We modify the model presented in [4] to answer this question. Let $v_{H1}$ represent value of consumption for the high-value consumer during her first visit, and $v_{H2}$ the value of consumption during her second visit. Define $v_{L1}$ and $v_{L2}$ similarly. The self-selection constraints now become

$$v_{H1} + v_{H2} - p_H \geq v_{H2} - p_L, \tag{7.9}$$

$$v_{H1} + v_{H2} - p_H \geq 0, \tag{7.10}$$

$$v_{L2} - p_L \geq v_{L1} + v_{L2} - p_H, \tag{7.11}$$

$$v_{L2} - p_L \geq 0, \tag{7.12}$$

The optimal prices are $p_H = v_{H1} + v_{L2}$ and $p_L = v_{L2}$. The revenue from price conditioning exceeds the revenue from flat pricing when

$$\pi v_{H1} + v_{L2} > \pi v_{H1} + \pi v_{H2}, \tag{7.13}$$

$$\pi v_{H1} + v_{L2} > v_{L1} + v_{L2}. \tag{7.14}$$

Making the obvious cancellations gives the following result: conditioning prices will be optimal when

$$v_{L2} > \pi v_{H2},$$

$$\pi v_{H1} > v_{L1},$$

in which case $p_H = v_{H1} + v_{L2}$ and $p_L = v_{L2}$.

Note that these inequalities are precisely the reverse of those summarized in Section 7.4.2 and described in [4]. Comparing those results to those presented here, we can summarize what happens for all four sign patterns in these inequalities:

- $v_{L2} > \pi v_{H2}, \pi v_{H1} > v_{L1}$. Conditioning profitable when second *visit* has higher value.
- $v_{L2} < \pi v_{H2}, \pi v_{H1} < v_{L1}$. Conditioning profitable when second *purchase* has higher value.
- $v_{L2} < \pi v_{H2}, \pi v_{H1} > v_{L1}$. Sell only to high-value type.
- $v_{L2} > \pi v_{H2}, \pi v_{H1} < v_{L1}$. Sell to both high- and low-value type.

In other words, a seller able to track consumers over repeated transactions and condition prices depending on previous purchase histories may have several different available strategies: flat-pricing to all consumers or just to the high-value consumers, or adopt pricing strategies that induce conditioning. In the latter case, the seller may choose to provide enhanced services to all consumers visiting the seller's store a second time, or just to the consumers who already purchased on that store. Which strategy is the best will depend on the values of the parameters in this economy, and in particular on $\pi$, $v_{H1}$, and $v_{L1}$. Based on its perceptions of how many high and low value consumers exist in that economy, and how much each type of consumer is willing to pay for the good, the seller can choose its offerings so as to make the second purchase or visit a better experience, depending on which is more profitable. For example, when $\pi v_{H1} < v_{L1}$, the seller will find it optimal to make all consumers purchase in the first period and then offer the enhanced services to the returning high-value consumers in the second period.

### 7.4.4 Making it costly (or not) to visit the seller

This analysis, however, triggers a question: we have not explicitly considered the costs of visiting the seller. Should such costs be included in the price of the good purchased by the buyer, *or* in the cost of visiting the seller even if there are no purchases? In the model presented in Section 7.3, it would appear that the costs of inserting personal information (for example, stopping at the checkout counter to provide credit card data) the first time one purchases with a certain merchant could be incorporated in the model into the price that the customer is paying in the first period. Similarly, the enhanced service associated to the second purchase might be interpreted as the time saved the second time around (e.g., no-stop checkouts thanks to "intelligent" wireless wallets that interact automatically with the checkout counter).

Interestingly, it turns out that different types of tracking technologies may lead to slightly different solutions in the model.

A first type of tracking technology is a technology that requires user intervention (for example, manual registration of personal information on a wireless payment card at a ubiquitous computing equipped grocery store). A second type is a technology that works automatically and does not need user intervention (for example, automated registration of personal data through exchange of cryptographic keys and digital signatures between the user's devices and the store's sensors).

## Adopting a tracking technology that requires user intervention

Let us consider first the technology that requires user intervention. Let us assume that the customer has to register every time she makes a purchase, because the seller is not storing any information. Then the profits for the seller from flat pricing will be either $2v_L - 2d_L$ or $2\pi v_H - 2\pi d_H$ , where $d_X$ stands for the disutility of providing information to complete a purchase (for example, the subjective value assigned to the time spent doing that). Note that for this base case we assume that this information must be provided every time there is a purchase.

Compare this to the profits from price discrimination: the self-selection constraints produce the following optimal prices, $p_L = v_L - d_L$ and $p_H = v_H + v_L - d_L - d_H$, and therefore the following profit: $\pi (v_H - d_H) + v_L - d_L$. By comparing these profits, one gets again the contradiction found in Section 7.3: conditioning, again, is not optimal.

Now consider what happens if the merchant stores the information so that the customer does not need to provide it again during the second purchase. Imagine that this is the only "enhanced service," that is, that the product itself is valued the same in both periods, and nothing more (no personalized offers, no targeted discounts) is being offered. The conditioning prices now will be: $p_L = v_L - d_L$ and $p_H = v_H + v_L - d_L$ (with a resulting profit: $\pi v_H + v_L - d_L$), while the profits from flat pricing will now be: $2v_L - d_L$ or $2\pi v_H - \pi d_H$. Conditioning will dominate flat pricing if

$$\pi v_H \geq v_L, \tag{7.15}$$
$$v_L + \pi d_H - d_L \geq \pi v_H.$$

These results are similar to the "second visit has different value" case discussed above. Inequalities 7.15 say that, even though the second purchase in this scenario has actually the same value, if the discomfort of the high type for spending time providing personal information is proportionally higher than the discomfort of the low type, then conditioning is optimal. This confirms that hassles (e.g. search costs) associated with making a purchase can be used to price discriminate among customers.

What happens when the "second visit has different value" in this setup? That is, what happens when the customer has to spend time logging in the first time regardless of whether she purchases or not the good? The above solutions do not change. In other words, when one approaches the price discrimination problem as a "cost of inserting personal information" problem rather than an "advantages from enhanced services" problem, it turns out that two cases are possible. In the first case, when the tracking technology requires time to be used (for example, because the user has to register manually), then the "costs of inserting personal information" approach does not highlight any difference between one case and the other. In the second case, when the second visit has higher value because in the first visit the customer spent time registering, the self-selection constraints become equivalent to the case where the customer registered and purchased during the first period.

## Adopting a tracking technology that does not require user intervention

Things are different when one considers the second technology — a tracking technology which does not cost time or efforts to the customer even during her first visit or purchase but still offers her some advantages the second time she is around. This might happen for example because a vendor has automatically assigned a ubiquitous computing device to the customer (say, on a "smart" shopping cart) and through that device can track the customer's behavior. The vendor might observe which products the customer is passing by in the store or placing in the cart. The next time the same customer comes to that store, the seller may provide special offers on the customer's device, personalized and targeted based on what the customer's preferences have been revealed to be, without her having previously spent time explicitly compiling a profile or actually purchasing. In this case, indeed, price discrimination on the base of the "second visit having different value" becomes a more appealing strategy for the seller.

We can also combine the two approaches proposed in Section 7.4.2 and here. In the setup proposed in this section an implicit assumption was that the only benefit from a tracking technology is the saved time the second time around, equalled to (not having to waste) $d_X$. Now we can imagine that the customer values both the time saved and also additional enhanced services such as personalized information or targeted offers.

By mixing the two approaches in the self-selection constraints we get the following optimal prices in the conditioning case: $p_L = v_{L2} - d_L$ and $p_H = v_{H1} + v_{L2} - d_L$. The profits from flat pricing are: $\pi (v_{H1} + v_{H2} - d_H)$ and $v_{L1} + v_{L2} - d_L$. Conditioning will be optimal if

$$\pi v_{H1} \geq v_{L1},$$
$$v_{L2} + \pi d_H - d_L \geq \pi v_{H2},$$

which is again a similar result to the one found above for the "second visit has different value" case. The results of this section therefore support the view that merchants can make strategic use of the heterogeneity in their customers' search costs (see also [32]) for profitable price discrimination.

## 7.4.5 Offering Multiple Goods

So far we have analyzed price discrimination strategies that impose a separating equilibria: low type consumers buy once, and high type consumers buy twice a repeated purchase good. Consumer tracking data, however, can also be used for price discrimination without this form of rationing, when the seller is able to offer new but related goods at each visit. This strategy has the advantage for seller (but a disadvantage for the buyer) of making price discrimination less visible — because purchase histories are used to vary prices of different goods. This strategy is particularly relevant to ubiquitous computing commerce environments in which multiple related goods may be offered in the same physical or virtual space.

Imagine that in period 1 consumers can choose between two goods offered by a monopolist producer: $A_1$ and $A_2$. One type of consumer (let us call her the high type) prefers $A_1$ to $A_2$: $v_{HA_1} > v_{HA_2}$. The other type (the low type) prefers $A_2$ to $A_1$: $v_{LA_2} > v_{LA_1}$. Let us also assume that the seller knows that there are, again, $\pi$ high consumers, and that those high consumers are willing to pay a price $B_H$ for a third good $B$, while low consumers only value that good $B_L$, with $B_H > B_L$. For example, $A_1$ and $A_2$ could be, respectively, a CD with music by Gershwin and a CD with music by Pink Floyd, and $B$ is a CD with music by Louis Armstrong.

What kind of pricing schemes the seller can adopt to elicit truthful revelation of each consumer's taste in period 1, in order to offer the third good at different prices in period 2? Again we adopt a mechanism design approach and try to solve for:

$$v_{HA_1} + B_H - p_H \geq v_{HA_2} + B_H - p_L, \tag{7.16}$$

$$v_{HA_1} + B_H - p_H \geq 0, \tag{7.17}$$

$$v_{LA_2} + B_L - p_L \geq v_{LA_1} + B_L - p_H, \tag{7.18}$$

$$v_{LA_2} + B_L - p_L \geq 0. \tag{7.19}$$

This system solves for $p_L = v_{LA_2} + B_L$ and $p_H = v_{LA_2} + B_L + (v_{HA_1} - v_{HA_2})$. For example, the seller may charge $v_{LA_2}$ for both goods in period 1, and then either $B_L$ or $B_L + (v_{HA_1} - v_{HA_2})$ for the second product in period 2 - depending on the customer's choice in period 1.

Note that now both types are consuming twice. The high type, however, by revealing her preferences in period 1, is charged an higher price than the low type in period 2 for the very same good. The profits are: $v_{LA_2} + B_L + \pi(v_{HA_1} - v_{HA_2})$.

Now, compare the conditioning profits to those obtained under

- flat pricing low ($\pi v_{HA_1} + (1 - \pi)v_{LA_2} + B_L$), and
- flat pricing high ($\pi v_{HA_1} + (1 - \pi)v_{LA_2} + \pi B_H$).

It turns out that conditioning is always better than flat pricing low, but is better than flat pricing high only when $(v_{LA_2} - v_{HA_2}) \geq (B_H - B_L/\pi)$ and the incentive compatible and individual rationality constraints above are satisfied (hence, for example, it must also be: $(B_H - B_L) \geq (v_{LA_2} - v_{HA_2}) \geq (B_H - B_L/\pi)$). These inequalities draw upper and lower boundaries of the parameters under which price conditioning with repeated purchases by both types is optimal.

The conclusion is that tracking customer data can be used to profitably price discriminate even when the cost function is linear and *no* enhanced services are offered, if consumers have different evaluations for different goods offered across two periods.

Note that under the proposed pricing strategy, when all constraints are met, no type has incentives to skip purchasing for a period, or using anonymizing technology. However, we have also implicitly assumed that the seller can commit to those prices.

One may notice that this form of price conditioning may be harder to detect for the consumer, since she is no longer dealing with a repeated purchase good. As the number of periods extends beyond two, it becomes increasingly difficult for any customer type to misrepresent herself for a different type, since this would imply suppressing at each period her real taste (or preferences).

Still, the power of information technology can also be used by consumers to monitor the seller's actions: in the famous Amazon.com price "experiment" (see [25]), reports that the same product was being sold at different prices quickly spread from an Internet chat room to the mainstream media. Note, also, that in this chapter we have not considered additional privacy concerns associated with tracking technologies but not related to pricing: see [1] for a discussion.

## 7.5 Implications

Ubiquitous computing technologies offer retailers new opportunities to interact with their customers. Aggregating and analyzing purchase and individual data, sellers can provide personalized services, and targeted offers, but also employ dynamic pricing strategies. In this chapter we have used micro economic theory to discuss under what conditions it may make sense for retailers to use ubiquitous computing tracking technologies to enforce price discrimination. Chapter 6 of this volume and [12] point out that identifying value-creating uses of ubiquitous computing technologies is not trivial: we have shown here that naïve price discrimination may in fact be sub-optimal for sellers under general conditions.

We have shown under what conditions price discrimination based on tracking data may become optimal. First of all, the seller may provide enhanced services [4] that create the proper incentives for consumers to self-select into those who accept the higher prices as a cost to access desirable services, and those who prefer to receive lower prices — and lower quality services attached to the product they purchase. Therefore, sellers may deploy ubiquitous computing in ways that make the shopping experience for the consumer more engaging [17] or augment products with services. We have considered other strategies, such as making it difficult for customers to hide previous behavior through privacy enhancing technologies, or providing tracking and enhanced services which do or do not require customer intervention to operate. In this respect, a ubiquitous computing merchant may make strategic use of the heterogeneity in their customers' search costs through different forms of tracking technologies.

We have also considered the strategy of using customers' revealed preferences for one good as a tool for price discrimination on another good — a natural application in ubiquitous computing environments rich in different, related products, such as "smart" grocery stores.

With regard to this, Acquisti [2] shows under what conditions it is optimal for sellers to use previous purchase histories to *recommend* new goods to customers and gain from the customers' following the recommendations. The conditions studied in [2] may well apply to the ubiquitous computing commerce scenario, again for the case of merchants providing several goods and able to correlate data from several customers' transactions. Such recommendations may be useful particularly to sell niche goods for which customers' experimentation would otherwise be too costly.

Our results (and those in [4]) indicate that industries where transactions can be mediated through computers and in which the marginal costs of providing products augmented with personalized services are low (but those services show significant variation in user valuation) can be candidates for value-creating uses of ubiquitous computing technologies.

Of course, the complexity of certain ubiquitous computing environments may make it difficult for customers to recognize different pricing strategies offered by the seller. However, technology (for example, intelligent agents — see [22]) may help consumers navigate through the complexities of the new pricing models made possible by ubiquitous tracking technologies.

# References

1. A. Acquisti. Protecting Privacy with Economics: Economic Incentives for Preventive Technologies in Ubiquitous Computing Environments. In *Workshop on Socially-informed Design of Privacy-enhancing Solutions, International Conference on Ubiquitous Computing (UBICOMP '02)*. 2002.
2. A. Acquisti. Inducing Customers to Try New Goods. In *Workshop on Information Systems and Economics (WISE '03)*. 2003.
3. A. Acquisti. Privacy in Electronic Commerce and the Economics of Immediate Gratification. In *Proceedings of the ACM Conference on Electronic Commerce (EC '04)*. 21–29, 2004.
4. A. Acquisti and H. R. Varian. Conditioning Prices on Purchase History. *Marketing Science*. Forthcoming. 2005.
5. R. C. Blattberg and J. Deighton. Interactive Marketing: Exploiting the Age of Addressability. *Sloan Management Review*. 33(1):5–14. 1991.
6. G. Calzolari and A. Pavan. Optimal Design of Privacy Policies. Technical report, Gremaq, University of Toulouse. 2001.

7. S. Carr. M-commerce Market Set to Multiply. *Silicon.com.* Archieved at: http://www.silicon.com. October 28. 2004.
8. Y. Chen and G. Iyer. Consumer Addressability and Customized Pricing. *Marketing Science.* 21(2):197–208. 2002.
9. Y. Chen, C. Narasimhan, and Z. J. Zhang. Individual Marketing with Imperfect Targetability. *Marketing Science.* 20(1):23–41. 2001.
10. O. Christ, E. Fleisch, and F. Mattern. M-Lab - The Mobile and Ubiquitous Computing Lab, Phase II. M-Lab Technical report. 2003.
11. E. Fleisch. Business Perspectives on Ubiquitous Computing. M-Lab Working Paper No. 4. University of St. Gallen. 2001.
12. E. Fleisch and C. Tellkamp. The Challenge of Identifying Value-creating Ubiquituous Computing Applications. In *Workshop on Ubiquitous Commerce, International Conference on Ubiquitous Computing (UBICOMP '03).* 2003.
13. D. Fudenberg and J. Tirole. *Game Theory.* MIT Press. Cambridge, MA.
14. A. Gershman. Ubiquitous Commerce: Always on, Always aware, Always proactive. In *Panel on Mobile Commerce: Vision and Challenges, International Symposium on Applications and the Internet (SAINT '02).* 2002.
15. O. D. Hart and J. Tirole. Contract Renegotiation and Coasian Dynamics. *Review of Economic Studies.* 55(4):509–540. 1988.
16. P. Kourouthanassis and G. Roussos. Developing Consumer-Friendly Pervasive Retail Systems. *IEEE Pervasive Computing.* 2(2):32-39. 2003.
17. P. Kourouthanassis and G. Roussos. Developing the User Experience in Ubiquituous Commerce. In *Workshop on Ubiquitous Commerce, International Conference on Ubiquitous Computing (UBICOMP '03).* 2003.
18. R. E. McCulloch, P. E. Rossi, and G. M. Allenby. The Value of Purchase History Data in Target Marketing. *Marketing Science.* 15(4):321–340. 1996.
19. J. Riley and R. Zeckhauser. Optimal Selling Strategies: When to Haggle, When to Hold Firm. *Quarterly Journal of Economics.* 98(2):267–289. 1983.
20. P. E. Rossi and G. M. Allenby. Marketing Models of Consumer Heterogeneity. *Journal of Econometrics.* 89(1-2):57–78. 1999.
21. G. Roussos. Consumers and Ubiquitous Commerce. In *Ubiconf 2004. April 19th, Gresham College, London.* 2004.
22. N. M. Sadeh, T-C. Chan, L Van, O-B. Kwon, and K. Takizawa. Creating an Open Agent Environment for Context-aware m-Commerce. In *Agentcities: Challenges in Open Agent Environments:*152–158. Springer Verlag. 2003.
23. S. W. Salant. When is Inducing Self-selection Suboptimal for a Monopolist? *Quarterly Journal of Economics.* 104(2):391–397. 1989.
24. N. Stokey. Intertemporal Price Discrimination. *Quarterly Journal of Economics,* 93(3):355–371, 1979.
25. D. Streifield. On the Web Price Tags Blur: What you Pay Could Depend on Who you Are. *The Washington Post.* September 27. 2001.
26. C. R. Taylor. Private Demands and Demands for Privacy: Dynamic Pricing and the Market for Customer Information. *RAND Journal of Economics.* 35(4):631-651. 2004.
27. D. Ulph and N. Vulkan. Electronic Commerce and Competitive First-Degree Price Discrimination. Technical Report. University College, London. 2000.
28. D. Ulph and N. Vulkan. E-commerce, Mass Customization and Price Discrimination. Technical Report. University College, London. 2001.
29. J. M. Villas-Boas. Dynamic Competition with Customer Recognition. *RAND Journal of Economics.* 30(4):604–631. 1999.

30. J. M. Villas-Boas. Price Cycles in Markets with Customer Recognition. *RAND Journal of Economics*. 35(3). Forthcoming. 2004.

31. M. Weiser. Some Computer Science Issues in Ubiquitous Computing. *Communications of the ACM*. 36(7):75–84. 1993.

32. F. Zettelmeyer. The Strategic Use of Customer Search Cost. Technical report, University of California, Berkeley. 1998.

# 8

# The Design of Pervasive Retail Experiences

Panos Kourouthanassis and George Roussos

## 8.1 Consumerism and Technological Change

To be a consumer is to know about needs and how to satisfy them by searching for, selecting, acquiring, using, and enjoying objects and services. Which particular objects individuals perceive as necessary and why is an issue open to argument: needs are frequently seen as natural and self-evident or more commonly as arbitrary and subjective. But need is also a fundamentally social concept, not in the trivial sense of social influences and socialization, but rather in two important ways: first, in the sense that needs are dictated by a particular choice of lifestyle, social interests and politics, and second, in the sense of setting a claim on particular social resources. Indeed, modernity has witnessed the manifestation of consumer culture as a major shaping force of social structure and for this reason, it is frequently judged by its ability to sustain desired ways of life and meet perceived needs [8, 23].

More importantly, consumer culture has emerged as a social system for resource allocation that is evaluated on the basis of its ability to meet the conflicting needs defined by autonomous social groups and communities for themselves. Indeed, consumer culture can be valued on its effectiveness to relate questions of lifestyle to questions of social organization and its implications for everyday life: where and how we live, the food we eat, the clothes we wear, the scarcities and inequalities we suffer, leisure and employment. At the interface of consumer culture and new technology lie new retail experiences. Indeed, successive generations of technologies have transformed the way individuals experience consumerism and indeed the consumer experience. In this chapter, we will discuss the new challenges and opportunities in consumer experience design brought about by the emergence of ubiquitous computing.

## 8.2 Creating Consumer Value

Among all retail sectors grocery is the most competitive, as it operates at minimal profit margins. It is thus important that grocery retailers exploit any possible efficiency improvement opportunities offered by technology, and indeed over the past fifty years they have pursued this objective with considerable success. In particular, the supply chain of grocery products — or else, Fast Moving Consumer Goods (FMCG) — has attained considerable operational gains through the implementation of a number of technologies including bar codes, resource-planning software, and optimized logistics. This need has also produced Efficient Consumer Response (ECR), a voluntary and industry-wide initiative to raise performance levels across the entire retail sector [14]. ECR aims to carry out a continuous and in-depth self-examination of processes and procedures for the industry as a whole, recommend improvements, and oversee the implementation of recommendations. ECR was initiated in the United States but its distinct advantages from a business perspective have rapidly extended its scope to the rest of the world, with national and regional initiatives in action.

ECR has identified three priorities: (i) to increase consumer value, (ii) to remove costs that do not add consumer value, and (iii) to maximize value while at the same time minimizing inefficiency throughout the supply chain. In practice, these priorities are used to identify and fulfil specific goals, for example providing consumers with the products and services they want, reducing inventory, eliminating paper transactions, and streamlining product flow. To meet these goals, distributors and suppliers are making fundamental changes to their business processes that can only be enabled through the implementation of novel information and communication systems.

In this context, the new information sources made available by pervasive retail can offer significant benefits for business. For example, decades after the introduction of information systems in production and logistics control, there are still significant inefficiencies in modern supply chains, which adversely affect the cost of retail operations. Upstream supply chain inefficiencies affect the relationships of all trading partners and result in high out-of-stock conditions at the point of sale, a high returns rate, and long lead times. Inefficiencies in the downstream direction affect negatively demand forecast accuracy, which results in low on-shelf availability and thus loss of revenue despite the fact that products are available on site. Moreover, information-sharing ineffectiveness between trading partners reduces the accuracy of demand forecast and the scheduling of the replenishment process.

A direct consequence of low demand forecast accuracy is that trading partners have to maintain increased inventory levels to address unpredictable increases, which in turn result in increased logistics costs. Common practice today is forecasting consumer demand by processing historical point of sale data, using decision support systems that utilize data warehousing and data mining techniques. However, using point of sale data to make forecasts results in lower accuracy because demand patterns are changing rapidly and such fluctuations cannot be captured at the point of sale but have to be identified earlier in the consumption process. Moreover, historical forecasts cannot effectively take into account the influence of promotions and other marketing instruments, since the success rate of such mechanisms is generally hard to quantify beforehand. A quantitative description of this situation according to a recent study by Andersen Consulting (currently Accenture), a management consulting and technology services firm, estimates that 53 percent of out of stock conditions are due to store replenishment inefficiencies. Even worse, a further eight percent of on the floor out of stock conditions occur despite the fact that the necessary supplies are in storage on site. Ubiquitous computing technologies applied to this problem space can provide the necessary consumption data early on in the replenishment process so as to allow for greater prediction accuracy which leads to reduced inventories and optimized supply chains, both upstream and downstream.

One contribution towards the ECR goals is the so-called Vendor Managed Inventory (VMI) approach where the vendor, rather than the customer, specifies delivery quantities sent through the distribution channel. This reversal in the procurement process has become possible only through the deployment of Electronic Data Interchange (EDI) systems, a computer-to-computer exchange protocol for business data. VMI has succeeded in reducing stock-outs and inventory buffers in the supply chain. Common features of VMI include reduction in supply chain length, centralized forecasting and frequent communication of inventory levels. From a fleet management perspective, delivery vehicles are loaded in a prioritized manner: items that are expected to stock out have top priority, then items that are furthest below the targeted stock levels, then advance shipments of promotional, and finally, items that are least above targeted stock levels. In addition to EDI, a second technology critical for VMI is the Universal Product Code (UPC), a standard for constructing bar codes to automatically identify products. This technology plays a core role in the automated creation and entry phases of the order cycle and can take days out of the total cycle time. The two technologies together can help develop collaborative relationships in which any combination of retailer, wholesaler, broker and manufacturer work together to seek out inefficiencies and reduce costs by looking at the net benefits for all participants in the relationship.

Overall VMI has been successful in significantly reducing inventory levels and the number of stock-outs. The latter issue is particularly important not only because of lost sales but also because shelf availability is central to supermarket strategy. Indeed, a significant proportion of supermarket profit margins are due to interest free periods for products already available on the selves. Thus, one of the main concerns of retailers implementing VMI has been the perception that reduced inventory will result in less product being available on the shelves at any one time and therefore loss of market share. A partial solution to the problem is to fill shelf space with other stock-keeping units (SKUs) from the same vendor but this approach does not fully address the problem.

## 8.3 The New Consumer

While suppliers and retailers have invested considerable effort to optimize their supply chains, they also have to respond to considerable social and market changes that directly affect consumer behaviors. Indeed, there are several forces in action that dictate a major shift in the current food retailers' core business processes. For example, competition in the FMCG sector is growing and forces retailers to continuously lower profit margins. At the same time, socio-demographic changes such as increased number of dual-income, single-parent and technology-familiar households have significantly altered shoppers' expectations, demands, and spending patterns during their traditional shopping experience [10]. Among other factors identified, a recent survey highlighted the decline of the "traditional family" [4]: it is estimated that by 2021 the average household size will be 2.21 persons compared against an average of 2.70 of 1981 in the UK. Moreover, an increase of 30% of one person households is expected followed by a decrease of 33% for married couples. Finally, it is estimated that the share of total retail expenditure accounting to groceries and food will decrease to 40% by 2004 compared to 50% in 1984.

These findings indicate that forging stronger consumer relationships and establishing successful consumer retention strategies will become increasingly important. Thus, appropriate consumer relationship building strategies will be the fundamental building block for the successful economic future of tomorrow's food retailers. A core component of such strategies is the development of attractive consumer experiences. It is worth observing that the overall consumer shopping experience is affected by a number of store-related factors which include ambience (temperature, scent, music, and so on) [3], service quality in the store [2], store perceived image [12], and situational elements such as crowding, time, and budget availability by the consumers and so on [6]. Failure to provide an effective consumer experience result in increased consumer stress levels [2], which translate into consumer rejection of shopping and have been seen to conspire to create apathetic shoppers — consumers who have no interest in, or actively dislike, shopping and appear to endure rather than enjoy the whole experience [17].

At the heart of the matter lies the fact that in the new consumer situation traditional factors of competition, for example price level, selection, and location, although still important, are no longer sufficient in order to achieve competitive differentiation. As a result, retailers must concentrate on enhancing the end-to-end shopping experience, aiming to win customer loyalty by inventing innovative ways of satisfying the new consumer needs.

## 8.4 Revisiting the Retail Experience

So far we have discussed in detail how the changing market situation and the emergence of a new type of consumer are exerting pressure on retail shopping. In this section we discuss solutions offered by the new technical development in computing and wireless communications technologies often referred to as ubiquitous or pervasive computing (see Chapter 1 for more details). We believe that appropriate use of these technologies can make significant contributions towards meeting the new market and social requirements identified previously.

According to traditional retail management theory, a shopping experience can be driven towards the maximization of efficiency or towards entertainment [13]. Yet, the current situation demands that both these objectives must be met, clearly a challenging task. Thus, it becomes imperative that stakeholders of the retail value chain should jointly discover the actual consumer needs and implement new shopping experiences. The rapid evolution of new technologies presented both opportunities and risks for those retailers eager to innovate. In fact, the retail sector is particularly IT-oriented, constantly experimenting with new technologies that promise to streamline and optimize core operations within the store or the warehouse and communication within the entire value chain.

In previous sections, we identified the relatively late collection of sales data at the POS as one of the main factors for the low accuracy in forecasting demand and as a barrier in developing effective replenishment strategies. For this reason, the next natural step for ECR is to extend the use of technology to the collection of data directly from the shelves and even more, to consider extending the supply chain to the consumer home. Indeed, the replenishment process starts when the consumer runs out of a particular product. Gaining such early information and using it in supply chain optimization can potentially increase considerably the accuracy of predictive replenishment strategies to a degree that is well beyond what is possible today. Ubiquitous computing technologies can fulfil exactly this requirement. Several projects have attempted to explore opportunities offered by ubiquitous computing technology in retail and here we will report on our experiences with MyGrocer, a second generation pervasive retail system and one of the early prototypes in this area (for a review of previous work in this area refer to [11]).

MyGrocer was primarily aimed at creating an early prototype and identifying some of the core issues in this context rather than develop specific technical aspects of ubiquitous commerce. The later is the focus of more recent work. For example, the Auto-ID Center, a research consortium of leading universities across the globe, is actively developing the required infrastructure to facilitate business data exchanges in this new retail environment, with the assistance of EPCglobal[1] (cf. Chapter 2). Moreover, the majority of leading

---

[1]EPCGlobal has defined three new standards as extensions of its existing UPC bar code and EDI initiatives with a view of facilitating optimizations to the supply

IT providers have already modified their systems to cater for the novel requirements of ubiquitous commerce, the SAP experience is discussed in detail in Chapter 3. The so-called "Super Market of the Future" developed by the Metro Group in Germany aims to quantify the operational gains from this new infrastructure and identify the exact cost of its deployment in a controlled environment. An ongoing research project at Intel Labs, Portland, is exploring cultural aspects affecting the deployment of pervasive retail systems (this project is briefly discussed in Chapter 10 ).

Nevertheless, extending the supply chain in this way has significant repercussions for the consumer who is now involved in the data processing pipeline. Ubiquitous commerce services use personal data associated with individual consumers in intimate ways that can be used to reconstruct their private activities at an unprecedented level of detail. Moreover, as evidence from our recent studies corroborates [11], the implementation of these technologies may cause fundamental transformations to the consumption experience due to the continuous replenishment process at home and, on the other hand, it creates a novel retailtainment experience on the supermarket floor. This change can be seen as a shift from particular retail ecology to another [20], and thus it should come as no surprise that consumers show considerable scepticism to ubiquitous commerce value propositions.

The argument developed in this section points to the significance of adopting ubiquitous computing technologies in FMCG retail. The success of such technological offerings depends heavily on their adoption by consumers, and thus the development of trust between the service provider, the consumer, and the systems is of paramount importance. Indeed, the role of trust in developing particular markets has been clearly identified in [7] and has been one of the core issues affecting the slow adoption of both electronic and mobile commerce in recent years [16].

## 8.5 Pervasive Retail Application Scenarios

Despite the fact that ubiquitous commerce was perceived as potentially having a major impact on improving retail efficiency, the different technologies available made possible the implementation of very different systems. Due to the diverging views of project partners, the first step in creating consensus was to develop and agree on three usage scenarios. To this end, a workshop was held where the different interests and options were discussed and consensus was reached on the development of three usage scenarios. These seemed to satisfy the requirements of all the participating organizations. The scenarios were subsequently used to collect functional requirements for the system.

---

chain. For example, in the so-called Electronic Product Code (EPC) uses Radio Frequency Identification (RFID) tags to store information about specific product items (rather than SKUs) and relate them to product descriptions written in Product Mark-up Language (PML) retrieved through the Object Name Service (ONS) [21].

The three scenarios agreed upon related to the usage of the system on-the-floor during a supermarket visit, on the move using a mobile device, and finally at home to monitor consumption:

**Supermarket Scenario.** The consumer enters the supermarket and selects a "smart" shopping cart equipped with radio frequency identification (RFID) readers and a tablet PC. She identifies herself to the system with her username and password. The system logs her in, responds with a welcome message, and then proceeds to present a "suggested" shopping list, based on monitored home inventory and actual consumption data. The consumer walks in the supermarket aisles and picks up products from the shelves. For example, she may decide to buy a shampoo, which she picks up and places inside her shopping cart. The cart identifies that the shampoo bottle has been placed in it and triggers the following event sequence: the product ID is sent to the back end system, which retrieves related information that is used to update the shopping list and the total cost of the shopping cart contents. Next, the consumer decides to buy a brand of hair conditioner that the retailer is promoting for customers with her profile. When the consumer places the product in the cart, the system displays the relevant offer on the screen together with instructions on the shortest path to the aisle and shelf where the associated products are held. Later, the consumer decides to remove one can of orange juice from her cart and replace it on the supermarket shelves. The system updates the shopping list with the new total amount and the new contents of the cart. When the items on the shopping list are exhausted, the consumer proceeds to check out. When she approaches the till, the system re-scans all the items in her shopping cart, calculates the total value of the products, displays that information on the till display, and prints out a receipt. The consumer pays at the till or charges everything to her account.

**Home Scenario.** The consumer returns home and places her shopping in her RFID enabled storage (including her fridge, cupboards, and so on). New product information is recorded by her home server and consolidated to the home inventory data. The home maintains data on inventory levels as well as consumption. Periodically, the consumer gives permission to her home server to upload her new shopping list to the system.

**On-the-Move Scenario.** While on her way to work, the consumer uses her mobile phone to check which products she needs to replenish before the weekend. After logging in, the system displays her current home inventory and/or her shopping list. The consumer decides to add new items to her shopping list for the dinner party she gives on Saturday night. The consumer is happy with her new shopping list. The system displays the total cost of her shopping list at her usual supermarket. The consumer is unhappy with the price and she decides to look for a better price, thus initiating a reverse auction. The system forwards her list to participating retailers and prompts the consumer to define the duration of the auction, which she does. The system sends a confirmation message that the process has been initiated. A short while later the consumer receives offers by different retailers and selects the best. The consumer selects "home delivery" and confirms the order. Later in the day, the system notifies the consumer via SMS to her mobile that baby diapers are going to run out in the following hours and requests confirmation of instant replenishment order. The consumer confirms and the order is placed.

## 8.6 A Case Study in Pervasive Retail

Several issues had to be addressed for the design and implementation of the system including (a) the design of a compelling interface, enabling seamless interaction between shopper and system, (b) the implementation of a product scanning mechanism that would minimize the shopper involvement, and (c) the design of an integrated information system that would enable the provision of retail services. The technical development of the system has been detailed elsewhere [19] and here we will only touch upon the design of two of the main elements of the user interface: the shopping cart and the sensing of product related actions (for example, placement and removal of an object in the shopping cart, consumption of goods at the home, and so forth).

### 8.6.1 Experience Design

The shopping cart was modelled around a touch-screen mounted on the shopping cart as seen in Figure 8.1. Five distinct areas were identified to facilitate the shopping experience:

- Shopping cart content: lists products placed in the shopping cart;
- Total cost: shows the total value of products in the cart and the total amount of reductions due to promotions and offers;

**Fig. 8.1.** Prototype shopping cart implementation: Shopping cart with tablet PC, wireless network, and RFID reader (left). User Interface: Login screen, shopping options including shopping cart content monitor, shopping list, total shopping cart content cost, offers and personalized promotions, additional product information, and finally, fast check-out (right).

- Shopping list: lists products that are marked as regular buys and those that have been indicated as for replenishment due to consumption;
- Offers and promotions: details offers and promotions for the particular shopper;
- Additional information: displays either detailed information on the last product scanned (for example weight, cost, nutritional value and so forth) or on the terms and conditions of the last triggered promotion.

Unlike general-purpose product browsing appliances where the design should address all possible user cognitive processes, adopting the so-called appliance argument offers several benefits. The consumer may still perform all the activities usually associated [22] with web browsing and shopping, that is, finding products, information and general browsing, transacting and communicating. However, the particular focus of the system implies that all of the user goals may be achieved much more efficiently. Whenever additional computing power or storage resources are required, such problems may be offloaded to a central server and results exchanged wirelessly.

Product related events are sensed via the use of radio frequency identification (RFID) technologies. Contrary to bar code, the current most commonly used technology for product identification that requires significant involvement on the part of the user RFID (a) senses events and captures related data in a way that does not require line of sight visibility between the tag and the reader, (b) is more resistant to hostile environments and can survive the effects of excessive levels of dust and moisture, (c) can store more information and thus may be programmed to hold a unique product identification number, and finally (d) provides for antitheft capabilities.

On the other hand RFID is a relatively new technology and thus more expensive and more difficult to produce in large quantities. This is a significant limitation and has restricted our ability to field test the system with multiple concurrent users. Indeed, the initial design was for the RFID field to fully cover the volume defined by the shopping cart sides (80x40x60 cm). However, as this was deemed economically unfeasible with regard to the cost of the shopping cart as well as the recharging of the cart batteries, we opted for a single RFID reader. Thus, the shopper has to bring each product within the range of the RFID reader to register the product identity. Although this solution does not provide a completely seamless experience, it still has several advantages over bar code scanning (no need to search for the bar code label and align it with the scanner to register it, and antitheft mechanisms).

### 8.6.2 Formative Evaluation of Pervasive Retail Scenarios

Collection of user requirements aimed at understanding both how to integrate pervasive retail with the systems of the supply chain actors as well as how to cater for the needs of the end users. To this end, research was carried out to assess the appeal of pervasive retail as a value proposition to the consumer as well as to identify barriers to acceptance. The approach adopted was qualitative in nature and used focus groups. Market Analysis, a market research firm, was commissioned to conduct the field research. The target audience consisted of: women between the age of 25-34 who are responsible for grocery shopping within their household who demonstrated some familiarity with information and communication technologies, either as regular users of personal computers and mobile telephony at home or at work; women with the same background but from the 35-50 age range; married couples with both partners between the ages of 25 and 34, both responsible for shopping and with similar background as groups one and two; and couples as in the previous group but from the 35-50 age range. During the discussion, the participants were first introduced to pervasive retail concepts through a presentation based on concept drawings with explanatory text, which the moderator used to discuss selected usage scenarios. Following the introduction, participants were encouraged to discuss their thoughts, feelings, and reactions to this novel approach to retail as well as to express their response regarding attitudes and purchase behavior in this environment. The discussions of all groups were recorded in audio and video with the permission of the participants. At the end of the discussions participants were given a voucher for one of the retailers participating in the project.

The pervasive retail proposition attracted significant interest from most participants as a shopping option in addition to the ones available today. In particular, the in-store scenario received the most favorable response with the main benefits perceived to be the improvement of the shopping experience which was understood to be faster, easier, and offering better value for money. The features that proved most attractive were

- constant awareness of the total cost of the shopping cart content which offers to the opportunity to accurately control spending during a shopping trip,
- access to complete and accurate descriptions of products including price, size, ingredients, suitability for particular uses, and so forth,
- the ability to compare the value of similar products,
- the provision of personalized, targeted promotions that reflect the individual consumer profile in addition to the usual generic promotions as well as the fact that the participants could access all offers available in the specific supermarket at a single contact point,
- the proposed in-store navigation system, especially in the case of hypermarkets where orientation is particularly complex,
- the smart check-out and the ability to bypass queues and reduce waiting time.

However, the findings highlighted one of the main concerns of the participants: the use of personalized purchase statistics by the retailer and collaborating service providers. A large number of participants were particularly concerned about the collection and storage of personal data, even though they were aware of the provisions (albeit not the practicalities) of the data protection act. Their negative reaction to data collection was triggered primarily after the eponymous authentication during the initial use of the shopping cart when, after entering personal identification credentials, they were presented with a personalized shopping list derived through the analysis of their purchase history. The two main issues arising related to the immediate recognition of the fact that for the construction of the personalized shopping list their data is recorded, preserved, and processed. This reaction was more pronounced when trust of third parties was also involved — a core property of fourth generation systems. The main source of concern was that private data, collected in the sheltered space of the home could be delivered to external sources without the explicit consent of the consumer. The vast majority of participants did not trust a service provider to protect their privacy, irrespective of whether it was a contractual obligation or not.

Another major concern related to the overall shopping experience, which was perceived to point towards a technology controlled, fully standardized life-style. Two issues interrelate on this point. On the one hand, participants rejected the claim that a software system could predict accurately their wishes just by collecting historical data and monitoring habitual purchases. Indeed, due to its ability to pre-empt their wishes, this aspect of the system appeared patronizing and overtly rationalized but most importantly contrary to the experience of being human. In fact, the majority of participants discarded the possibility of a computer system that could successfully predict their wishes, while some of them were offended by this suggestion. On the other hand, the participants of the study perceived that the pervasive retail system reviewed promoted primarily the interests of the supplier while the consumer only received marginal benefits.

Finally, several participants observed that adoption of pervasive retail would result in a fundamental transformation of the traditional family roles. They emphasized that product selection and maintenance of appropriate home

**Fig. 8.2.** Access to retail m-services via cellular wireless mobile devices: user authentication (left) and shopping list editing (right) on wireless enabled personal digital assistant and cellular mobile telephone (both Java 2 Micro Edition capable).

inventory levels are a means to establish roles within the family unit and the responsibility to carry out these activities an integral part of the identity of the person or persons in charge. Elimination of this responsibility was perceived to undermine the status quo and pervasive retail was consequently treated with mistrust and hostility.

### 8.6.3 Privacy Protection and Consumer Trust

While the value proposition of MyGrocer did indeed attract substantial interest by consumers, at the same time it was also evident that, if implemented as described in the user scenarios, several aspects of the system would create considerable friction and would pose barriers for the wider adoption of the system. A short-term solution of this problem was to invite loyalty club members to test the system in the second phase of systems testing (detailed in the following section), a fact that offered two distinct advantages: it capitalized on the established trust relationship between consumer and the supermarket and allowed for the regulation of the relationship via a contractual agreement. Indeed, participation in a loyalty program often implies a relationship built over a longer period of time, which fosters mutual trust and helps develop a set of reasonable expectations. Furthermore, having agreed on a contract, the two parties clearly understand their rights and responsibilities to each other and have an explicit set of rules for interacting. It is thus easier to explore the extension of the relationship to include the new ubiquitous commerce services. In practice, this approach proved very successful and allowed for the evaluation of the deployed system in conditions where security and privacy were not the dominant factor.

Arguably, some of the research findings of the previous section should be seen within the context of the study, especially with respect to the evolution of retail practice. To this end, we will briefly discuss the timeliness of the emergence of supermarkets as the dominant retailing option and of the adoption of credit cards in this country. Until the early 1980s most grocery shopping was done in small, neighborhood shops with very few large supermarkets, primarily located in the two main metropolitan areas in the south and the north. Over the decade, this situation changed in accelerated pace, with most of the local shops disappearing and by the end of the decade almost completely being replaced by super and hypermarkets. Today, even in rural areas most grocery shopping is done in supermarkets that belong to one of the five national chains. The end of the 1980s also witnessed the rapid adoption of credit cards for electronic payment. Deregulation of consumer loans at the beginning of the decade played a key role in making credit cards common place and accessible to most within a few years. Since the mid-1990s, supermarket shopping and payment by credit card is as common as in any other Western European country or the US , although middle-aged Greeks still prefer to use cash and would opt to shop from a smaller grocer if possible. At the same time, the traditional family roles have also changed significantly. With the urbanization of the population in the 1950s more women entered higher education and joined the professions. Today, especially in urban areas and with younger couples, the norm is that both partners work outside the home and share the responsibility of running the household. In particular, it is likely that either the husband or the wife would be responsible for the replenishment of home supplies, although women take up this role more often than men, certainly in middle-aged couples.

This work highlighted several aspects of researching ubiquitous computing systems that may have wider implications. Unlike more traditional information systems where interaction is mediated by a computing device, for example a desktop or mobile computer, in ubiquitous computing things seem to happen transparently in space that cannot be approximated through a real or even a representational one. Thus, users are confused by their lack of appropriate language to describe it and will need other abstractions to be offered to replace the device. In our case, consumers attempted to express their opinions by anthropomorphizing system behavior so as they could relate it to their existing experiences.

One aspect that appears to be highly relevant (but we were unable to investigate in depth) is the question of how pre-existing attitudes towards privacy affect consumer views of ubiquitous commerce. Previous studies have indicated that there are considerable variations in how people deal with such issues and there is a reasonable expectation that some of these attitudes would directly affect their perceptions of ubiquitous commerce.

The novelty of ubiquitous computing means that for more significant observations to be made, one has to allow for an extended period of interaction with the system. Unlike system functionality, habits and practices take much longer to develop and often what seems novel and threatening at first glance quickly becomes part of the routine. Longer-term implications of use cannot be discovered without ethnographic studies. Of course, the problem with this approach is the very high cost for deploying and maintaining the required infrastructure at the required scale and time frame.

This last observation points to another aspect of trust that is often overseen. Indeed, trust in information systems is often seen in the tradition of cognitive psychology, which was also the basis for machine learning and artificial intelligence in the early 1960s. While this approach has made considerable contributions to computer science and systems engineering, we expect that it may not facilitate further development of our understanding of trust. Indeed, in the technical literature, trust is considered as a purely cognitive process. It is often treated as a utility function that system users try to maximize for their own benefit. We believe that this approach is better suited as a measure of trustworthiness, which is quite different from trust, and moreover that trust is a non-cognitive function that cannot always be approximated well by mathematical constructs. Hence, in the intimate computing context of ubiquitous commerce, the development of concepts of trust on this basis is of restricted use.

Approaching trust within its social context may provide a more productive alternative. It appears that this is particularly relevant in cases where there is little information on which to make a judgment of the trustworthiness of the other party and thus the decision to trust or not depends mainly on non-cognitive elements. Clearly this aspect of trust played some role in the case of our studies where the information to make an unambiguous and provable trust judgment were not available. In fact, the system frequently created significant levels of stress to the participants, which they could not justify in concrete and objective terms.

### 8.6.4 The Enacted View of Ubiquitous Commerce

There are different ways of conceptualizing ubiquitous commerce, and hence different ways of understanding what is needed for its success. One perspective is the 'objective' view, in which technologies are seen as singular entities with specific powers and consequences. Thus, in the vein of technological determinism, these powers and consequences are regarded as predictable. And in the vein of strategic choice, success is seen as depending on decisions made by management in selecting and deploying technologies. As argued by [15], however, it is crucial also to recognize the 'enacted' view of technologies.

According to this view, the digital economy is an open-ended sociotechnical production: a mass of particular actions taken as individuals and groups make their own uses of technologies. The result may be dynamic, unpredictable, and strongly mediated by the idiosyncrasies, needs, and preferences of individuals and groups. The enacted view argues that if we ignore individual human agency in the actual and day-to-day use of technologies, then we achieve an artificial and unhelpful understanding of their success. Hence, we need to attend to 'technologies-in-use', that is, the actual results of introducing technologies into particular situations, contexts, tasks, and communities, rather than just to 'espoused technologies' that is general expectations about the functions of systems.

In discussing ubiquitous commerce we believe that the enacted view of technology adoption has a critical role to play. To help conceptualize and argue about systems viewed thus, we propose that three principles that may be used to guide the design of appropriate systems and help interpret behaviors when this technology is seen in its use context [18]. The three principles are

- *Reciprocity and Understanding.* The principle of reciprocity and understanding concerns the negotiation and knowledge of identity of a peer in a trust relationship as well as the need for mutual comprehension.
- *Context and Locality.* This principle implies that relationships of trust are situated in particular contexts, relationships, roles, and communities, and that the decision to trust or not to trust may change depending on the perceptions of different contexts.
- *Communication and Interaction.* This principle recognizes the importance of non-cognitive aspects in building trust.

In this view, the reciprocity and understanding principle bears on issues of privacy protection, personalization, and consumption monitoring. It implies that collecting personal data by tracking the activities of individuals will be unacceptable if it is not reciprocal. That is, not knowing who is the organization collecting the data, how the data will be used, how to correct errors in the data, and whether to expect a return describes the relationship as non-reciprocal and introduces asymmetry, making it unacceptable for the consumer. The fact that our profile is formed under circumstances that are well beyond out control, we cannot influence and that are invisible to us introduce considerable stress to the relationship, irrespective of whether the profile is accurate or not. Moreover, this principle implies that consumers need to understand the service provider as well. Thus, although ubiquitous computing technology may allow business to offer new ubiquitous commerce services, consumers may choose to engage in business activities with parties for whom they have access to a comprehensible company identity and thus a clear set of expectations of trust.

Another aspect that creates considerable tension is the fact that persons using the system are seen as having a single dimension, that of the consumer. This view is not restricted only to the space where the actual shopping activities are carried out but extends into their own home. But following the principle of context and locality, consumers in ubiquitous commerce cannot be expected to be comfortable with a single identity profile in relation to ubiquitous and pervasive services. Rather, we can expect a strong preference to maintain different identities attached to different functions, roles, communities, and spaces and to exercise control over these. This would explain the overall negative reaction of the participants of the focus groups to pervasive retail since users of the system were characterized and treated singularly as consumers.

The communication and interaction principle implies that rather than focusing singularly on the trustworthiness of a system, the design should also address the affective aspects of interaction between ubiquitous commerce services and the consumer and the emotional impact of system usage. It accepts that since emotions are akin to strategies — even while they remain inarticulate and non-deliberate — they can be brought into the realm of rationality and have to be taken into account for the development of a trust relationship.

Last but not least, our findings have specific implications for the current discussion on the value of pervasive retail systems. With several major retailers currently making significant investments in RFID infrastructures, the issue of user acceptance is widely discussed. The common approach to this is that consumers will find the value proposition of ubiquitous commerce so attractive that they will disregard any privacy concerns. Such comments anticipate that adopting the strategic approach will indeed provide the required mechanisms to commercialize this technology. We find that two issues indicated by this study are in conflict with this view. First, pervasive retail systems are clearly viewed as being for the benefit of the business rather than the consumer.

Looking at the benefits and costs for all involved parties, it is easy to see that consumers have marginal benefits that would probably not be justified by the huge investment required to develop and use the infrastructures. Moreover, most benefits to the consumer are indirect and thus not visible and so they are easily discounted. More importantly, it is unlikely that consumers will be persuaded to use the system without allowing some degree of control over it. Indeed, controlling the flow of personal data was seen as a core element in developing a trusting relationship between consumer and retailer.

In the long term, developing a trusting relationship between ubiquitous commerce and consumers is critical for its wider acceptance. To be sure, there are several examples of technologies that were eventually rejected by the market due to the attempt to capitalize on public apathy and withhold information about their true operation. Attempting to develop ubiquitous commerce by following this approach may well have the same result.

Rather surprisingly, we did not find any major differences between the perceptions of the system across the four groups. Differences were mainly in the elected ways for expressing their concerns, but the concerns themselves were on very similar issues. There were only two areas where significant differences were found: the implications for family roles for older women and overall trust in information technology.

### 8.6.5 System redesign and deployment

Following the results of the formative evaluation study, extensive modifications were made and the supermarket scenario was selected as a more feasible alternative to be considered for system implementation. A new study was conducted focused on the particular characteristics of this scenario. The aim of the study was to understand how pervasive retail influences the shopping experience compared against the traditional supermarket environment. Members of the supermarket loyalty club were selected to take part in the study. The participants were 60 men and women responsible for shopping in their families in the 25-65 age range who had varying degrees of expertise in using personal computers and mobile telephones. Loyalty club members are familiar with the terms of use of their personal information by the supermarket and have accepted it in a trade-off for better value through discounts, gifts, and so on.

The trials were carried out in one of the stores of the supermarket chain that participated in the project where two aisles were separated and clearly marked as the location of a research study. A selection of products was equipped with RFID transponders, and the systems infrastructure was installed in the back end room. Participants were contacted over the telephone and 45-minute slots were booked for each individual. Upon arrival, participants were first introduced to the system and then invited to use the system independently. They were able to select products placed in the two aisles used for the study and receive offers and promotions according to their profile.

Finally, participants were asked to complete a questionnaire to evaluate the system services, express their views of their experience, and compare it against traditional shopping.

Several aspects of the system received favorable responses, especially the features that help save time and money. Minimizing check-out time appears to be the most attractive feature, with second the capability to continuously monitor the total value of the shopping cart content. Other services that attracted significant interest were the ability to inspect additional product information and the automated construction of a regular shopping list. Indeed, the ease of access to offers and promotions and the navigation features of the system were valued highly by the vast majority of participants who, at the same time, considered the expedited check-out features to be particularly desirable as they considered waiting time to be a significant factor in their decision to shop at a particular store. Moreover, the display of the cumulative value of the shopping cart and detailed information about offers and promotions was seen as improving the effectiveness of the shopping experience.

**Fig. 8.3.** Prototype pervasive retail application: Log-in (top left), product selection (top right), scanning (bottom right) and fast checkout (bottom left).

Participants expressed their perceptions of different aspects of the system including usefulness, usability, trust, intention to use, and service quality. The majority (49 out of 60) of participants regarded pervasive retail as a useful addition to current supermarket shopping options, expressed the view that it significantly improves the shopping experience, and found the system to be user-friendly and intuitive to use. Having resolved the issues of fair use of personal information by selecting members of the loyalty club, no other signif-

icant issues relating to trust were raised and, in fact, a significant number of
the participants stated that they would trust the system to do their shopping
and that they would trust it more than they trust Internet shopping. Overall, participants were satisfied with the service quality of the system, and the
majority (54 out of 60) expressed their willingness to use it when it becomes
available.

The most interesting results related to the changes of the shopping experience of the participants. The most striking response was that pervasive
retailing has a high entertainment value, with the majority (53 out of 60)
of participants stating that they found the experience enjoyable, while more
than half considered pervasive retail an exciting activity. In addition to this,
participants overwhelmingly agreed that the use of the system reduces their
stress level and sense of time pressure while shopping. We will return to this
point later but, first, we would like to point out that the entertainment value of
pervasive retail makes it a particularly good candidate for new ways to shop,
since it addresses most of the drivers for change in food shopping experiences.

## 8.7 Discussion and Conclusions

Pervasive retail is no longer only a vision: over the past few years it has
gradually become a reality. This can be mainly attributed to the recent technological advances that made the deployment of pilot initiatives technically
and economically viable. In effect, 62 of leading retailers in North America
and Europe have expressed their plans to deploy new IT-enabled convenience
schemes for consumers (such as info-kiosks, RFID enabled check-outs, navigation assistance and so on) within the next 3 to 5 years according to a survey
carried out by IBM and the National Retail Foundation [9]. It should be
noted that over the past few months we have already observed an increasing
number of retailers willing to embed innovative technological solutions and
shopping schemes into their store environment. Price Chopper is planning to
deploy self-service info-kiosks providing access to accurate product information; Wal-Mart is working with its top 100 suppliers to deploy new RFID tags
for tracking crates and pallets in the supply chain beginning in January 2005;
Marks & Spencer will install new self-checkout schemes in eight additional
stores following a successful three-store pilot. The benefits deriving from the
deployment of ubiquitous commerce systems are apparent. Retailers will have
a tool that enables them to "work with their consumers," making them an indistinguishable part of their operations and reaching them in a way that they
become a real stakeholder, part of their vision for an optimized value chain.
The direct benefits for the retail value chain deriving from the incorporation
of leading edge technologies include among others:

- Real-time information provision regarding the products' lifecycle within
  the value chain, optimizing the forecasting process of future demand.

- Real-time information provision regarding the shopper's consumption behavior, providing the ability to identify and model shoppers' emerging needs.
- Introduction of personalized marketing/promotional programs, including accurate monitoring of promotions' effectiveness.
- Elimination of out-of-shelf/out-of-stock conditions.
- Elimination of thefts within the store.

However, the most important benefit deriving from the deployment of ubiquitous commerce systems is the creation of new shopping experiences, and consequently, greater enthusiasm for the consumers. This is particularly true especially in our era where recent advances in manufacturing, distribution, and information technologies combined with the urbanization of modern society have created the so-called new consumer, who is more knowledgeable about comparable product costs and price; more changeable in retail and brand preferences; shows little loyalty; self-sufficient, yet demands more information; holds high expectations of service and personal attention; and is driven by three new currencies: time, value, and information. Although there are still several challenges to the wider deployment of such integrated shopping schemes — especially those relating to issues of personal identity, security, and privacy but also standardization and engineering — the results of our prototype implementation indicate that consumers would accept the introduction of innovative information systems when they become commercially available.

Our research revealed that the issue of trust and privacy is extremely important, considering the fact that we constantly need information regarding the consumer's current location in-store, past consumption patterns, household information, demographic data and so on in order to provide fully personalized services. An initial critical appraisal of this situation would indicate that application designers must make some compromises on the extent they offer personalized services. Traditionally, data protection legislation in most EU countries prohibits the capture and storage of any person-related data and only allows exceptions for clearly defined purposes, after which the data must be destroyed. In our case, we allowed consumers to deactivate the provision of personalized services and at the same time participate in the system without providing their full set of personal information. However, this is not the solution to the general problem of trust and privacy. We expect that users will eventually be willing to adopt such applications only if they perceive that they are getting better shopping experiences in return for letting go some of their privacy. Finally, the full involvement of the end-users during the design and development of the ubiquitous commerce system ensures the adoption and actual use of it after its commercialization. Our experience from MyGrocer revealed that the production of mock-up demos (in the form of concept sketches and non-functional interface screenshots of selected system functionality) and their exposure to real supermarket shoppers helped us identify potential barriers of acceptance and provided us with the necessary feedback to redesign the system according to the actual user needs and expectations.

# References

1. Accenture. *Guide to CPFR Implementation*, ECR Europe. 2001.
2. R. Aylott and V.W. Mitchell. An exploratory study of grocery shopping stressors. *International Journal of Retail and Distribution Management* 26(9):362–373. 1998.
3. J. Baker. The role of the environment in marketing services: The consumer perspective. In J.A. Czepeil, C. Congram and J. Shanahan J. (eds) *The Services Challenge: Integrating for Competitive Advantage*. American Marketing Association, Chicago, IL. 1986.
4. D. Carter and I. Lomas. Store Of The Future. *Proceedings of ECR Europe 2003*. Berlin, Germany. 2003.
5. N. Davies and H.W. Gellersen. Beyond prototypes: Challenges in deploying ubiquitous systems. *IEEE Pervasive Computing* 1(1):26–35. 2002.
6. R.J. Donovan and J.R. Rossiter. Store atmosphere: An Environmental Psychology Approach. *Journal of Retailing* 58:34–57. 1982.
7. F. Fukuyama. *Trust: Human Nature and the Reconstitution of Social Order*. Free Press, New York. 1996.
8. M. Gottdiener. *New Forms of Consumption: Consumers, Culture, and Commodification*. Rowman & Littlefield Publishers. 2000.
9. IBM Institute for Business Value. Enhancing the customer shopping experience. *IBM/NRF Store of the future survey*. 2002.
10. Y.K. Kim. Consumer Value: An Application To Mall and Internet Shopping. *International Journal of Retail and Distribution Management* 30(12):595–602. 2002.
11. P. Kourouthanassis and G. Roussos. Developing Consumer-Friendly Pervasive Retail Systems. *IEEE Pervasive Computing* 2(2):32–39. 2003.
12. M. Levy and B.A. Weitz. *Retailing Management*. McGraw-Hill, New York. 2003.
13. D.M. Lewison. *Retailing*. Prentice Hall. 1997.
14. A.J. Martin. *Infopartnering: The Ultimate Strategy for Achieving Efficient Consumer Response*. John Wiley & Sons, London. 1995.
15. W. Orlikowski and C.S. Iacono. The truth is not out there: An enacted view of the Digital Economy, In E. Brynjolfsson and B. Khim (Eds.) *Understanding the Digital Economy: Data, Tools and Research*. MIT Press. 2001.
16. Pew Research Center. *Pew Internet and American Life Project Trust and Privacy Online: Why Americans Want to Rewrite the Rules*. Available at http://www.pewinternet.org/reports. August 20, 2000.
17. R. Reid and S. Brown. I hate shopping! An introspective perspective. *International Journal of Retail and Distribution Management* 24(4):4–16. 1996.
18. G. Roussos, D. Peterson and U. Patel. Mobile Identity Management: An Enacted View. *Int. Jour. E-Commerce*. 8(1):81-100. 2003.
19. G. Roussos, D. Spinellis, P. Kourouthanassis, E. Gryazin, P. Pryzbliski, G. Kalpogiannis and G. Giaglis. Systems Architecture for Pervasive Retail. *Proceedings ACM SAC 2003*. Melbourne, Florida, USA. 631–636. 2003.

20. T. Salvador, G. Bell and K. Anderson. Design Ethnography. *Design Management Journal* 10(4):35–41. 1999.
21. S. Sarma, D.L. Brock and Kevin Ashton. *The Networked Physical World Proposals for Engineering the Next Generation of Computing, Commerce and Automatic-Identification.* Whitepaper WH-001. Auto-ID Centre, MIT. Cambridge, MA, USA. 2002.
22. A. Sellen. The Future of the Mobile Internet: Lessons from Looking at Web Use. *Appliance Design* 3:20–25. 2002.
23. D. Slater. *Consumer Culture.* Polity Press, Cambridge. 2002.

# Part III

# Society

# 9

## Legal Challenges to Ubiquitous Commerce

Olli Pitkänen

### 9.1 Introduction

Legal systems must take into account numerous interests and seek to balance diverging and often conflicting principles. Indeed, one of the primary aims of such systems is to develop legal structures to facilitate business by diminishing risks and establishing an environment of trust, thus enabling effective business methods. In this context, the function of law is to establish a framework where future legal conditions can be negotiated and a common basis for fair business exchanges developed. For example, contract law enables business parties to assess the liabilities they take on under an agreement; property laws clarify the rules for allocating assets and who and who may dispose of them; competition and consumer protection laws strive to ensure that market mechanisms work properly and the rights of individuals are respected; data protection; the moral rights of the author; the freedom of speech, and other comparable laws implement the fundamental values that modern societies are built on. A good law makes the future legal circumstances more predictable. Furthermore, good laws reduce transaction costs as individuals and organisations spend less time in negotiations of every aspect of a business relationship. For this reason and from a business perspective, legal structures generally play a critical role in commerce by reducing risks and thus enforcing adherence to fair business methods. On the other hand, when designed erroneously, laws may also constrain business by developing an inefficient or even non-functional environment.

In this chapter, I discuss legal challenges to ubiquitous commerce in particular. By *legal challenges* I refer to difficulties in legal reasoning or situations that in some way have led the legal process to an unsatisfying outcome. One such case is when legislation may prohibit certain business models: data protection laws like the European Directive on the protection of personal data (Directive 95/46/EC) ban certain usages of personal information. A business model that would depend critically on the use of personal data in a way prohibited by the legislation will clearly lead to business failure. Although it is unlikely that a business model which is solely based on assumptions well outside the current social norm would go very far, it is rather common that considerable constraints in business practices are the result of specific legal structures. Hence, fostering market conditions conducive to business and constraining business practice are often only the opposite faces of the same coin.

Finally, it is worth pointing out that especially in novel business environments, particularly those that became feasible through the use of technology, existing legal structures may easily become outdated, contradictory, or difficult to apply to new and complex situations. Even structures that have served society well for a long time and have a long track record of success can suddenly turn into negative forces for market development. In such situations, the effect is easily observed in increased transaction costs and the slow-down of the development of value networks. In the worst case scenario, companies become vulnerable to risks that could be avoided or contained if the legal challenges were better understood [5]. Indeed, poor understanding of legal challenges may lead governments or standards bodies to regulate markets in an unsatisfactory way and even to create obstacles to services that might be important and useful both for users and the society at large.

## 9.2 Ubiquitous Commerce Technologies

In this chapter I will first outline several technical issues that will be essential to ubiquitous commerce and will bear considerably on emerging legal challenges[1]. Ubiquitous computing is being brought about by a convergence of advanced digital computing and wireless communications technologies and the Internet, where computation is embedded into physical spaces and artifacts that combine to create largely autonomous intelligent information systems (for a more extensive discussion of the vision of ubiquitous computing and commerce, see also Chapter 1 of this volume). From a legal perspective, the implication is that interpretation of law is harder and often uncertain as it has been developed to apply to a radically different context. One case where the new computing paradigm appears to open new questions is in contractual agreements, since in a ubiquitous computing system it is often possible that the user of a computationally augmented artifact is actually unaware of the content of the agreement or even the fact that they are participating in a transaction since system operation is completely transparent. Thus, it is not always clear how to establish legally binding contracts in ubiquitous commerce situations using the current requirements of law. Although there are similarities between mobile and ubiquitous computing, the latter has much wider implications. One can always turn off a mobile phone or a handheld computer and thus retain their privacy or simply become unreachable. Yet,

---

[1]Some of these challenges have also been identified in our recent work on mobile commerce[5, 6].

in most cases, ubiquitous systems cannot be turned off, as they are composed of several different devices often outside the control of the user or because they are often so tightly embedded into physical spaces, that are completely hidden and undiscoverable.

One of the core ingredients of ubiquitous commerce is context-awareness, which allows for systems to modify their behaviour according to the particular user situation. Context includes all physical and social circumstances and facts that define a particular user situation or user generated event. Typically, context includes location and thus proximity to particular objects or spaces, user and device identity, time, history of actions, and current activity [3]. In the short term, it appears that location information will be one of the most important elements of context. Contrary to the Internet, which has removed several limitations of the physical world, ubiquitous computing requires knowledge and use of such attributes as well as of their inherent characteristics and constraints to operate effectively. Clearly, to collect context information it is necessary that systems employ sensor and actuator devices to collect data from the environment and the user. Thus, a core requirement of ubiquitous commerce systems is the collection of personal information and sharing of information between service providers, a clear challenge for privacy and data protection law.

Indeed, information is the currency of ubiquitous commerce. In Chapter 5, Gershman and Fano introduced a variety of consumer services that either add value to the customers' own information or enable customers to benefit from information produced by other users of the same service. Technologies that enable creation, harvesting, transfer, modification, and storage of information in ubiquitous commerce systems will be critical for their success. On the other hand, it will also be necessary to manipulate information while adhering to specific rules often imposed by the technology itself but more often so as to comply to social rules implemented in law.

## 9.3 Legal Challenges

In this section, we will discuss specific legal challenges that affect ubiquitous commerce grouped by legal theme according to current practice.

### 9.3.1 Privacy

By its very nature, a significant proportion of information managed by ubiquitous commerce systems is private. People object if information on their location, behavior, habits, interests, transactions, finance, social situations, and health, among others, is communicated without their consent. Therefore, a priority for ubiquitous commerce systems is privacy and confidentiality protection. On the other hand, many companies and public agencies are keen to access such data. For example, a commercial company would be able to direct marketing to the right individuals much more accurately if it held detailed information about their habits and health. Some customers might be willing to benefit from the situation while others are so concerned about their privacy that they would not even consider letting this information be utilized under any circumstances.

The European Union has set rather strict rules regulating the use of personal data via the data protection directive. However, in other regions, for example in the USA, the discussion about privacy protection has not led to comparable statutes thus far, often opting for self regulation of markets. It remains unclear which approach ultimately will prove to be more attractive: although privacy is perceived as an extremely important aspect of legal systems and must be protected appropriately, too strict a privacy protection legislation may lead to unintended results with useful services for consumers being simply unsustainable in the marketplace.

### 9.3.2 Intellectual Property Rights

Intellectual property rights (IPR), including copyright, patent, database protection, and so on, form the legal basis of business models that are built on selling information or providing information-based services. In particular, copyright issues are important to ubiquitous commerce services that aim to profit from using information assets. Moreover, companies that may benefit from associated products, for example device manufacturers and wired or wireless service providers, can find business opportunities by enabling the mechanisms that support enforcement of copyright protection rules [4, 5].

Nevertheless, intellectual property rights do not necessarily protect all types of information: legal rules are often outdated and have been developed to address a different set of requirements. Ubiquitous commerce sets a different context and indeed stretches the limits of legislation developed in a pre-computerised world.

### 9.3.3 Contracts

Contract law affects all parties involved in ubiquitous commerce for the simple reason that each commercial transaction is in fact a contract. Contracts also play the role of documents where agreements are recorded for situations that are not covered by law. For example, if copyright law does not adequately addresses a certain situation, it is often overridden by a contract. Yet, transaction costs increase rapidly with the number of issues that must be explicitly agreed upon.

An area of particular concern is the generalization of fundamental contract concepts like *offer*, *acceptance*, and *consideration* to software agents running on mobile computers and negotiating with each other transparently for their owners. Even the simpler case where individuals are directly involved in contract negotiations via a ubiquitous commerce system, some fundamentals of contract law may need revision: for example, it can be very difficult to identify beyond doubt other parties involved in a certain transaction, due to the use of mediators or intermediaries.

In recent years, the European Union has been active in developing directives that harmonize contract law for electronic business across Europe. This legislation tends to be technology neutral, and thus applicable to all kinds of electronic contracts regardless of the particular technology employed. But it is most likely that it is impossible to make totally technology neutral legislation. This is especially challenging when a paradigm shift is required, which is the case when a fundamentally new generation of technology arrives notably ubiquitous computing. Even though lawmakers have attempted to avoid the constraints of existing technologies, they can hardly avoid thinking in terms of personal computers, displays, and web pages. For example, the European Directive on electronic commerce (2000/31/EC) states that in connection with an information society service, the customer must have access to specific and considerable amounts of information. When using a desktop computer and the web, accessing this information is not an issue. Things change rapidly, though, when using a deeply-embedded ubiquitous computing device, that can have very limited display capabilities, and thus it might be impossible that this information be always displayed prior to agreement to the terms and conditions of the contract.

### 9.3.4 Other Legal Areas

There are a number of other legal areas that are affected by ubiquitous commerce technologies. For example, labor law affects professionals when ubiquitous commerce changes their working conditions. In many countries, labor laws are badly outdated. They are hard to apply in situations where working hours, company or group formation, and other conditions are extremely flexible.

Tax law faces similar challenges to labor law. Traditional tax law is hard to apply in new kinds of transactions on ubiquitous commerce. In this context, it is unclear which of the fiscal entities involved has jurisdiction to tax a certain transaction. Competition law and industry specific regulations may restrict businesses especially if they are in a strong position in the marketplace. In ubiquitous commerce, these rules may force companies to open up their systems and interfaces to enable competition in unpredictable ways, especially in terms of their effects on business and revenue models.

Finally, ubiquitous commerce by its nature ignores borders. Transactions can easily be completed between parties anywhere in the world. If a service is indeed provided over the whole globe, international aspects of law become vital for a customer who travels abroad while using the service . Although considerable effort has gone and is still going into harmonising law, many areas will remain different, reflecting different cultural and local priorities and traditions.

## 9.4 Application Scenarios

Since there is little experience with ubiquitous commerce applications and large scale commercial deployments are a few years away, a readily available alternative to studying the associated legal challenges is to assess scenarios that describe future situations[6, 7]. For example, one could follow the work of the IST Advisory Group (ISTAG) of the European Commission that has-taken a higher-level approach in identifying future Information and Communication Technology developments in Europe. As a part of this work, ISTAG launched a scenario planning exercise in 2000. The scenarios were developed at the European Commission's Joint Research Centre in collaboration with the Information Society directorate and with the active involvement of several domain experts across Europe. The aim has been to describe in practical terms the vision of living with the so-called 'Ambient Intelligence' (AmI), a concept roughly equivalent to ubiquitous computing, for the general public in 2010 [2].

The four published ISTAG scenarios are quite similar from a legal point of view. They all portray a world in which computing and communication devices are present everywhere and have access to huge amounts of personal information. Furthermore, a common pattern in all scenarios is situations where machines make decisions on behalf of human beings. For example, *Maria* is a scenario about a busy business person travelling abroad and using highly automated and integrated communications infrastructures (cf. Appendix B). From the legal point of view this scenario is notable because almost all transactions — both private and public — are automated. In fact, most decisions are made by machines and there is hardly any human interaction required. However, heavy use of context-aware services as described in the scenario consume considerable amounts of personal information. Location information in particular is needed for almost all services.

The ubiquitous computing technologies described in the ISTAG scenarios represent specific challenges to privacy, since the interconnected computing devices employed require access to a large amount of private information to be able to provide the services. Clearly, there is great potential for privacy compromises. Yet, the ISTAG scenarios do not reflect on any such problems: all systems are working perfectly and honor users' privacy. But there are no mechanisms in place to ensure that. A system with massive amounts of personal information pervading all aspects of everyday life is very easy to misuse, either intentionally or in error, with data used wrongfully or distributed too widely. In fact, it is often the case that the best solution from a purely technical point of view is quite unacceptable from a privacy protection perspective, and this is also true for mechanisms that protect access to information flows. For example, access control mechanisms that prohibit unauthorized use of information are too complex to implement and decrease the overall performance and usability of a system. Therefore it is often tempting (and cost effective) to leave such mechanisms out or at least make them as lightweight as possible.

Unless a paying customer insists or the law demands so, a system provider can easily ignore privacy protection.

Moreover, there seems to be a dichotomy between stated attitudes and actual behavior of individuals facing decisions affecting their privacy and their personal information security. While there is some evidence that a large proportion of individuals are concerned about the security of their personal information and are willing to act to protect it, experiments reveal that very few individuals will actually take any action to protect their personal information, even when doing so involves limited costs. Since users of systems and services do not necessarily insist on privacy protection until after specific problems occur, it becomes the responsibility of legal systems to protect individuals and society as a whole [1].

In the European Union, several directives and other statutes, notably the Directive on privacy and electronic communications (2002/58/EC), have been introduced to protect privacy and personal data. However, the autonomic nature of ubiquitous computing has implications that cannot be adequately addressed by existing legislation. An example of this situation relates to the use of location data to provide essential context for many ambient intelligence services. Processing such location information falls under the provisions of the directive that requires explicit consent by the user. In an ubiquitous commerce environment where a number of services by different service providers are used in tandem it is difficult to notify and receive the consent of users to process location data every time this is necessary. In fact, the directive requires that the user accepts separately the use of their data by each service and even more, services must provide continually the"possibility, [of] using a simple means and free of charge, of temporarily refusing the processing of such data for each connection to the network or for each transmission of a communication" (2002/58/EC). Indeed, it appears that this aspect of the directive completely excludes the possibility of federated service provision. Moreover, if users are required to accept separately the use of their private data by each service, then in practice, it is most likely that users simply would not use the services rather than accept this management overhead. Surely, usability improvements and automatic mechanisms can make the situation much easier, but ultimately the user must have control and the ability to refuse the processing of location data in order to fulfill the requirements of the directive. Finally, while the directive aims to harmonise legal systems and guarantee certain levels of protection within the EU, obviously it does not apply in countries outside its boundaries.

This is exactly one of the issues raised by the ISTAG Maria scenario (cf. Appendix B), where a European citizen is travelling outside Europe. Her personal data mainly originates from the Union but is needed for services offered in Asia. Presumably Maria is willing to use those personalized services and therefore accepts the transfer of her personal data between at least her home country and the Asian country in question. In accordance with the directive and European national law, she has to explicitly accept this transfer. Although this requirement protects her privacy effectively, it also introduces significant challenges to the designers of the service. Moreover, it reduces the efficiency of the AmI concept as envisioned by ISTAG, namely that "Ambient Intelligence works in a seamless, unobtrusive and often invisible way." The need to receive explicit consent from the user makes this goal hard to achieve. In fact, the Maria scenarios completely shy away from this issue.

ISTAG scenarios also describe how immigration and border control procedures as well as cross-border negotiation processes have been automated. However, the current situation is that in most cases humans make the final decisions: immigration officials decide who is allowed to enter the country, individuals representing legal entities make agreements on behalf of the organizations, and so on. Those human beings are able to make the decisions often using incomplete information and taking reasonable risks, they are authorized to use due deliberation, and eventually they are also responsible for their decisions. It is a long process for computer systems to become able to analyze such deliberate complex problems, provide answers with incomplete input information, and take balanced risks. There are fundamental difficulties in making a machine legally liable for its decisions.

When developing scenarios, it is often difficult to estimate how much change can occur in any given period of time. The ISTAG scenarios appear very optimistic that the legal systems involved could change to this degree by 2010. Especially with respect to privacy and data protection, the legislation in Europe has gone in a more restrictive direction in the recent years. While protecting most important values, it has not made this kind of a scenario easier to achieve. Perhaps only the easiest, most straightforward cases can be automated, and most of the scenarios will be legally feasible, if it is presumed that human beings are still making all but the trivial decisions.

In this chapter I concentrated on the ISTAG scenario but there is nothing special about it. Indeed, I have also assessed a large number of scenarios related to future ubiquitous technologies and commerce developed by other groups. In these different situations, in most cases the same challenges as those reviewed here are highlighted, namely privacy, intellectual property rights, and contracts.

## 9.5 Conclusions

Legal challenges affecting the development of ubiquitous commerce systems will be related to aspects of *privacy, intellectual property rights, and contracts*. Several implications of this view have been discussed here and are supported by analysis of specific application scenarios. In relation to ubiquitous commerce, privacy will possibly be the most critical area as ubiquity and context-awareness will bring computer networks closer to the most intimate places and walks of life. Challenges to privacy are much greater in ubiquitous commerce than in any other situation faced by modern societies ever before.

Intellectual property rights, and in particularly copyright, will also be a legal area where a number of challenges will emerge. Issues related to content adaptation will be significantly more challenging than in previous technology generations. In addition to legal protection, the future information products will be increasingly protected by digital rights management systems. On the other hand, provision of high quality services should distribute content flexibly and adapt on the basis of context.

There are significant challenges to fit these different aspects together. In the case of contracts there are several issues: first, on ubiquitous networks it is not always easy to find out who the contracting parties are. Second, it can often be difficult to state what the subject of a contract is. It can also be complicated to determine the exact point in time when parties have committed to the contract. Finally, for services operating over a ubiquitous computing network it can be very hard to verify which law regulates a transaction and thus which authority has jurisdiction over disputes. A fundamental characteristic of networks supporting ubiquitous computing that underlies all these issues regarding contractual challenges is the fragmentation of networks themselves.

Finally, other legal areas will also be affected. In general, International law will play an important role due to the global scope of service provision and high user mobility. Labor law and tax law will also face challenges due to the new kinds of transactions and changing work patterns.

# References

1. A. Acquisti and J. Grossklags. Privacy Attitudes and Privacy Behavior: Losses, Gains, and Hyperbolic Discounting. In: J. Camp and S. Lewis (Eds) *The Economics of Information Security*. Kluwer Academic Publishers. 2004.
2. K. Ducatel, M. Bogdanowicz, F. Scapolo, J. Leijten and J.C. Burgelman (Eds). *ISTAG Scenarios for Ambient Intelligence in 2010*. Final Report, IPTS-Seville. 2001.
3. J. Hong and J.A. Landay. A Context/Communication Information Agent. *Personal Technologies*. Special Issue on Situated Interaction and Context-Aware Computing. 2001.
4. R. Merges, P. Menell and M. Lemley. *Intellectual Property in the New Technological Age*. 2nd edition. Aspen Law & Business. 2000.
5. O. Pitkänen. *Managing Rights in Information Products on the Mobile Internet*, HIIT Publications. Helsinki Institute for Information Technology, Finland. 2002.
6. O. Pitkänen, M. Mäntylä, M. Välimäki and J. Kemppinen. Assessing Legal Challenges on the Mobile Internet. *International Journal of Electronic Commerce* 8(1):101–120. 2003.
7. B. Wendell. *Foundations of Futures Studies*. Volumes I-II. Transaction Publishers. 1997.

# 10

# Thoughts on Retail System Design to Support Polimorphic Actions Among Clerks: That'll Be $20 — But if You Buy Two, I'll Knock off 10%

Tony Salvador, Kenneth T. Anderson, and John W. Sherry

> Give me a stock clerk with a goal, and I will give you a man [sic] who will make history. Give me a man without a goal, and I will give you a stock clerk.
> – J.C. Penney

## 10.1 Opening

Our goal in this chapter is to broaden the conceptualization of technological innovation in retail environments with a keen eye toward re-enabling the role of the human worker. The authors all work with Intel Corporation in the People and Practices Research group[1] , a group of social scientists whose role is to challenge, question, and guide the corporation's prevailing viewpoint. We use mostly ethnographic data collection, analysis, and synthesis techniques to understand how people adopt and use technologies in their daily lives — or how they don't. The techniques we use include observation, shadowing, participant observation, and nondirective, situated interviews; we often work with local anthropologists and other social scientists. As a group, over the years, our research has led us to more than 25 countries, into hundreds of homes and businesses, and we have spoken with, worked with, lived with and observed thousands of people. This chapter draws on upon this wide body of research in which retail establishments were one element consistently explored in our work over the years, sometimes with a more intense focus, other times as peripheral to our main area of study.

We note that where technologies have been adopted in retail establishments, they have been used to rationalize operations — often with the (perhaps inadvertent (perhaps not)) effect of constraining human behavior. Chapter 5 by Gershman and Fano in this volume speaks to the potential for retail

---

[1]See http://intel.com/research/exploratory/papr for more information about this group and its work.

establishments to profit by removing human variability from their systems. We offer a complementary perspective that with ripening technologies and the right attitude and perspective, technology can be designed explicitly to enable and collaborate with the worker, encouraging a human-machine retail system that values the clerk. This chapter offers three windows on this topic. In terms of word-count, we spend a pleasant proportion of the chapter presenting examples of retail transactions from our field notes. To move us into the design space, we take a theoretical view based on the concept of agency [3] and specific types of actions that foster agency; for this we rely on recent work by [1]. Finally, we have a little fun with two simple concepts that highlight exactly our point of intentionally considering how new technologies can be used.

## 10.2 Back Stories

Early in his book *Reinventing the Bazaar* [4], John McMillan quotes the sociologist George Simmel: "Exchange is 'one of the purest and most primitive forms of human socialization,' in that it creates 'a society in place of a mere collection of individuals.'" One would expect, therefore, that as individuals form various societies of various descriptions, the means and types of exchanges would also vary. And indeed, they do. It is with some irony, then, that we find relatively significant use of technology in retail settings coincides with an increased standardization of transactions whereas stores with a lower level of technology adoption seem to offer a greater variety of transaction styles. Moreover, the role of the clerk becomes increasingly standardized, less improvisational, and more scripted in the former as compared to the latter situation.

McMillan writes: "The mechanisms that underpin transactions are intricate — and they are in everlasting flux. People are ingenious at finding ways to make exchanges that bring mutual gains." In the grand scheme of things, this too seems a valid statement. At issue for us, however, is to distinguish the locus of this ingenuity. For large corporate retail operations, the ingenuity seems to exist far from the actual transaction — far in terms of time, place and people involved, that is, central headquarters. Conversely, for small retailers, the locus of ingenuity is on the spot, at that time, in that shop involving that customer and that retail clerk. Perhaps not coincidentally, it is the larger retailers that tend to adopt more technology, and it is the smaller ones that either actively eschew the use of technology in their shops, or who simply have not found the need for it. As a result, they retain the locus of ingenuity. Here's an example:

Pete and Tony were going on a week of trekking on Lesvos, a larger and overall somewhat less touristy Greek island in the northern Aegean Sea. Arriving in Mytellini by ferry, they made their way to the start of the trek, Skala Eressos, a small and mostly quiet seaside town, which seems to attract local

Greek families, German families and lesbian women who have adopted the poet Sappho, hailing originally from just up the road, as a kind of patron saint. There is a beach, some seaside restaurants and some shops along the main street. It was very hot. After dinner, walking along the main street, they saw a tourist shop renting motorcycles and thought it wouldn't be at all a bad idea to leave the packs in Skala Eressos, walk to Sigri, the next day's destination, and then rent motorcycles to come back and retrieve the packs. They thought it would be sort of fun anyway — the roads are not full of cars, the hills beautiful, and the days long. Tony approached the clerk:

"Excuse me, but you do rent these, don't you?"

"Yes, certainly."

"Do you also rent them in Sigri?"

The clerk responded, but with little hesitation: "Why don't you tell me exactly what you are thinking."

Tony and Pete told him that they were walking to Sigri and wanted the round-trip to begin and end there. He thought for a moment. "We can do that. We can bring the scooter to Sigri for you and pick it up later. It will cost you twenty euros extra."

Up until that moment, that service didn't exist. It was a new service, offered on the spot, by this clerk, to two tourists who had this idea to walk from Skala Eressos to Sigri and who saw an opportunity to not have to carry their packs over the hills in the hot Grecian summer sun. The clerk knew enough about his business, the resources available to him in Skala Eressos as well as in Sigri, and what it would cost him in fuel and time. Having a full understanding of his business, he exercised a little ingenuity and evolved an exchange on the spot.

OK, that's a tourist town. Maybe he's used to it; maybe that's the nature of his business. In Santiago de Chile, Claudio, John and Tony are walking through the weekly Feria in Pealoln, a relatively resource-limited district of Santiago and most certainly not a tourist destination. The Feria comes to this location every Monday and occupies several streets. It moves seven days a week, going to a different designated spot on each day to cater to the residents in their area. Each vendor — from those selling bolts of clothing to plastic jugs to bike parts to fruit to fish and meat — sets-up and takes-down at this location every Monday. They are assigned a spot; they bring their own tenting, shelves, items, etc. They can show-up or not and not get fired. They are free to set and negotiate prices. That they don't take checks or credit cards is reflective more of the customer base and its resources more than it is an active decision or choice. In many of the transactions, people knew their customers. In fact, our guide, Claudio, was well known to many of the vendors who shouted and greeted him as he walked by. In fact, one of the vendors *gave* us all drinks (because we were with Claudio, of course) and took no payment.

Ingenuity is one part of how exchanges can evolve. Having the understanding, the authority, and the autonomy to make the decisions are also necessary components for exercising ingenuity. There are innumerable ways to retain the ability to exercise ingenuity. It's important to consider a range of examples to get a feel for a more complete set of possibilities. Another example:

Saturday Market is a market of artists selling their art and craft under the Burnside Bridge in Portland, Oregon. Artists sell only what they make, ranging from tie-dye clothes to funky jewelry to whimsical fish sculptures. Saturday Market is a bit of a misnomer, as it operates Saturdays and Sundays from spring through Christmastime. Each artist is assigned a particular location — a chalked outline on the pavement beneath the bridge, for which they pay a nominal fee. They bring everything else — their own tables, tents, poles, racks, shelves, cash boxes, artwork, etc. Each artist is responsible to set-up and take-down their "shop" each weekend. Each artist is independent; they can show-up every weekend, or skip some, though they are encouraged to attend each weekend. They can sell their work or simply display it. They can negotiate the price; they can take special commissions; they can give their things away if it pleases them. Some take checks, some don't. Some accept credit cards, but it's a cumbersome process and most avoid the hassle.

Compare these last two experiences (Saturday Market, Feria) with the experience of shopping at a Big Red store. "Big Red" is a multinational retail corporation with nearly 2000 enormous stores in the US. As we approach one store, two sets of sliding doors part, automatically bathing us in artificially cool air as we draw one of the identical red carts from the cart depot. Walking in to the store, we see a veritable Feria of products — and more — all so neatly and systematically arranged its borders on the surreal - especially compared to the Feria. It is quite the experience, one to which many in the US have become accustomed and no longer notice.

It goes almost without saying that Big Red Corporation would be unable to operate effectively and efficiently without the technological infrastructure undergirding its operations. Similarly obvious is that markets around the globe, like the Feria, operate every day without anything close to a similar level of technological infrastructure.

What is less obvious is the role of the clerk in each example and the resulting transaction experience. At Big Red, it's the inventory management systems in conjunction with point of sale systems dictating where, when, and how to place products on what shelves and informing both the clerk and the customer of the price at check-out. The stores, each being based on one of a few "models," offer nearly identical experiences, whether in Seattle or Tampa. Moreover, the clerks are performing nearly identical jobs. An Atlanta clerk could, we assert, work just fine in the Seattle store. Most of the human actions meaningful to the transaction are mediated by the technology, controlled and managed centrally. In contrast, at the Feria and Saturday Market, the clerk and the customer jointly mediate all the actions meaningful to the transaction. To work at the Feria is not to work at Big Red.

But what does it mean to work at Big Red? What does it mean "to work" at the Feria? What does it mean more generally for a person to "work" as a clerk in a retail establishment? How do information systems intersect what it means to work in such environs? How should new technologies encourage new definitions of work?

## 10.3 Agency

We've talked above about the "locus of ingenuity," which frankly we just made up to get us through the examples. A rather more thoroughly discussed - and hopefully useful — perspective with which to consider the role of workers and information systems in retail establishments is that of "agency." Habermas [2] defines agency as the ability to control and/or make a difference through decision making power. Humans alone possess and can express agency and information systems (machines) do not and cannot; machines are designed to serve human needs.

Agency can be bounded and constrained in various ways. The Greek scooter renter is relatively unbounded. The mot vendor at the Feria can decide and act on his decision to give us free drinks; the fish sculptor can decide without repercussion to give away the salmon leaping over the falls. The clerk in Big Red, however, is relatively bounded, having relatively little ability to express agency. Ironically, the information system at Big Red is doing the bounding — even if as an extension of the designer. The information system is, therefore, imposing its will on the interaction.

This is exactly as Latour [3] defines agency: the ability to impose one's own will in a given network of interacting actors. An actor is any node in an interacting network — human or machine. Phrased slightly differently, agency is not expressed at the "nodes," that is, only by the actors, but rather as transformations that result from the interaction of all the actors in a network. Agency is, therefore, an emergent property of the total system.

From a design perspective, each definition leads one to consider different roles for technology. The former, of Habermas, assumes that technical systems, once designed and installed, serve a rather passive role of "doing what they'd been told to do." To the extent that the system is designed to enact certain specific processes in certain specific ways, they increasingly dictate the actions and possible actions of the human worker.

At Big Red, the inventory system is aligned with the times when there is an expectation of having the fewest customers in the store; the system informs the clerks not only of when to stock the shelves — so as to provide minimum disruption to the customers - but also exactly what shelf, how many items of a kind to place on the shelf, how many deep and how many facing across the shelf. One store manager told us that on a snowy day, he made an executive decision to put shovels in the aisle — a deviation from the system's instructions and a certain risk.

On the other hand, thinking of agency as emerging from the interactions of the actors in the network, the Latour definition, opens the design space by considering the information system as an equal partner in the emergence of agency; that is, the total system is responsible. Taking this view into account, we use, although only temporarily, a definition of agency which is the ability of the retail worker to act appropriately but relatively unencumbered by the dictates and wishes of the establishment. This definition is a more succinct and useful-for-design definition of agency indicative of this partnership and respectful of the worker, while offering "hooks" to guide a design process. For example, this perspective gives us the latitude to consider how technologies can be designed to support an interaction of workers and information systems in such a way as to enable and empower the worker while also attending to the operational imperatives of the business. It forces us to shift our perspective from *technology to rationalize* to *technology to energize.*

To this point, we've argued that clerks' agency, or the lack thereof, is a critical differentiator among retail establishments and that relatively low clerk agency co-varies with high rates of technology adoption. We've also argued that agency is dependent on a clerk's ability to "act unencumbered." We need to do one more thing: before we can go ahead and consciously design to encourage clerk agency, we must also define what it means to act and add that to our definition of agency.

Collins & Kusch [1] define two types of actions: polimorphic and mimeomorphic. Basically, polimorphic actions are those that can only be understood — or done — by other people who are functionally members of the same society (*poli-* from the root for *polis*, of the people, and not only, but also a pun on the root *poly-*, as in many). Mimeomorphic actions are those that if replicated by someone who didn't understand the action would still look the same as if someone who did understand was performing the actions. As stated by Collins & Kusch, polimorphic actions are defined such that only the enculturated can see sameness, whereas enculturated and non-enculturated can see sameness in mimeomorphic actions. It's like this: your teenage children hang-out with their friends after school. They do things. You have no idea what they're doing or why and, in fact, you would be unable to hang out with them and "be one of them." Their actions are polimorphic. On the way home there's a road crew stopping traffic; the actions of the worker with the walkie-talkie and the stop sign are mimeomorphic — it doesn't matter who's doing the job, one of the teenagers or a lifetime road crew worker — it would look the same to you.

Action and behavior map onto social and natural kinds. Non-intentional acts such as blinking your eye — can be described in terms of natural kinds. We're not interested in these. Polimorphic actions can only be described in terms of social kinds. These behaviors happen in the context of, are guided by, and initiate from social interaction. In retail, the social kinds are inscribed by the actor-network of the retail establishment and by the mores of commercial/market transactions in general. The corporation needs actively to consider the design of retail transactions to support the increase of polimorphic actions.

We arrive to our final definition of agency as: "the ability of the retail worker to act appropriately but relatively unencumbered by the dictates and wishes of the establishment by *engaging in a greater proportion of polimorphic actions as compared with mimeomorphic actions.*" It's easy to design systems to encourage mimeomorphic actions — we've been doing it for 100 years since Taylor [8]. This definition is useful because it shifts our perspective; one can now imagine designing information systems explicitly to encourage polimorphic actions by clerks. It remains for us to consider the types of technological innovations that explicitly support polimorphic actions in retail environments.

## 10.4 Technology Examples

The emergence of increasingly viable ubiquitous computing technologies suggests new possibilities for the design of retail transactions. Weiser's [9] paper is perhaps most well known for introducing the concept of ubiquitous computing. Since then, these technologies have come to include three main capabilities: a) the ability to 'label' people, places and things with passive (no power of their own) radio-frequency identification 'tags,' b) the ability to distribute remote and independent 'sensors' to detect environmental stimuli, such as noise, temperature, emissions and so forth, and c) the ability to combine these two capabilities into small fully functional computing devices that can form networks of communicating sensors and tags (cf. [6]). Computing capabilities formerly confined to specific locations can now be distributed throughout the environment. One of the first thoughts of what to do with this new technology is to continuously track products from manufacture (indeed, before manufacture) through to the customer purchase, with the envisioned further rationalization that inevitably would manifest itself. There are sound financial reasons for this approach. There's also evidence that this approach will further tip the balance away from polimorphic actions.

For example, there is an ideal that customers will be able to simply walk into a store, select some items and walk out having paid. No lines. No wait. No clerk at all. Even with today's robust systems, errors occur and are revealed at check out with surprising regularity, as reported by customers we've interviewed. When we simulated this fully automated check-out using new ubiquitous technologies, customers were pleased. They were pleased because we told them everything worked just fine. However, when we also simulated these reportedly common and to-be-expected errors, including the payment of regular — not sale — prices, customers demanded accountability and recourse with human intervention [7]. One solution would be to design systems that purposefully support human intervention. ECR (Efficient Consumer Response, discussed in [5]) though not explicitly removing the clerk, does automate many clerk functions (and more) to remove non-value costs in the total system. We have no argument with this, per se; what we pose for consideration is to give appropriate weight to potential roles for clerks — roles in large part have been relegated to automation. At least, designers ought to consider whole systems, including the intangibles such as trust, as addressed by [5].

If we accept the result that human intervention will be required, then we argue why not capitalize on that resource? At Amazon.com, customers can write book reviews and post them with the product. At Powell's Books, in Portland, Oregon, staff personnel write short, 50 word reviews that they place on the shelves with the respective books. The two should be combined based on the electronic tagging of items. A clerk ought to be able to assemble on site reviews of items from the Internet as well as from physically present customers and other clerks.

In our work, we visited an outdoor store in Portland, Oregon. One item for sale was a rain-jacket; the price: USD $495.00. Now, this is a rather steep price for a rain jacket. We asked what justified the exorbitant price, and the clerk told us about the strength of the seams and other physical attributes of the jacket — nothing but generalities about its actual use and utility.

We wanted to talk to people who'd actually bought the jacket and used it on a mountain in the rain (the clerk hadn't). The clerk could be a nexus for this information being as he was at the juncture of customer and jacket. When a customer comes in again to make another purchase, the information system could suggest to the clerk that he/she ask the customer about the customer's experience with the jacket. The clerk can then have the discussion with the customer — making the clerk more of a general expert and truly listening to the customer — which customer actually like. In this example, the Information system does what it does best: process automatic information. The clerk does what he does best: have a conversation. The result is polimorphic actions by the clerk initiated by the information system.

It's 11 am on a Tuesday morning in March in a large department store in a suburban shopping mall. There are a few women (and us) mulling around. A slow time in the store, and yet, the store is fully open. In this case, the clerk sees two women studying some items and goes over to them. After some discussion, the clerk knows one of the women is considering the purchase, but hesitating. The clerk could make a discrete inquiry of the information system and given a result, make an offer on the spot — bringing a bit of the bazaar back to the store. In this case, it was the human who recognized the purchase interest of one woman, the time of day, the number of people in the store and so on, and initiated an interaction with the information system. The clerk's performance could, of course, be managed and the clerk's skills enhanced over time, thereby further supporting the clerk's polimorphic actions, while the system maintains the pricing information and tracks profit margins, etc: something the information system does well.

Of course, a good clerk would have also found something of interest for the other customer as well — perhaps an accessory, something to go with the outfit she had on. In New Delhi, India, two travelers were participating in a carpet purchase from a reputable dealer. One was the customer, the other along for the experience. Throughout, the dealer would ask both their opinions, but focus on the actual buyer. At the end, after the negotiation and the settlement, the dealer says to the other traveler: "Now, how about you, what can we get for you?" The traveler insisted there was no interest in a carpet at which point the dealer brought out some uniquely embroidered pashminas. In contrast to the price paid for the carpet, the pashmina was the equivalent of a peppermint patty at the check-stand in a supermarket. The dealer sold a pashmina through his astute powers of observation (and a customer with apparently cash to burn).

The dealer's skill was in manipulating the customer's perception of what he wanted. The dealer would likely say he helped the customer make an informed decision because the customer didn't even know the dealer had any pashminas for sale. The dealer is engaged in polimorphic actions — the dealer is using his skills and knowledge of the social situation to engage in a transaction. The customer is doing the same. To those who say caveat emptor, we say: polimorphic actions.

## 10.5 Summary

These two examples are relatively simple. Yet they make the point that the human and the machine can work in concert to support agency as defined by an increasing proportion of polimorphic actions. We've defined agency uniquely as emphasizing polimorphic actions over mimeomorphic actions; increasing agency means increasing the proportion of polimorphic actions. In retail settings, clerks with an increasing repertoire of polimorphic actions are clerks with increased agency.

New information technologies are continuously available. Or so it would seem. While much of this new technology is initially conceived for streamlining supply chains, that's not the limitation of the technology — that's the limitation of the designers. To design systems that support agency, one must explicitly consider the role of the human in the human-machine system. It won't just happen. And that's the unethical part.

## References

1. H. Collins and M. Kusch. *The Shape of Actions: What Humans and Machines Can Do.* MIT Press. London. 1998.
2. J. Habermas. *Toward a Rational Society: Student Protest, Science and Politics.* (J. J. Shapiro, Translation). Beacon Press. Boston. 1970.
3. B. Latour. On recalling ANT. In J. Law and J. Hassard *Actor Network Theory and After.* Blackwell Publishing. Oxford. 1999.
4. J. McMillan. *Reinventing the Bazaar: The Natural History of Markets.* W.W. Norton and Company. New York. 2002.
5. G. Roussos and T. Moussouri. Consumer Perceptions of Privacy, Security and Trust in Ubiquitous Commerce. *Personal and Ubiquitous Computing.* 8(6):416–429. 2004.
6. K. Sakamura. Making Computers Invisible. *IEEE Micro.* 22(6):7–11. 2002.

7. T. Salvador, S. Barile and J. Sherry. Ubiquitous Computing Design Principles: Supporting Human-Human and Human-Computer Transactions. *CHI Extended Abstracts*:1497–1500. 2004.

8. F.W. Taylor. *Principles of Scientific Management.* Unabridged republication of the work published by Harper & Brother Publishers in 1919. New York. Dover. New York. 1998.

9. M. Weiser. The Computer for the 21st Century. *Scientific American.* 265(3):94–101. 1991.

# 11

# Privacy Protection and RFID

Simson Garfinkel

Nobody bothered to tell me that my new identity card contained a wireless identification chip that allowed me to be tracked at a distance. The only thing that I knew was that my employer, the Massachusetts Institute of Technology, had switched to a new ID card. On the surface, the reason for the change was the Institute's ongoing effort at rebranding: the old ID cards brandished the Institute's old logo featuring two white men hard at work on a big piece of equipment — now politically incorrect — while the new ID has a modern and somewhat neutral collection of lines and dots that all sort of spell out "MIT."

Inside the card was another change – one that was hidden from view and hardly publicized. A small wire antenna attached to a tiny silicon microchip with a unique identification number was sandwiched between the card's top and bottom plastic layers. MIT, like many organizations, had opted to purchase identity cards that could be read at a distance with special "proximity readers." It was a radio frequency identification system, known more commonly by the initials "RFID."

## 11.1 The RFID Prox Card

In addition to the cards, MIT has also deployed special wireless readers around campus. My laboratory, for instance, has readers installed in all of the stairwells. During the day the stairwell doors are unlocked, but at 5pm they bolt shut. To gain entrance I need to take my wallet out of my pants pocket and wave it a few inches in front of the reader for a few seconds. At some point I hear the reader "beep," a loud electronic bolt snaps, and the little light on the reader turns from red the green. Overall, the system is much more convenient than trying line up a conventional metal key with a tiny little hole. The Institute likes the system as well, since cards can be individually enabled or disabled for particular doors with just a few minutes notice. There's also a permanent record made every time I use my card. This can be useful for police investigations after a theft.

Today MIT's RFID-enabled identity cards are used solely for accessing laboratories and other restricted areas. But once all of the Institute's undergraduates have the cards, we may find more potential for their use. Compared with the magnetic strip that's also on the ID card, the RFID chip can be read faster and at a distance, making RFID both more convenient and more reliable.

RFID is more reliable than magnetic strip systems because the RFID reader never comes in contact with the object being read. Earlier this year, for instance, the magnetic strip on my MIT card was scratched. All of a sudden the card wouldn't work in some of the readers on campus. The scratch probably came from a piece of dirt that was in one of the remaining swipe-card readers on campus. But since RFID readers don't get dirty or otherwise contaminated with repeated use, they can't damage an RFID card. Neither will keys, magnets, grime, or other items that might find their way into my wallet.

Because of the convenience and reliability, we might see other uses for RFID on campus as the cards become more widespread. For example, MIT has a "Tech Cash" program that allows me to use my ID card to purchase food all over campus. It's possible that Tech Cash will move over to an RFID-based cash-register at some point. Already the MIT garages allow faculty and staff to use their Massachusetts Turnpike "FastLane" tags, another RFID-based system, to check their cars into and out of a growing number of garages on campus. It's much easier to simply drive through a lane than to open one's window and swipe a card through a reader.

On the other hand, the RFID chip inside my identity card poses risks that mag stripes never did. The primary risk is covert reading. While the readers in the stairwell only have a read-range of a few inches, that's because MIT bought relatively low-cost readers with relatively small antennas. The same vendor sells more expensive readers that have a read range of nearly two feet, and students at my lab have experimented with a new design that increases the read range to four feet or more. And while the current readers beep and flash a light when a card is successfully read, there's nothing on the card itself that beeps: snip a few wires and there would be nothing to alert the person holding a card that their presence had been detected and recorded.

There are also persistent questions about the security of RFID systems. One real problem is an attacker who is sufficiently motivated can listen to the code that an RFID chip transmits and copy it onto a chip of their own. This kind of attack is called cloning, and it resulted in billions of dollars in fraudulent cell phone charges back in the 1980s. It turns out that cloning is a risk for RFID-based systems as well — or at least for many of the systems that have been deployed.

It is possible to build an RFID system that is resistant to cloning. The trick is to give every RFID chip in the system its own unique password, and then to have a copy of every chip's password at some central computer. This password is then used as part of a cryptographic protocol called challenge-response.

Mobil uses such a technique in its SpeedPass RFID payment system. But most proximity card systems don't implement challenge-response. To demonstrate this fact, in the spring of 2003 an undergraduate at University of Waterloo in Canada built an RFID cloner as part of his senior project. The whole system cost him less than $100 to create. After he created the handheld device he was promptly prohibited from bringing it into his lab, for fear that he might copy the card of a high-placed official and compromise the lab's physical security [14]. Of course, the real cloners that the lab should worry about was not the one that the student, Jonathan Westhues, had created and publicized, but the cloners that the lab didn't know about.

## 11.2 RFID: Promise and Threat

These two stories demonstrate both the promise and threat that RFID poses for ubiquitous commerce. On the one hand, RFID-based systems could make it much easier for people to make payments and otherwise participate in the electronic economy. Waving a Speedpass fob to buy gas or an RFID-enabled credit-card to pay your bill is just one possibility. Another idea, promoted by Nokia, is a cell phone with a built-in RFID reader that could read tags utility meters or subway posters [9]. For example, if you saw a poster for a movie that looked interesting on the subway you could scan the poster's RFID chip with your cell phone and get more information about the movie — and possibly even an electronic coupon good for a discount at a nearby theater. This data wouldn't be on the poster, of course. Instead, a special application running inside the phone would take the 96-bit serial number on the poster and submit it to some web-based service, which might then consult the movie theater's database and find out if there were still seats available for the next show.

RFID also has the potential to end one of the most urgent threats to consumer health and safety in the modern world: the threat of counterfeit pharmaceuticals. At $2 per pill or more, many popular pharmaceuticals are literally worth their weight in gold. But in recent years a growing number of criminal organizations have started creating fake look-alike drugs, putting them in convincing packages, and selling them into the pharmaceutical supply chain. The problem is big and getting bigger. According to a recent report by the US Food and Drug Administration [3], "Although exact prevalence rates in the US are not know, outside the US drug counterfeiting is known to be widespread and affect both developing and developed countries. In some countries more than half the drug supply may consist of counterfeit drugs. For example, recent reports have detailed that more than 50% of anti-malarials in Africa are believed to be counterfeit. In virtually all countries, counterfeit drug operations have been uncovered in recent years."

RFID will be a powerful weapon in the fight against drug counterfeiting in the future. With RFID, each bottle, blister pack, injectable vial, inhaler, and other package manufactured by a drug maker could be equipped with its own unique serial number — a number that can be read and instantly verified with the drug maker's website. What's more, RFID could allow tracking of individual bottles within a case. If 72 legitimate bottles in a sealed case left a distribution point but only 65 showed up, the receiver could reject the shipment, for fear that 7 of the bottles had been replaced with counterfeit. Next-generation RFID tags could even directly detect product tampering — for example, recording where and when a vial was opened.

Tiny RFID "immobilizer" chips in more than a hundred million automobile keys have already reduced auto theft rates in both Europe and the US. The chips, introduced by Philips Semiconductor [8] in Germany in 1994, match with a tiny RFID reader that is built into the ignition lock of high-end automobiles. If the car's computer doesn't see a properly-programmed key in the reader, the computer won't let the ignition start the car. According to Phillips, auto theft rates for cars containing immobilizers dropped 90% after the technology's introduction. A similar study by the US-based Highway Loss Data Institute found that theft of Nissan Maximas dropped by 50% the year after immobilizers were installed; overall, auto theft in the US is down 76% from 1990, thanks to a combination of technology and better police enforcement [5].

On the other hand, many consumer activists have painted RFID as a dangerous technology that could help bring about an anti-consumer explosion in personal information collection. In the supermarket, cameras linked to shelf-based RFID readers could automatically snap photographs of us when we pick up merchandise. RFID chips embedded into our clothing — put there for added visibility into the supply chain — could alert a store when we enter and leave, giving the store's computers our name and taste in clothing. As we walk in the store, the shelves and displays could literally call out to us, telling us that pants that are both better and cheaper than the ones we are wearing can be found over in Aisle 7.

Even worse, these advocates say, RFID could be a technology that enables a totalitarian "Big Brother"-style government to grab hold and remain in control. Chips forcibly implanted into our bodies could quickly become the new identity card, making it easy for the government to track dissidents and mete out increasingly stringent punishments for people who refuse to think correctly. RFID readers embedded in the highways could track the movement of our cars — already tags are voluntarily being carried by millions of drivers to automatically pay for tolls, and in the future RFID chips will be embedded in tires, as well. RFID readers placed strategically throughout the city could create a permanent record of our face-to-face meetings, associations, and even our contemplative solo walks along the riverfront.

What's so compelling about these scenarios is that many seem well on their way to being realized — and are being actively promoted by the RFID industry itself. The idea that shelves might literally call out to consumers was publicized in a March 2002 article appearing in Forbes magazine [10].

The shelf calls out to the shopper, "Honey, you could get those pants [you are wearing] for less in Aisle 7." Until recently this illustration was proudly featured on the website of Alien Technology, one of the leading makers of RFID chips. Between March and July 2003, Procter & Gamble and Wal-Mart ran a secret trial of RFID technology at an Oklahoma store in which RFID tags hidden in Lipfinity packages were used to trigger remote-controlled cameras [1]. (Procter & Gamble, for its part, claims that there were signs at the store notifying consumers of the trial, and that the cameras were only present because the people conducting the trial were in another city and had no other way of seeing what was going on.)

Likewise, RFID chips really are being implanted into people. The chips, which have been used to track animals for more than a decade, were originally proposed as a way to track wandering Alzheimer's patients. Lately, though, they've been promoted as a security solution — a kind of implantable biometric. Here the leading player is VeriChip, a subsidiary of Applied Digital Solutions. One of VeriChip's most public customers to date is Mexico's Attorney General Rafael Macedo de la Concha and 160 employees of Mexico's new anticrime computer center in Mexico City [6]. In theory, bad guys won't have the chips so they will be denied access to the anticrime center and its computer files. Even the RFID chips in car tires are on their way, thanks to the US Transportation Recall Enhancement, Accountability, and Documentation (TREAD) Act. Passed in the fall of 2000 after the US news media publicized deaths relating to Firestone tire failures on Ford Explorer Sport Utility vehicles, that act requires that the automotive industry track its tires and be able to recall them when there are safety issues. Unfortunately, stickers, paint, and practically anything else you put on a tire is likely to wear off. The only way that the industry has found that it can satisfy the tracking requirements of the act is by embedding tiny RFID chips in the fabric of the tires themselves.

## 11.3 But What Is RFID, Really?

One of the reasons that there is so much confusion over RFID is that the phrase "Radio Frequency Identification" covers an impressive array of different technologies and systems.

On the face of it, the letters "RFID" refer to any system that sends out identification codes over radio waves. The underlying technology dates back to the Second World War, when wireless identification systems called Identification Friend or Foe (IFF) were placed onboard military aircraft. Within a few years Harry Stockman demonstrated a system powered completely by reflected power [11]. In the 1960s the first anti-theft product surveillance systems were commercialized. In the 1970s the Department of Energy investigated using another form of the technology to safeguard materials at nuclear weapons sites. The technology really took off in the late 1980s and early 1990, with low-cost RFID devices being used as the basis of inventory tracking systems, wireless entry systems for offices, and implantable tags for tracking laboratory animals, livestock, and pets.

Most RFID systems have two parts: a reader and a tag. The reader generates a strong RF field at a specific frequency. The tag is energized by this field. A tiny computer on the tag powers up and starts transmitting a code back to the reader. The length of the code depends on the system being used: implantable systems tend to have 64-bit codes, while systems based on the new Electronic Product Code have 96-bit codes. RFID systems can also implement a challenge-response system in which the reader transmits a challenge number and the tag sends back the result that is mathematically based on the challenge number and a secret key.

RFID tags can be passive, in which case they are completely powered by the RF signal, or they can be active, in which case they have an embedded battery. Active tags can be read at much greater distances — typically 10 to 100 meters — but batteries have a maximum lifetime of a few years. Passive tags typically can't be read at distances of more than a few meters — and sometimes much less — but they can theoretically work for decades. Naturally, active tags are much larger than passive tags, owing to the size of the battery. Active tags also tend to have better read rates as long as their battery is still charged, but then they fail. Most automatic toll payment systems rely on active tags with a five-to-seven year battery.

Another important factor that determines reading distance is the size of an RFID tag's antenna: the larger the antenna, the greater the range. An antenna of 20-30cm might be readable at a few meters, while the almost-microscopic antenna on the Hitachi mu-chip gives the device a reading distance of just a few millimeters — great for allowing automatic document processing, but not sufficient for reading RFID-enabled bills that might be in someone's wallet.

Although most RFID systems use unlicensed portions of the electromagnetic spectrum, different devices operate at different frequencies, resulting in different performance characteristics. Implantable RFID chips and proximity cards have traditionally operated between 125 and 134.2 Khz, where reading ranges are short but where the RF signal is not significantly absorbed by water. Systems envisioned for tagging items at supermarkets will probably operate in the 800Mhz (Europe) or 900Mhz (US) range, where read ranges are longer and data rates are considerably higher, allowing an entire case or shopping cart of tagged items to be read in a second. One serious problem that has yet to be overcome is that radio waves at these frequencies can be stopped by water or a thin layer of metal: milk or soda cans in a shopping cart can prevent other items from being read. Although many RFID proponents think that this problem will eventually be solved, solutions are by no means guaranteed.

## 11.4 The 21st Century Bar Code?

Many see RFID tags as a 21st century replacement to the bar codes that became ubiquitous in the last 25 years of the 20th century. And indeed, RFID tags offer many advantages over traditional optically-scanned tags. Whereas optical bar codes need to be in plain view to be read; RFID tags can be read through fabric, paper, cardboard, and other materials that are transparent to the frequency of operation. This means that tags can be literally embedded in products — for example, in the heel of a shoe — meaning that they can't be accidentally or intentionally separated from the item that they are being used to track.

In theory, RFID tags offer considerably more security than optical bar codes. RFID tags can be assigned a password, limiting who has the ability to read or write them. Optical bar codes are promiscuous, in that any reader can read any compatible optical bar code that comes in range. RFID tags can also be electronically put-to-sleep or completely deactivated. The only way to deactivate an optical bar code is by obliterating or obscuring it.

But the most important difference between RFID tags and optical bar codes is the amount of information that they hold and the ease of programming them. Traditional optical bar codes are limited to 13 digits of information, and two-dimensional bar codes are limited to several hundred; RFID tags can in theory store hundreds or thousands of bytes of information. As a result, while optical bar codes are usually used to label an item with its manufacturer and product code, RFID tags invariably assign every object its own specific serial number. One of the design goals of the Electronic Product Code system is for no two objects in the world to have the same code.

For example, the UPC "041508 800822" refers to a case of a dozen 750ml bottles of San Pellegrino sparkling natural mineral water. Each bottle inside the case has a UPC with the code "041508 800129." A shipping container might contain a thousand cases, all with the same code.

Each RFID tag, by contrast, can have its own unique identifying code. A shipping container of RFID-tagged San Pellegrino cases would have thousands of separate unique codes. One way of assigning these could be to use a standard UPC/EAN code as a prefix and to append a unique serial number. Such a system would allow easy integration with existing inventory systems, while simultaneously allowing new applications that make use of the unique ID.

Giving each package a unique serial number has the potential of giving manufacturers and distributors unprecedented visibility into the supply chain. With RFID every product can be tracked from the factory, to the truck, to the distribution center, to the back room, to the store shelves, and finally to the checkout counter.

This visibility means that manufacturers will find it easier to pinpoint the source of "shrinkage" within their supply chain. If ten cases of razors are scanned entering the truck and only five cases are scanned leaving, the company will know that it should begin its investigation with the truck driver.

Equally important, separately serialized products and cases will let manufacturers verify that the product created for Hong Kong isn't diverted to, say, New York City. This is important because different markets are usually sold products at different prices. RFID could make the process of diversion much more difficulty.

Counterfeit goods are another problem that increasingly threatens many companies. Counterfeit goods not only cost sales, inferior quality counterfeits can damage a brand's reputation. And, of course, in the case of counterfeit drugs, these malicious products can cost lives. If every legitimate product is serialized and registered, then a country's border control can make sure that each licensed item only enters the country once. Serialization also stops another kind of counterfeiting — when a factory that is specially licensed to make a product makes more than it is supposed to and sells the extra on the black market. With RFID those "extra" products will either not have chips, they won't have chips that have codes that are properly recorded, or else they will have duplicate serial numbers. Each of these cases has a specific signature that will make its way back to the manufacturer and eventually enable to responsible party to be identified.

Finally, when things go wrong, RFID enables product recalls. Today companies generally do not track lot numbers and expiration dates on things like milk cartons and other food products. Recalls are thus labor-intensive processes that require "walking the aisles" and manually identifying the suspect goods. In the future, grocers will be able to use an RFID scanner to rapidly locate tainted goods on store shelves; suspect serial numbers could be programmed into cash registers to prohibit consumers from purchasing items that are blacklisted.

For consumers, some examples of the benefits of Auto-ID technology include making possible paperless product registration, exchanges, warrantee service, and returns. An RFID reader in a refrigerator or pantry could notice if a item is removed and not returned: such items could be automatically reordered. Consumers could also benefit from automatic searching of recalled products. Drugs sold in blister-packs could have little wires going back to an RFID chip that would notice when each pill was popped-out. Such a technology could be used to monitor patients' compliance with a drug regime.

Amusingly enough, one application occasionally suggested for RFID in the house — finding lost house keys — will probably not be a near-term application. Finding lost keys would require not only equipping a keychain with an RFID tag, but also equipping each room in a house with multiple RFID readers to allow for triangulation. Even then, the system might not be able to find keys that had fallen behind or into a couch or similar RF shields, unless the keys are equipped with active tags.

## 11.5 Privacy Issues

Ubiquitous deployment of RFID tags in consumer products poses several challenges to consumer privacy. Because human beings are not sensitive to radio signals, RFID tags could be covertly read by secret readers. Although 13.56 MHz tags cannot be read from more than two meters away, unshielded passive 915 MHz tags can be read from many meters. Such technology could be used to track the movement of individuals or, if the individual is known, to covertly figure out what people are carrying.

Even without deploying covert readers, it is possible for an attacker to covertly monitor the communication between a reader and a tag. In some cases the reader's interaction with the tag, detectable from many tens of meters, can be used to figure the tag's serial number without even hearing the tag's response. We can imagine several scenarios in which these properties could be exploited. A practical joker could covertly inventory, say, the undergarments of nearby pedestrians. Although this might be funny on the street, it could become an extremely effective harassment tool in some workplaces. Stores could deploy their own covert RFID readers to inventory the contents of shoppers' bags as they enter — or perhaps to identify individuals as they window shop. More seriously, the unique codes transmitted from promiscuous RFID devices could be used to detonate remote-control bombs, allowing specific individuals to be targeted.

Covert readers are not limited to streets and stores. Household electronics and other kinds of products might covertly inventory which other products are in the consumer's house, and then report this information back to a central repository — assuming that these "moles" have network access. Such information might be used to target the consumer for special offers or to deny the consumer offers that he or she might otherwise receive.

Several technical measures have been proposed for dealing with the potential privacy problem of RFID technology. The industry's leading approach is called "kill," in which RFID tags are removed or disabled at the time a consumer purchases an item. Kill is part of the Electronic Product Code specification. Alternatively, the unique part of the product serial number could be erased, leaving only the prefix. Yet another approach is to simply attach the RFID to a tab or label that is removed after the item is purchased.

Yet another approach would be to equip RFID tags with passwords, and have these passwords changed at the time of purchase. This would allow the consumer to read his or her tags but would prevent others from reading the consumer's tags without permission.

Finally, RFID tags can simply be shielded — either with metal cases, or with the RFID "blocker tag" developed by RSA Security. The blocker tag is a noisy RFID tag that prevents other tags within its sphere of influence from being read at all.

But all pro-privacy RFID countermeasures depend, more or less, on the consumer being aware of the existence of the tag and having the technical ability and the necessary patience to deactivate or reprogram an RFID tag. A serious concern is that consumers might not exercise these technical measures for any of a number of reasons. For example, the manufacturer or merchandiser might fail to tell the consumer about the presence of the tag, and might equally fail to kill or remove it at checkout. A company might do this because they see the tags as an anti-theft security measure that is better not to publicize. Alternatively, the company might simply not have the equipment to "kill" the tags and might not want to publicize this fact. Companies might even think that there is little consumer concern with the technology.

An alternative solution to assuring consumer privacy with RFID would be to use policy implemented through regulation and licensing requirements. Much current thinking on informational privacy issues is based on the Code of Fair Information Practices, developed by the US Department of Health, Education and Welfare in 1973 (cf. Appendix A and [13]). The code has been subsequently expanded in by the OECD in 1980 [7], the European Union in 1995 [2], and the government of Canada in 1999 [12].

I believe that many of the issues raised by the use of RFID can be solved by extending Fair Information Practices so that they specifically address the problems raised by RFID technology. I call this adoption the "RFID Bill of Rights."

The RFID Bill of Rights consists of five guiding principles for the creation and deployment of RFID systems. Users of RFID systems and purchasers of products containing RFID tags have:

1. The right to know if a product contains an RFID tag.
2. The right to have embedded RFID tags removed, deactivated, or destroyed when a product is purchased.
3. The right to first class RFID alternatives: consumers should not lose other rights (e.g. the right to return a product or to travel on a particular road) if they decide to opt-out of RIFD or exercise an RFID tag's "kill" feature.
4. The right to know what information is stored inside their RFID tags. If this information is incorrect, there must be a means to correct or amend it.
5. The right to know when, where, and why an RFID tag is being read.

Together, items #1 and #5 mandate that there should be no covert RFID systems. One approach is to have a logo that must be prominently displayed on any product that contains an RFID tag and in any area that is under surveillance by RFID readers. Likewise, organizations that wish to declare a space "free" of RFID readers could have similar placards; freedom could be assured through the use of RFID reader detectors or RFID jammers such as the Blocker Tag.

Item #2 overcomes the fear that stores might find it inconvenient to provide consumers with a means for deactivating their tags. Tags that comply with the Auto-ID Center's standard will be required to incorporate a password-protected "kill" feature. Rather than forcing consumers to find their passwords, a more consumer-friendly approach would be for manufacturers to use standardized kill passwords, or else to either kill tags or erase unique serial numbers as part of the checkout process. [1]

Item #3 seeks to avoid penalizing consumers who decline to partake in RFID-enabled services. It is easy to imagine how poorly-designed RFID system could be coercively deployed if consumers are not given a choice regarding its use. For example, if the only way to ride on a particular highway is by paying the toll with an RFID tag, then even consumers that are opposed to the tag might nevertheless use it, if there is no other way for them to commute to work.

Item #4 is a straightforward application of fair information practices to RIFD systems, similar to the application of these principles to smartcards that I proposed in 1999 [4].

Item #5 is likely to be the most controversial. There are many ways that consumers can be informed that their RFID tags are being read. For example, a prominent placard could be placed in the vicinity of a reader. Readers could emit a tone or flash a light when a reading takes place. Alternatively, the tag itself could emit a tone or flash a light. In addition, a tag equipped with memory could count the number of times that it has been read. Of course, a passive tag would not have an accurate time source to remember when the reading took place, and a simple count may not by itself add enough information. In general, though, most of these options would add cost to the tag, either in the form of a battery, or in the form of increased functionality.

Yet another alternative is providing concerned consumers with RFID reader detectors. Such detectors could be cheaply made and equipped with, real time clocks, and position-aware technology such as GPS. Although such detectors might not be a primary means for enforcing item #5, they could prove to be a powerful means for finding organizations that do not comply with these principles.

These principles could be legislated or could be adopted on a voluntary basis. If voluntary, conformance with the principles could be ensured through licensing of logos, protocols, or intellectual property required for proper RFID operation.

---

[1] One potential problem with a widely-known "kill" password is the notion that a saboteur might enter a store for the purpose of killing all of the store's RFID tags. To protect against such actions, stores could be equipped with RFID sensing systems that will quickly report any such activity. Killing an RFID tag requires exercising anti-collision algorithms to find a particular tag, addressing the tag, and finally sending the "kill" command with sufficient power to affect a kill. Because of this involved procedure, even a high-speed RFID tag killing system would not be able to kill more than five tags per second. Such a system would have a distinct radio signature and would be easily found by a store with RFID readers in every aisle.

## 11.6 Conclusion

RFID is a powerful technology, and it is a technology that is likely to see world-wide deployment within the coming years. Attention to Fair Information Practices and related public-policy issues today will assure that these systems are designed and deployed in a manner that is compatible with evolving privacy principles.

## References

1. K. Albrecht. Scandal: Wal-Mart, P&G Involved in Secret RFID Testing. Archived at: http://www.spychips.com/broken_arrow.htm. November 10. 2003.
2. European Commission. *European Union Directive 95/46/EC of the European Parliament and of the Council of 24 October 1995 on the protection of individuals with regard to the processing of personal data and on the free movement of such data.* http://europa.eu.int/comm/internal_market/en/dataprot/law/
3. Food and Drug Administration. *Combating Counterfeit Drugs.* U. S. Department of Health and Human Services, Food and Drug Administration Rockville, Maryland 20857. 2004.
4. S. Garfinkel. *Smartcard Holder's Bill of Rights.* Archived at: http://www.simson.net/smartrights.html.
5. R. Ingrassia and A. McQuillan. City car theft is on the skids. *New York Daily News.* Archived at http://www.cnn.com/2000/LOCAL/northeast/08/01/mny.car.theft/. August 1. 2000.
6. P. Lewis. RFID: Getting Under Your Skin? *Fortune Magazine.* http://www.fortune.com/fortune/ontech/0,15704,675442,00.html. August 1. 2004.
7. Organization for Economic Co-operation and Development. *Guidelines on the Protection of Privacy and Transborder Flows of Personal Data.* 1980.
8. Philips Semiconductors. *Identification - Identification Applications - Car Immobilization.* Archived at : http://www.semiconductors.philips.com/markets/identification/applications/vaccess/immobilization/index.html. 2004.
9. RFID Journal. *Nokia Unveils RFID Phone Reader.* March 17. Archived at http://www.rfidjournal.com/article/articleview/834/1/1/. 2004.
10. C.R. Schoenberger. The Internet of Things. *Forbes.* March 18. 2002.
11. H. Stockman. Communication by Means of Reflected Power. *Proceedings of the IRE.* 35:1196–1204. 1948.
12. The House of Commons of Canada. *Personal Information Protection and Electronic Documents Act.* Bill C-6, 2nd Session, 36th Parliament, 48 Elizabeth II. 1999.
13. U.S. Department of Health, Education and Welfare. *Records, computers, and the Rights of Citizens.* Report of Secretary's Advisory Committee on Automated Personal Data Systems. 1973.
14. J. Westhues. Hacking the Prox Card. In S. Garfinkel and B. Rosenberg (Eds) *RFID: Perspectives, Policy, and Practice.* Addison-Wesley. 2005.

# A

## The Code of Fair Information Practices

The Code of Fair Information Practices as developed in 1973 by the Secretary's Advisory Committee on Automated Personal Data Systems, Records, Computers, and the Rights of Citizens at the U.S. Department of Health, Education and Welfare is based on five principles:

1. There must be no personal data record-keeping systems whose very existence is secret.
2. There must be a way for a person to find out what information about the person is in a record and how it is used.
3. There must be a way for a person to prevent information about the person that was obtained for one purpose from being used or made available for other purposes without the person's consent.
4. There must be a way for a person to correct or amend a record of identifiable information about the person.
5. Any organization creating, maintaining, using, or disseminating records of identifiable personal data must assure the reliability of the data for their intended use and must take precautions to prevent misuses of the data.

# B

# The ISTAG Maria Scenario

After a tiring long haul flight, Maria passes through the arrivals hall of an airport in a Far Eastern country. She is travelling light, hand baggage only. When she comes to this particular country, she knows that she can travel much lighter than those days less than a decade ago, when she had to carry a collection of different so-called personal computing devices (laptop PC, mobile phone, electronic organizers, and sometimes beamers and printers). Her computing system for this trip is reduced to one highly personalized communications device, her PCom that she wears on her wrist. A particular feature of this trip is that the country Maria is visiting has since the previous year embarked on an ambitious ambient intelligence infrastructure programme. Thus her visa for the trip was self-arranged, and she is able to stroll through immigration without stopping because her P-Comm is dealing with the ID checks as she walks.

A rented car has been reserved for her and is waiting in an earmarked bay. The car opens itself as she approaches. It starts at the press of a button; she does not need a key. She still has to drive the car, but she is supported in her journey downtown to the conference center-hotel by the traffic guidance system that had been launched by the city government as part of the 'AmI-Nation' initiative two years earlier. Downtown traffic has been a legendary nightmare in this city for many years, and draconian steps were taken to limit access to the city centre. But Maria has priority access rights into the central cordon because she has a reservation in the car park of the hotel. Central access, however, comes at a premium price; in Maria's case it is embedded in a deal negotiated between her perserv and the transaction agents of the car-rental and hotel chains. Her firm operates centralised billing for these expenses and uses its purchasing power to gain access and attractive rates. Such preferential treatment for well-heeled visitors was highly contentious at the time of the introduction of the route pricing system, and the government was forced to hypothecate funds from the tolling system to the public transport infrastructure. In the car Maria's teenage daughter (Amanda) comes through on the audio system. Amanda has detected from the 'En Casa' system at home that her mother is in a place that supports real time audio communication. However, even with all the route guidance support, Maria wants to concentrate on her driving and says that she will call back from the hotel.

Maria is directed to a slot in the underground garage of a newly constructed hotel building operated by the Smar-tel Chain . She is met in the garage by the porter, the first contact with a real human in our story so far! He helps her with her luggage to her room. Her room adopts her 'personality' as she enters. The room temperature and default lighting are set and there is a display of selected video and music choices on the video wall. She needs to make some changes to her presentation – a sales pitch that will be used as the basis for a negotiation later in the day. Using voice commands she adjusts the light levels and commands a bath. Then she calls up her daughter on the video wall, while talking she uses a traditional remote control system to browse through a set of webcast local news bulletins from back home that her daughter tells her about. They watch them together. Later on she 'localises' her presentation with the help of an agent that is specialized in advising on local preferences (colour schemes and the use of language). She stores the presentation on the secure server at headquarters in Europe. In the hotels seminar room where the sales pitch is to take place, she will be able to call down an encrypted version of the presentation and give it a post presentation decrypt life of 1.5 minutes.

She goes downstairs to make her presentation. This is a high stress event; not only is she performing alone for the first time, the clients concerned are well known to be tough players. Still, she doesn't actually have to close the deal this time. As she enters the meeting, she raises communications access levels to block out anything but red-level 'emergency' messages. The meeting is rough, but she feels it was a success. Coming out of the meeting, she lowers the communication barriers again and picks up a number of amber level communications including one from her cardio-monitor warning her to take some rest now. The day has been long and stressing. She needs to chill out with a little meditation and medication. For Maria, the meditation is a concert on the video wall, and the medication a large gin and tonic from her room's minibar.

# Index